PROFILE
of
Castletown

Lily Publications Ltd.,
PO Box 33, Ramsey, Isle of Man,
British Isles IM99 4LP

Tel: +44(0) 1624 898446
www.lilypublications.com

LILY

Derek Winterbottom

ISBN: 9781899602391

Produced and designed by Lily Publications Ltd
Printed and bound by Gomer Press, Wales.

© Lily Publications Ltd 2010

Published by Lily Publications Ltd
Registered office: PO Box 33, Ramsey, Isle of Man, IM7 3HD.
Tel: +44 (0)1624 898446
Fax: +44 (0)1624 898449
Email: info@lilypublications.co.uk
Web: www.lilypublications.co.uk

A CIP catalogue record for this book is available from the British Library.

The contents of this book are believed correct at the time of printing. Nevertheless, the printers cannot be held responsible for any errors, omissions or changes in the details given in this book or for the consequences of any reliance on the information provided by the same. This does not affect your statutory rights.

Contents

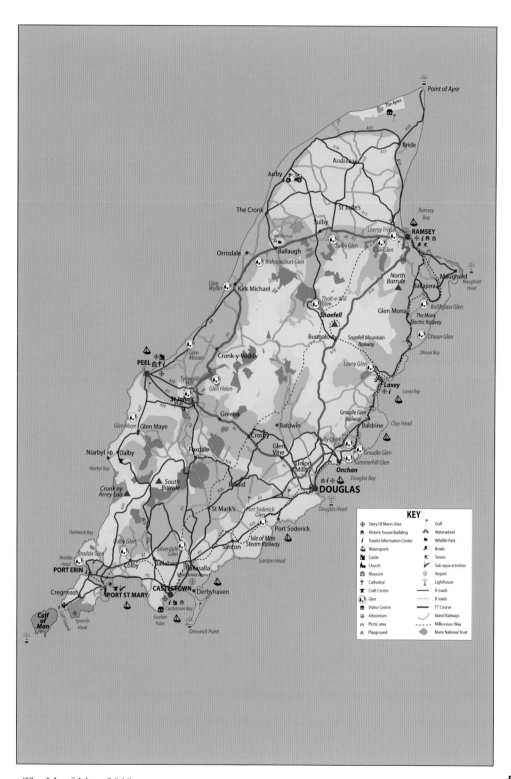

Castletown harbour. (Lily Publications)

Preface

I was informed recently by a well-known Island printer that he turned out nearly one softback book or pamphlet a week on various aspects of the Isle of Man's history, and this takes no account of the several well-established publishers who are also producing Manx books at a steady rate. My excuse for adding to the pile with this book is that, remarkably perhaps, it is the first substantial history of Castletown and I hope it will therefore be useful in filling an obvious gap. Of course, many people have studied and written about the history of the town in specialist articles, and I am indebted to them for much of what I have written here, though I have also tried to do some original research myself.

I am grateful above all to Frank Cowin, RBV, who has been interested in the history of the town, especially the castle, since he was a boy, and whose detailed verbal comments on my first draft amounted to a masterclass which lasted for six hours without a break. Sir David Wilson showed me clearly that the early history of the Castletown area has to be treated with much caution and his wife Eva Wilson helped me with her intimate knowledge of the town in later years. She has been a driving force behind Castletown Heritage and its newsletters, which I have found very useful during my research. Roger Rawcliffe, Michael Hoy MBE, Colin Meakin, Brian Trustrum and Ron Ronan have all been generous with help and information, and, as always, I owe a lot to the knowledge and expertise of the staff of the Manx National Heritage Library, the Tynwald Library and the Henry Bloom Noble Library in Douglas.

As a resident of faraway Onchan, I hardly knew one Castletown street from another before I began my research, so I have been able to approach the task without any sort of bias or preconception. Realizing that there was no history of Castletown as such, Roy & Sue Tilleard decided to commission this one, and I am grateful to Roy for help with details concerning both Lorne House and Callow's Yard. Walking around the town on a dazzling summer's day recently, I could not help thinking how attractive it looked, and how successfully – in the end – it has preserved the best of the past while also preparing for the future. How this has been achieved is the story told in this book.

Derek Winterbottom
June 2010

Low tide at Castletown. (Lily Publications)

Chapter One

BEFORE THE CASTLE

When the runway at Ronaldsway aerodrome was extended in 1935 the contractors unearthed the extensive archaeological remains of ancient settlements, which included six circular structures showing signs of having been badly burnt. There were also many graves and artefacts such as combs, needles, bone pins, finely decorated bronze ornaments and a finger ring, all of which were placed in the Manx Museum.[1] When the airport runways were further extended in 2008 an intensive study was made by archaeologists of an area about the size of 20 football pitches, including the site discovered in 1935. Dating is problematical but from the evidence found there it is likely that people made their homes near what is now the beach at Derbyhaven from Mesolithic times through to the Viking Age and later. The land was highly cultivatable and the creek at the mouth of the Silverburn river, together with the two bays beyond, provided safe shelter for boats.

Close to the Dumb stream on the outskirts of Castletown there was also an Iron Age round house taking the form of two concentric circles about 180 feet across. The outer ring would have been a stockade for animals and the inner ring consisted of the main house constructed with brushwood and wattle walls supported by wooden posts and boasting a central fire-hearth made of marble slabs. There is a model of this house in the Manx Museum.[2]

From the end of the ninth century onwards the Island was colonized by Viking seafarers from Scandinavia who soon established control over the native Manx and asserted kingship of a sort over Man and many of the Western Isles, though they do not seem to have made the Castletown area their headquarters. Instead their main centre was probably St Patrick's Isle on the west coast, which was closer to Ireland where there were allied Viking settlements in Dublin and elsewhere. In 1945 Dr Gerhard Bersu excavated a site close to the sea at Balladoole, near Castletown, which proved to be the pagan ship-burial of a prominent Viking warrior on part of an earlier Christian cemetery set within a prehistoric enclosure. He was buried with many items including high-quality riding equipment, indicative of very superior social status. According to Sir David Wilson, 'The man in the Balladoole boat burial, although he had apparently lived in the region for some time, must…have been an important first-generation Norse settler in the Island.'[3]

Under the Viking leader Godred Crovan (1079-1095) the 'Kingdom of Man and the Isles' emerged as a powerful force as a result of his victory at the battle of Sky Hill near Ramsey, after which he granted most of the south of the Island (presumably considered the most fertile land) to his loyal followers. When he died his sons quarrelled among themselves, which provided an opportunity for the Island to be taken over by Magnus 'Barelegs', the youthful King of Norway. He landed on St Patrick's Isle about 1098 and we are told by the authors of the 'Chronicles of the Kings of Man and the Isles', written at least two hundred years later, that 'seeing the great beauty of the Island, it was pleasing in his sight and he chose to live in it. He constructed fortresses there which still bear his name.'[4] These fortresses were so well known to the monks who wrote the Chronicles that, apart from telling us that they still bore Magnus' name, they did not bother to tell us where they were. This is very tantalizing because neither the buildings nor the names have survived. It is almost certain that one of the fortresses was located on St Patrick's Isle, together with a residence of some kind, which was used by Magnus. Did he construct one of his fortresses on the present Castle Rushen site? We do not know. What is reasonably certain is that Peel has the right to claim the first significant Isle of Man fortress and there are some grounds for considering St Patrick's Isle the first seat of government in the Island.

In 1103 Magnus was killed while fighting in Ireland and Godred Crovan's son Olaf 1 was recognized as king in Man. He took the momentous step of founding Rushen Abbey in 1134 by granting land to the English Abbey of Furness whose monks built a small sister-house there. Between 1192 and 1230 the abbey, by then part of the Cistercian Order, grew rapidly in power and influence and farmed over a thousand of the Island's most fertile acres, though the church and monastery remained small, housing only about 20 monks. The abbey enjoyed the right to appoint the priests at the parish churches of Lonan, Santan, Arbory, Rushen and Malew and the abbey church was a mortuary chapel for some of the kings of Man. The siting of Rushen Abbey so close to the Castletown bays inevitably increased the importance of the area.

Olaf I enjoyed a long and generally peaceful reign but in 1153 three of his nephews plotted against him and one of them, Reginald, pretending to approach the elderly king in order to salute him at a meeting at Ramsey, instead cut off his head with one blow of his axe. Olaf's son Godred II returned from Norway and avenged his father by capturing his rebellious cousins, killing one and blinding the other two. Firmly established as King of

Man and the Isles he then defeated the Viking ruler of Dublin and was accepted as king there. However, through over-confidence he began to rule despotically and made enemies who appealed to Somerled, the ruler of Argyll, for assistance. Godred and Somerled fought a naval battle in 1156 which was indecisive, though it eventually resulted in a division of the Kingdom of Man and the Isles, with Godred retaining Man, Lewis, Harris and Skye, while Somerled controlled Islay and Mull. According to the 'Chronicles', Godred died in 1187 on St Patrick's Isle, which suggests that Magnus' fortress and residence were still in use then as the centre of government.[5]

Godred's illegitimate son Reginald I was chosen to succeed him in preference to Olaf, his legitimate son who was only ten years old, a decision that sowed the seeds of a lengthy civil war in the future. Olaf was banished to Lewis but in 1224, aged 47, he made a bid for power and sailed with a fleet of thirty-two ships to the Castletown bays. He then forced Reginald to agree to share the kingdom with him and sailed back to Lewis. This use of the bays emphasises their suitability as shelter for large fleets, and if the wind was blowing from the wrong quarter, it was possible to carry ships from one bay to the other across the narrow piece of land, only 330 feet wide and with a rise of 32 feet, which became known as Reginald's ford or 'Ronald's way'.[6]

The next significant use of this location came in 1228 when Reginald, having been deposed by the Manx in favour of Olaf, enlisted the support of Scottish lords and sailed into the bays, from where his men disembarked and, according to the 'Chronicles', 'laid waste the entire southern part of the Isle of Man and plundered the churches, killed as many men as they were able to capture, and the southern part of Man was practically reduced to a desert'. Later that year Reginald destroyed Olaf's ships at St Patrick's Isle and 'he then sailed round the land, and seeking peace from his brother he stayed at the port called Ronaldsway for about 40 days'. The final showdown between the two brothers occurred 'at the place called Tynwald' where Reginald was slain. 'Many fell in the conflict', the 'Chronicles' report, 'Then came freebooters to the southern part of Man and ravaged it and left it almost without an inhabitant'.[7]

In 1235 Olaf made a treaty with Henry III of England by which, in return for forty marks and a good deal of corn and wine, he paid homage and committed himself to guarding the English and Irish coasts on behalf of Henry, as well as providing 50 ships when they were needed. This meant that a secure base in the south of the Island would have been useful to safeguard English ships taking the southerly route past the Island. Olaf was succeeded in 1237 by his fourteen year-old son Harold II who further strengthened the treaty with England. Tragically, while returning to the Island from Norway in

The ruined chapel on St Michael's Isle dates from the early 12th century and is the oldest building in the immediate Castletown area. (Lily Publications)

1248 with his new bride Cecilia, the daughter of King Hakon, his ship was wrecked in a storm off the Shetlands and all aboard were drowned. This disaster resulted in a period of confusion during which Harold's brother Reginald II was proclaimed king but he was murdered 24 days later, probably by agents of his cousin Harold who illegally claimed the throne in preference to Olaf's youngest son, Magnus. Hakon of Norway backed the claims of Magnus, summoned Harold to Norway, where he was imprisoned, and sent Magnus, accompanied by Hakon's ally John of Lorn and a Scandinavian fleet, to the Island, where they landed at Ronaldsway in 1250.

The Manx were quite prepared to accept Magnus as king but it seems that power went to the head of John of Lorn who acted as though he were king himself and greatly offended the Manx by his pretensions. In the end John was forced to fight a rearguard action against the Manx on St Michael's Isle and he and Magnus were driven off and returned to Norway. For the next two years the Island was probably under the control of governors sent by Hakon of Norway but in 1252 Magnus returned to the Island on his own authority, 'whereupon all the Manxmen received him gladly and made him their king'.[8] For much of 1253 and 1254 Magnus was an honoured guest at the Norwegian court, where Hakon formally confirmed him as King of Man.

CASTLE RUSHEN

The first surviving documentary evidence for the existence of Castle Rushen comes from the 'Chronicles of the Kings of Man and the Isles' which tell us very clearly that when King Magnus II died in November 1265 he died at Rushen Castle ('apud castellum de russyn') and that he was buried in St Mary's Abbey, Rushen.[9] Armitage Rigby, the architect employed by Lord Raglan to restore the castle in the early twentieth century, was of the opinion that it was Magnus who 'commenced the erection of the stone castle about 1250'.[10] It is possible that Magnus and John of Lorn decided to build a fortification when they arrived at Ronaldsway to claim the throne in 1250, or Magnus might have built it after his acceptance as king in 1252. One of Magnus' major acts as king was to make a formal grant of St Patrick's Isle to the Church, possibly around 1257, and this may be linked to the fact that he had by then built an alternative place of residence and seat of government at Castle Rushen.[11] Given the lack of evidence, we can only guess.

Parts of the original stone fortress still lie at the heart of the present castle and in Rigby's view it probably consisted of a simple stone tower 'about 46 feet square inside'[12] An early 12th century chapel already stood nearby on St Michael's Isle but soon after the castle was constructed it seems that the monks of Rushen Abbey were responsible for the building of another small chapel very close to the walls. Dedicated to St Mary it was presumably intended as a place of worship for the garrison and those encamped around the castle. As with the castle itself, precise dating is problematical but it is likely to have been built by the time of Magnus' death in 1265.[13] It therefore predates by a considerable way the parish church for the Rushen locality at Malew. This was built in the early part of the next century, and it was in the churchyard there that the inhabitants of Castletown, as it gradually developed, were buried.

It is ironic that Magnus II was responsible for the construction of Rushen Castle because he proved to be the last of the Scandinavian royal dynasty founded by Godred Crovan. During his reign the two most important powers in the Irish Sea region were the kings of Norway and Scotland, and Magnus allied himself with Hakon of Norway and joined him in an attack on Scotland in 1263. This resulted in the indecisive battle of Largs but the elderly Hakon died soon afterwards and Alexander III of Scotland threatened to invade Man. Magnus felt obliged to travel to Dumfries and pay homage to Alexander as his overlord. When Magnus died in 1265 leaving only an illegitimate son, Godred, Alexander used this as an excuse to claim the kingship for himself, an arrangement endorsed by the new King of Norway at the Treaty of Perth in 1266.

The first castle as it might have appeared soon after 1250. (Manx National Heritage)

By this time the Isle of Man was firmly established as a Christian community with strong links to the papacy in Rome, and the establishment of Rushen Abbey in 1134 had been followed by the construction of a cathedral on St Patrick's Isle from the 1150s onward and the establishment of a small nunnery in Douglas around the end of the century. There were about seventeen parishes, each with a parish church, and a residence for the bishop at Kirk Michael. There were no towns or even villages, while homesteads, mainly small rectangular houses by now, were based on about 700 quarterland farms. 'Feudalism' as it developed elsewhere in Europe was unknown in Man and the new square tower at Rushen was the only stone castle as yet. The population, which probably consisted of only a few thousand, spent most of their time fishing, farming, and fighting.

Alexander III appointed bailiffs to govern the Island but in 1275 the Manx rebelled against Scottish rule and recognized the late King Magnus' illegitimate son Godred as king. Swift retribution followed when a Scottish fleet arrived at Ronaldsway, and before sunrise on October 8th the Scots attacked the Manx in the darkness, putting them to flight and killing 537 Islanders.[14] However, when Alexander died in 1286 he left only a grand-daughter to succeed him and she died in 1290, so the Scots asked Edward I of England to judge which of the twelve claimants to the throne should be

Castle Rushen as it might have been about 1392 after rebuilding by the two Earls of Salisbury. (Manx National Heritage)

recognized as king. He chose John Balliol, who accepted Edward as his overlord, which was not popular with the Scots. When Balliol renounced this arrangement Edward invaded Scotland, defeated Balliol at Dunbar and removed the iconic coronation Stone of Scone to Westminster. The Isle of Man was taken from the Scots by Simon de Montacute, an English noble, and the kingship passed into English hands. The Scots rallied round a new hero, Robert Bruce, who, during the reign of the weak Edward II decided to win back the Isle of Man and launched an invasion in 1313.

According to the Chronicles 'On the 18th May Lord Robert, King of Scotland, put in at Ramsey with a large number of ships and on the following Sunday went to the nunnery at Douglas, where he spent the night, and on Monday laid siege to the Castle of Rushen, which was defended by the Lord Duncan MacDowell against the said Lord King until the Tuesday after the Feast of St Barnabas the Apostle [June 21] on which day the said Lord King took the castle'.[15] Clearly the garrison put up a reasonable defence in order to hold out for about four weeks. After Bruce had left the Island, however, Edward II's Irish Sea fleet landed and repossessed the castle, but then Bruce demolished Edward II's invading army at Bannockburn in 1314 and he gave the Island to his follower the Earl of Moray who reclaimed it in 1317.

Moray died in 1332, by which time the young English king Edward III was keen to win back lost ground from the Scots and he waged a successful campaign against them in 1332 and 1333 which included sending a fleet from Bristol which seized back the Isle of Man in the king's name. Ignoring the rights of Moray's heir, Edward in 1333 created as King of Man his close friend and supporter William, Lord Montacute, the son of Simon de Montacute, and he also made him Earl of Salisbury in 1337. By the early 1340s Salisbury seems to have asserted his control over Man and according to the English chronicler Geoffrey le Baker he was actually crowned King on the Island. Aware of the continuing danger from Scottish invasion Salisbury decided to build a more impressive stronghold on the Island. Both St Patrick's Isle and the existing castle at Rushen were the two main possibilities, and he chose to strengthen Castle Rushen.

Work probably began soon after Salisbury assumed control of the Island and the stone came from the nearby Scarlett quarry and was set in very hard and gritty mortar. The existing fort was encased in new walls and provided with flanking towers to the south and west and an eastern tower with a twin-towered gateway, all much higher and far more impressive than the original building. Beyond this central 'keep' new curtain walls were built, roughly octagonal in shape and at a distance of about 15 yards from the keep, and opposite the entrance to the keep was the gatehouse to the outer walls containing a large guard-room and kitchen with a vaulted chamber beneath. So close were the new walls to the sea that water lapped up against them at high tide.[16]

According to the Castletown antiquarian and historian Archdeacon Stenning, writing in the 1960s:

> Between the gatehouse and the inner keep was the great drawbridge of the keep across a very deep trench. This drawbridge is unique, in that it normally stood erect in the magnificent arched recess in which it is fixed, and there was a lowering mechanism used when egress from or ingress to the keep was necessary. The keep gateway, too, was guarded by two very strong portcullises, one each side of the very strong door, and the usual 'murder' holes through which could be dropped red-hot stones and molten lead. Inside are two guard-rooms. The gateway opens into the inner court. Access to the rest of the castle from this point was limited to one very narrow spiral staircase in the thickness of the wall, its entrance just inside the gateway, on the right. In the courtyard too are the inner well about 20 feet deep and a stone staircase leading up to the buttery. This is an old staircase, but not the original.[17]

On the first floor of the castle there was a small and dimly lit hall with a dais at one end and the entrance to the kitchen at the other. Further rooms and a staircase led to the second floor, where the arrangements of the first floor were almost exactly duplicated. This would have made it possible for the Lord, when in residence, to have his establishment on one floor and the Governor on the other. A single spiral staircase led to the third floor and each of the east, west and south towers contained one room, with the room in the south tower being used at some point as an oratory chapel. A final spiral staircase led to the roof, from which the surrounding landscape and coastline, as well as many miles out to sea, could be seen on a clear day.

These considerable extensions no doubt took many years to build. The first Earl of Salisbury died in 1344 after being wounded in a tournament at Windsor and his successor as second earl and Lord of Man was his fourteen-year old son, also named William. He ruled the Island for 48 years and although the history of this period is not well documented, it does seem to have been a fairly peaceful time — possibly because William finished the work his father had begun at Castle Rushen, so that by the second half of the century he had a pretty well impregnable fortress from which he could defend the Island if necessary and also keep the Manx under firm control. According to the English chronicler Capgrave, French privateers arrived in 1377 and 'the Frenchmen took the Isle of Man, all save the Castle which Sir Hugh Tyrrel manfully defended: but the men of the Island were fain to give the Frenchmen [money] that they should not burn their houses'.[18] Scottish raiders always remained a threat, and a force under the Earl of Galloway attacked St Patrick's Isle in 1388 and caused considerable damage to the cathedral. Earl William was not as close to Edward III as his father had been and did not play a great part in national events. Nor is it likely that he visited the Isle of Man very often, so it is probable that up to 1392 the new castle was inhabited by a succession of Governors appointed by Salisbury, together with a military garrison.

In 1392 Salisbury decided to sell the kingship of Man to Sir William Scrope for 10,000 marks — a very large sum. Why he did this when the Island had been recognized by the kings of England and Scotland as an autonomous lordship with accepted claims to minor royal status is not clear, but he had no son to succeed him and he may have needed the money. Scrope was ruthless, ambitious, a loyal supporter of King Richard II and regarded as an upstart by the English aristocracy. In order to strengthen his hold on the Island he decided to fortify St Patrick's Isle and obtained a papal Bull dated 1396 authorizing him to build a castle which would defend the cathedral from further attacks. In fact he built a red sandstone gatehouse and part of the curtain wall which encloses the cathedral, St Patrick's church, the round tower and the bishop's house. It is clear that Scrope did not intend this to be his place of residence, however, because no suitable accommodation was built there to rival Castle Rushen. In 1397 the new Peel Castle was put to use by Scrope as the place to hold a distinguished prisoner, Thomas Beauchamp, Earl

Castle Rushen with additions made to its towers and curtain wall, c.1392 to 1405. (Manx National Heritage)

of Warwick, one of the King's main enemies.

Richard II, strongly supported by Scrope, whom he created Earl of Wiltshire, attempted to do what Henry VII achieved a century later – namely reduce the powers of overmighty barons and elevate his own authority as king. Had he succeeded in doing this England might have been saved the convulsions of frequent Civil Wars during the fifteenth century. However, he made the big mistake of unjustly banishing his cousin Henry of Lancaster, who was the heir to his throne, and then of promptly leaving England to campaign in Ireland. In his absence Henry returned to England with an army in 1399, defeated the royal troops and forced parliament to dethrone Richard and proclaim himself king as Henry IV. One of the first targets of the new regime was Scrope, who was quickly executed in Bristol, and Henry bestowed the Isle of Man on his chief supporter, the Earl of Northumberland. When he in turn rebelled against Henry in 1405 his lands were declared forfeit and in 1406 a royal grant awarded the Island and its kingship to Sir John Stanley, to be held in perpetuity as long as he and his descendants provided two falcons at the coronation of future sovereigns of England.

It was probably during the time of Scrope and Northumberland that further additions were made to Castle Rushen. The height of the towers was increased and a much higher and stronger curtain wall was constructed. It is possible that the military architect responsible for these changes was John Lewyn, who did work for Scrope at Bolton Castle and who designed a new keep for Northumberland at Warkworth. [19]

THE STANLEYS, 1406-1504

The Stanley lordship essentially lasted, with breaks, until Revestment in 1765 and throughout this period Castle Rushen stood at the centre of the Island's governance. The administrative structure inherited by Sir John Stanley probably consisted of a Governor and a Council composed of four members – the comptroller, the receiver, the water bailiff and the attorney-general, all appointed by the Lord. Their responsibility was to maintain his authority, defend his legal rights, and collect the revenues owed to him. There were also two deemsters, or judges, who together with the Council held law courts in the Lord's name. The Governor also appointed a 'coroner' as chief officer in each of the six sheadings and also his assistants, called 'lockmen' in each parish. Captains of each parish were also appointed to organize local militias. The Governors appointed by the Stanleys were mostly Englishmen from the lesser gentry of the north-west and they often held office for a considerable time, suggesting that they found the post and its duties congenial. During the fifteenth century the Governors were Michael Blundell (1406), John Litherland (1417), John Walton (1422), and Henry Byron, a man described as being 'of great prudence and severity', who was appointed in 1428 and seems to have held on to the post for several decades.

Sir John Stanley made his way in the world by his wits and his skill as a knight and also by a very advantageous marriage to Isabel, the daughter of Sir Thomas Lathom of Knowsley in Lancashire. His support of Henry IV brought him, apart from the Isle of Man, the lordships of Mold and Hope in North Wales and the position of Lieutenant of Ireland, and he was made a knight of the Garter. He died in 1414 without ever visiting the Isle of Man. His son, also Sir John Stanley, played a far less prominent part in national affairs but paid much more attention to the Island. He first visited it during his father's lifetime and received pledges of obedience from the leading men of the Island, who recognized him as his father's heir. After his father's death he returned to the Island in 1417, prompted by a revolt against the Governor, John Litherland, which was duly suppressed. He was back again in 1422 after another attack on the next Governor, John Walton, when he summoned a special sitting of Tynwald at Kirk Michael and tried the culprits, who were condemned to death. Also on this occasion Stanley received the homage of the bishop and confirmed the Island's laws, being officially referred to as 'Sir John Stanley, by the Grace of God, King of Man and the Isles'. [20]

In the same year Stanley attempted to lift the veil of obscurity which surrounded the role of Tynwald and the Keys in the Island's government by ordering the deemsters to pronounce on the situation. The best they could do was to say that the origin of the Keys was uncertain but that since the time of Godred Crovan the Keys had been 24 freeholders who acted as representatives of the people. Together with the King and his Council the Keys constituted 'Tynwald', a law-making body which could probably be traced back to the Viking rulers of the Island in the tenth century. Throughout the fifteenth and sixteenth centuries the Keys were not a fixed body but were called together, rather like an impanelled jury, when the Lord or the Governor required them. In 1423 Stanley was on the Island again and this time it is on record that he summoned the two deemsters and the 24 Keys to Castle Rushen and asked them to clarify what they considered the Island's constitution to be and how it worked in practice.[21] In 1429 the new Governor, Henry Byron, presided over a Tynwald Court which abolished trial by battle in favour of trial by jury and the following year, at a 'Court of all the Commons of Mann, holden at the Castle of Rushen betwixt the gates', six men from every sheading were chosen by the people of the sheading and the 24 Keys were chosen by the Governor from the resulting 36 men. This potentially democratic arrangement was not, however, maintained and subsequently the Keys were usually nominated by the Governors.[22]

Sir John Stanley II, partly perhaps because he did not involve himself very heavily in English high politics, had given considerable time and thought to the Island and its method of government and he must have resided in Castle Rushen on several occasions. He died in 1437 to be succeeded by his son Thomas who married into the upper aristocracy and by 1439 he was a member of the small group who ruled England in the name of the boy king Henry VI. He was created a peer as Lord Stanley in 1455 and died in 1459 without visiting the Island as far as we know. He left two sons, Thomas the second Lord Stanley and his younger brother Sir William, both of whom played a leading role in the closing years of the civil wars in England between the 'Yorkists' and the 'Lancastrians', largely, it must be said, by managing to change sides at just the right moments. In 1472 Thomas took as his second wife Lady Margaret Beaufort, a direct descendant of Edward III, whose son Henry Tudor had a strong claim to the throne and was the leader of the Lancastrians.

At the battle of Bosworth in 1485 both the Stanley brothers came to the field as reluctant supporters of the Yorkist Richard III, but seeing the way the battle was going, they attacked the royal troops and made a major contribution to Richard's death in action. According to tradition his royal coronet fell beneath a bush and it was retrieved by one of the Stanley brothers, probably Thomas, who placed it on the head of the victorious Henry Tudor, hailing him as King Henry VII. In return Thomas was created Earl of Derby, a title taken from the county town of Derbyshire but also referring to the Lancashire hundred of Derby (now West Derby, near Liverpool) where the Stanleys held great estates. So by 1485 the Lord of Man was one of England's richest and most powerful noblemen, married to the mother of King Henry VII, and right up to his death in 1504 he continued to play his cards skilfully, collecting more power and land along the way. He does not seem to have visited the Island but his family affairs were very efficiently governed from his houses at Knowsley and Lathom as well as the tower built by the first Sir John Stanley in Liverpool. Close watch was kept on the administration of the Isle of Man and in particular the flow of revenues due to the Lord, all of which was the immediate responsibility of the Lord's Governor, operating from Castle Rushen.

THE RENT ROLLS 1504-1603

The first Earl of Derby was succeeded in 1504 by his grandson Thomas who, after leading an attack on the Scots at Kirkudbright, sailed to the Isle of Man in 1507 where he dazzled his Manx subjects with the number of his servants, the magnificence of his household and the gold that he wore upon his person. He took up residence in Castle Rushen for a short time and probably discussed there with Ralph Rushton, his Governor, the results of an inquest held in 1504 into the Lord's traditional rights and the laws of the Island. A prominent member of the Court of Henry VIII, it was he who decided, no doubt wisely, that he would style himself 'Lord of Man' and quietly drop the title 'King', being well aware of the fate of overmighty subjects in Tudor England. He died in 1521, probably only in his late thirties, when his heir, Edward, was only eleven. This was a disaster for the Derby inheritance because Edward became the 'ward' of Henry VIII's ruthless minister Cardinal Wolsey, who controlled his estates for the next nine years, allegedly extracting from them the colossal sum of £5,500.

After Wolsey's death in 1530 Edward became the ward for one year of the Duke of Norfolk, whose sister he was required to marry, raising with her three sons and four daughters. He never visited the Island but he was entrusted by the King with the defence of north-west England and he maintained garrisons of at least 35 men at Castle Rushen and at Peel to guard against possible attacks by the Scots or the French. Moreover in 1533 he sent 40 archers to the Island from Lancashire and 100 men in 1540. Credited with a good knowledge of artillery warfare, it was probably Earl Edward who was responsible for the building of the 'glacis' on the south and east sides of Castle Rushen, which was intended to prevent cannon fire being directed at

The circular fort on St Michael's Isle, first constructed in the 1540s and rebuilt a century later. (Author)

the lowest and most vulnerable part of the walls. At much the same time the circular fort on St Michael's Isle (often known henceforth as 'Fort Island') was built, as well as a similar defence on Pollock Rock at Douglas and a battery at Peel.

Meanwhile, 'Castletown' was beginning to establish itself as a sizeable community. It is likely that a few scattered dwellings surrounded the castle from its earliest days and during the fifteenth century their number grew enough to be considered a large village, probably populated by the families of soldiers, mostly from Lancashire, who had been brought over by the Stanleys. Around 1507 the Derby administration introduced the 'Setting Books', which contained the names of all landowners in the Island as well as the rent owed by them to the Lord. In addition, from 1511 the 'Wast Books' were compiled, recording the admissions, entries and titles of landowners and all rents and fees paid to them. Jim Roscow, a Castletown resident and keen local historian, undertook a great deal of painstaking research into these documents and other surviving rent-rolls during the 1990s and published his findings in two important articles, one dealing with the sixteenth and the other the seventeenth century. They give a good indication of how 'Castletown' developed and much of the information that follows about the town during these two centuries comes from his researches.

A good deal of the land surrounding Castletown was marshy, and Scarlett was cut off from it by a small lake known as 'Rushen Loch', so the initial

Castle Rushen after the building of the 'glacis', c.1540. (Manx National Heritage)

settlement of necessity was situated round the castle and hemmed in to the
north by the harbour and the Silverburn river, which at this time had no
bridge. The first year for which there is a detailed list of the dwellings in the
town is 1506, when there were 72, all of them described as cottages (which
would have been thatched) except for two, considered large enough to be
called 'houses'. By the end of the century there were only 99 dwellings in
total so it cannot be said that there was very much growth in the number of
buildings during the sixteenth century, though the population probably
increased a good deal. Either the Lord or the Church owned all the land in
the Isle of Man at this time and the Lord's control over the domestic affairs of
his subjects could be considerable. In 1535, for instance, Earl Edward wrote
to the widow of Deemster Norris, who had died two years earlier, saying that
he desired that she should marry one of his soldiers, John Keighley. If she did
this, he would allow the couple to live in the late deemster's properties
'which said tenement is now in my disposition to order and dispose at my
pleasure'.[23]

Immediately outside the castle there was a market square and on the
opposite side to the castle there stood a stone-built dais which served as a
market cross from which a bell was rung to signal the start of trade. Also in

the square were a gibbet, stocks and a whipping post and at the seaward end of it there was Diall Hill, a mound with a sun dial on top which was probably constructed between 1506 and 1511.[24] Just off the south-west corner of the square was situated the Governor's House and the Lord's stables, and also West Street, then a dead end because it soon ran into Rushen Lough. One of the most intriguing buildings on this street was 'the Bagnio', the Lord's bathhouse. The main road leading from the Market Square to the hamlet of Ballasalla was the central thoroughfare, which by 1577 was required to be eighteen feet wide, and there were cottages and gardens on either side as far as Paradise Croft. Turning off the east side of the main street was Mill Street, a name derived from two small mills used for grinding corn which had been established there since the late 15th century, with the leases held then by William Stakell and Reynold Skillocorne and in 1506 by William Hopper. All tenants of the town were legally required to grind their corn at these mills, part of the revenues of which went to the Lord.[25]

Another turn-off from the main street farther south was Water Street, leading to a marshy extension of the harbour which became known as 'the Duckpond'. The harbour itself extended much more inland then, covering the area where Hope Street is now. There were no quays along the river bank in the sixteenth century and ships would have needed to settle on the river bottom when the tide was out. Larger vessels would use what was then the Island's main port, Derbyhaven, which presumably was given that name soon after Thomas, Lord Stanley, was elevated to the earldom of Derby in 1485. By ancient custom all able-bodied men throughout the Island were required to keep 'watch and ward' by day and night at long-established lookout stations and the ones that served Castletown were at Ronaldsway and the hill behind Poolvaish farm as well as on the top of South Barrule.

From St Mary's chapel a lane ran along the shoreline towards Knock Rushen, leading to a well which was much used by the people of the town. The chapel itself was still the only town church and it is possible that it had also begun to function as a small school even in the early part of the century before the great events of the Reformation and the dissolution of Rushen Abbey. As early as 1532 Earl Edward had received complaints that the Manx Church charged heavy and unreasonable taxes on a range of items such as death duties and tithes and he set up a commission under his Governor, John Fleming, who reduced many of them. In England Henry VIII took the momentous decision to reject the authority of the Pope and assume the headship of the English Church and closed down the monasteries and priories between 1536 and 1539.

The English Acts of Dissolution made no mention of the Isle of Man yet in 1540 the abbot and remaining six monks at Rushen Abbey, as well as the prioress and nuns of Douglas and the friars of Bymaken were all required to leave. Rushen Abbey, so long a flourishing and powerful neighbour to Castle Rushen and its town, fell into disuse and ruin. St Mary's chapel in Castletown had been founded and maintained by the monks of Castle Rushen but for many years it had been placed by them under the control of a vicar under the authority of the bishop, so the chapel was probably little affected by the abbey's dissolution. According to Roscow the chapel 'was occasionally used as a meeting place for the Court, presumably when bad weather prevented them meeting within the castle gates.'[26] The chapel also became more active than before as the centre for a school, though Roscow's researches suggest that the school was not situated within the chapel itself. He writes:

> The 1523 rent-roll shows a site with no named rent payer which paid 7d rent for a chamber west of the Chapel of the Blessed Mary. This chamber was later noted as the schoolhouse so a possible explanation for the blank tenant entry is that the students were responsible for paying the rent between them. This continued in the 1557 roll and in the 1560s the same chamber was listed, at the same rent, as 'the chamber of the Blessed Mary called the school house'. From the plot sequence the school was among the buildings at the south of the market square and in 1585 the 7d rent was still number 31 in the roll sequence..

However, in 1587 the entry was put much farther down the rent-roll and one Robert Prescot was named as the tenant of what was now described as 'a chamber near the swinestye lately called the schoolhouse'. From this Roscow deduces that 'the school had moved to another location, probably in Church Street.'[27] Meanwhile the Ingate and Outgate records of Castle Rushen mention that in 1578 a salary of four pounds per annum was paid to 'Peter ffarrand', the schoolmaster.[28] So there can be little doubt that there was a school in Castletown throughout the century with a salaried schoolmaster by the 1570s, but we know little more in detail than that.

At this time the two Island deemsters, or judges, operated in two separate jurisdictions, the North (the sheadings of Glenfaba, Michael and Ayre) and the South (Garff, Middle and Rushen). The southern deemster held his law courts 'between the gates' (i.e. in the barbican) of Castle Rushen and this meant that Castletown received a considerable number of visitors when the court was sitting. These were accommodated at various inns, which were inspected by officials called 'harbingers'. In 1577 the harbingers were John Parre and Gilbert Quyn and there were 31 licensed innkeepers on the official list, offering 41 beds. Chief among these early hotelkeepers were Henry Lucas who had four beds available, and John Clerke who had three. The rest

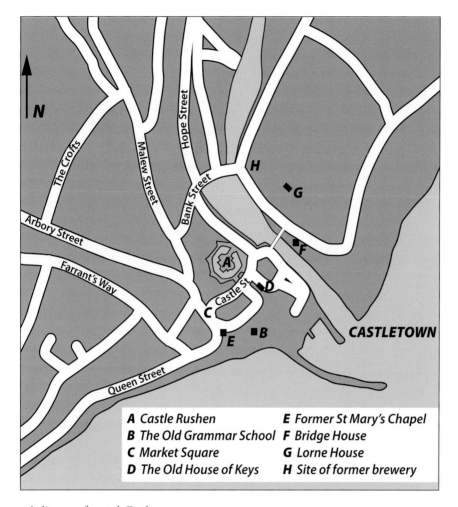

A diagram of central Castletown.

had only one or two.[29] Ale was on offer at these inns and indeed it was a regular feature of the average person's diet at this time. Brewhouses are frequently mentioned in the rent rolls and they generally consisted of a room with a fireplace which was specifically dedicated to the brewing and storing of ale. The ale was brewed first in lead and later in brass pans and a licence was required from the Lord (with fee).[30]

Earl Edward was a religious traditionalist and no great enthusiast for the Protestant Reformation, which he was slow to introduce in the Isle of Man. English clergy were allowed to marry in 1549 but Manx clergy could not do so until 1610. Requiems for the dead were still being said on the Island in 1594 and while England had been provided with new Protestant prayer books, most people on the Isle of Man used Manx Gaelic and could not

27

speak, let alone read, English. It seems that the first resident Protestant priest in the Island was Thomas Allen who came to Castletown in the 1550s to escape from the Protestant purges of the Catholic Queen Mary.

When Earl Edward died in 1572 he was succeeded by his son Henry, who had been a companion of the boy king Edward VI and had been brought up a Protestant. In 1555 he married Margaret Clifford, a great-niece of Henry VIII, who in fact became second in line to the throne as other Tudor heirs died out or were executed. This meant that her two sons by Henry, Ferdinando and William, had strong claims to the throne if Queen Elizabeth, who was not yet married, produced no heirs. Earl Henry lived on a princely scale and he ordered the construction of a substantial domestic house within the walls of Castle Rushen for the use of himself and his family should they choose to visit the Island one day.[31] In fact they never did and he died in 1592 having overstretched even his impressive resources, so that he left considerable debts to his son Ferdinando. Only one year later Ferdinando also died, aged 35, probably from peritonitis, and this caused major problems in the Stanley family because he had no son but three daughters, to whom in his will he left a large share of the Stanley lands, while his younger brother William succeeded to the Derby title. William, in fact, had actually been appointed Governor of the Island in 1593 and the rent roll of 1593 shows him paying 40 pence rent for the Governor's House.[32] So here is the first Stanley to become Lord of Man who was a resident in Castletown for more than a few weeks.

After Ferdinando's untimely death a legal dispute followed between the new Earl William and his brother's very determined widow Alice who claimed the Lordship of Man and other Stanley honours on behalf of her daughters. Since the 'Spanish Armada' of 1588 England had been at war with Spain, and Queen Elizabeth's advisers regarded it as too much of a risk not to have the Isle of Man firmly under control, so in 1594 the Crown resumed the Lordship pending a legal settlement of the disputed Stanley inheritance. The Queen appointed Sir Thomas Gerard as 'Captain' (or Governor) in 1595 and gave him the task of recommending how best the Island could be defended, and he asked for more arms and ammunition to be sent over from England with which he fortified Castle Rushen and Peel Castle. In 1596 he left to take part in an attack on Cadiz and the Queen replaced him with Peter Legh without reference to Earl William. Indeed, in 1598 the Privy Council declared that Henry IV's grant of the Island to Sir John Stanley in 1406 was null and void for technical legal reasons and returned the Lordship to the Crown. This was a ruthless move made by the English Government at a time of great national danger and is yet another reminder of the political reality that when backs are to the wall, might often supplants right. Elizabeth died in

1603 but she is traditionally credited with having given Castle Rushen the famous clock with one hand whose dial is now displayed on the south wall. It bears the inscription 'Eliz. Reg. 1597' but the present mechanism dates from the early eighteenth century.[33]

Some of the main changes in Castletown's life during the 16th century have been indicated by Jim Roscow who found that:

> New land was acquired from the bog, the number of plots increased and the number of rentpayers nearly doubled. By the end of the century properties were being purchased and inherited. The availability of a grammar school in the town meant that there was the opportunity of bright young men to get well-paid employment within the Lord's administration at the castle. The rise in population and the increase in buildings had given rise to a growing number of trades, and second sons from farms, who could not expect to inherit the family estate, began to take up trades within the town. The passing on of property to Manx names in the rent-rolls for the late sixteenth century reflects the attraction of the town, which had not been the case at the start of the sixteenth century when Lancashire names predominated.[34]

So by the end of the Tudor period Castletown was certainly a thriving community with an increased population, even though the number of its dwellings had not grown a great deal over the past hundred years. Castle Rushen would have appeared then much as it appears today and it was the busy centre of a garrison town, the home of the Governor and his administration and the place where law courts were held by the southern deemster. The castle had been visited by Earl Henry for a short time and used by Earl William when he was Governor and several other members of the Stanley family had held the post of Governor during the century. These were Henry (1527-1532), George (1536-1545), William (1545-1552) and Henry again (or another Henry) (1552-1570) and finally Randulph who succeeded Earl William for one year (1594-1595). This adds up to 41 years of the century, showing that the post of Governor was regarded as a valuable and honourable position for junior members of the Stanley family who would have had a considerable impact on life in the town. The Stanley connection also meant that the post of Governor would have seemed reasonably prestigious and attractive to the fourteen other men from outside the charmed circle of the Stanleys who held the post during the century and who were at the centre of Castletown life. Whether the Stanleys would recover their Island Lordship depended upon the attitude of England's new Scottish king, James I.

THE BURNING OF THE WITCHES, 1617

Earl William and dowager Countess Alice naturally pressed their cause with James and argued that they had been dispossessed unfairly. James referred the matter to his senior judges who in 1607 confirmed the Privy Council's decision of 1598 but pointed out that the Stanleys had nevertheless been recognized as Lords of the Island between 1406 and 1598 by successive English sovereigns and hinted that the King should perhaps follow in the spirit of justice rather than the letter of the law. For the time being James effectively gave charge of the Island to his minister Robert Cecil who was the uncle of William's wife Elizabeth, and by 1609 Cecil had engineered a compromise by which Alice's three daughters gave up their claims in return for large cash settlements and the Lordship of Man was granted to William and his wife jointly and to their descendants. Hence Cecil neatly arranged a share in the Island for members of his own family.

This long-running dispute was a blow to the financial strength and political power of the Earl of Derby. The 1609 agreement meant that the former Stanley lands and the Lordship of Man were still held by the Earl but heavy legal costs together with the payments made to his three nieces and their mother, as well as the debts incurred by his father, put him under severe financial strain. William devoted most of his time and energies to his English estates and left the Isle of Man to the care of his wife, Elizabeth. Neither of them came to Castletown but she was very much in charge of the Island's affairs between 1612 and her death in 1627 and petitions from the Island during these years were routinely addressed to her. After Governor Peter Legh left Castle Rushen in 1599 the Crown appointed as his successors Cuthbert Gerard (1599), Robert Molynieux (1600) and John Ireland (1609) while Sir Frederick Liege (1623) and Edward Holmewood (1626) were appointments of Countess Elizabeth.

It was during the period when Countess Elizabeth was responsible for the government of the Island that the shocking affair took place of the burning to death in the Market Square in Castletown of a woman and her young son accused of witchcraft. A papal Bull in 1468 condemned witchcraft and this led to the persecution of alleged witches throughout Christian lands for years to come, though there are only three cases on record of witches being condemned to death in the Isle of Man. One was Alice Ine Quay but she was reprieved in 1569 after her case had been reviewed by a jury of 'six honest women'. However, King James I wrote a treatise against Demonology in 1597 while still King of Scotland and he lost no time in passing an Act against witchcraft in 1604, the year after he succeeded to the English throne. In 1617 Margrett Inequane and her son were accused of witchcraft, apparently because she had been caught trying to work a fertility rite in order to ensure good crops. According to one Island historian:

> After being found guilty in the Ecclesiastical Court by a jury of six drawn from the parishes affected by their alleged practices they were, according to law, handed over to the temporal power by the Bishop's chief executive officer, the General Sumner. In 1617 mother and son appeared in the Head Court before the deemsters and a jury of twelve out of several sheadings, with the advice of Chapter Quest men. When they had deliberated on their verdict the foreman of the jury for Life and Death was asked by the deemster, according to the ancient custom, Vod y fer-carree soie? (May the Chancel-man sit?) Cha vod – (He may not), was the reply, for the Jury, like their fellows in the ecclesiastical court, had found the accused guilty, and the Bishop or Chancel-man, who occupied a place among the judges, left the Court to avoid being involved in the shedding of blood. Thereupon the dread sentence was pronounced: 'That she be brought by the coroner of Glen Faba to the place of execution, there to be burned until life depart from her body'. A like fate befell Margrett's son, who, with his mother, died at the stake erected near the Market Cross at Castletown'.[35]

Though the burning of witches in other parts of the British Isles occurred all too frequently during the sixteenth century this was the last time the death penalty for witchcraft was imposed in the Isle of Man, perhaps because of the moderating influence played by the Manx ecclesiastical courts and the reluctance of Manx juries to convict. A Kirk Arbory woman accused of being a witch in 1666 was spared the death penalty and instead performed three public penances, while the last witches to be tried formally on the Island, Ealish Vrian of Ballaugh in 1712 and Jony of Kirk Braddan in 1717, were imprisoned for thirty days and fourteen days respectively.[36]

LORD STRANGE, 1627-1643

On the death of Countess Elizabeth in 1627 Earl William made the unusual decision to retire from public life and the management of his affairs and lived somewhat reclusively in a modest house in Chester. He formally gave responsibility for running his estates, including the Isle of Man, to his eldest son James, aged just over twenty. James used the title Lord Strange because the eldest son of the first Earl of Derby had married the heiress to the ancient barony of Strange of Knockin in the late 15th century and so brought this second peerage into the family. In 1626 James married Charlotte de la Tremoille who was a daughter of the Duc de Thouars and a grand-daughter of

William, Prince of Orange, the Protestant hero and effective leader of the United Provinces of the Netherlands. Their grand wedding ceremony took place at The Hague, attended by several Protestant ruling princes. James was not a favourite at the Court of the new English king, Charles I, because Charles had married a Catholic French princess, Henrietta Maria, and together with Archbishop Laud he was intent on pursuing 'High Church' policies in England. James and his wife were not in tune with this and tended to remain at home in Lancashire, raising their six children and concentrating on restoring the Stanley estates to profitability.

As part of his plans to raise more money James attempted to change the system of land leases on the Island, known as 'the straw tenure'. In 1406 Sir John Stanley would have been regarded as the owner of all the land not in the possession of the Church, and all landholders were his tenants. However, over the years the leases had tended to be renewed automatically and tenants began to regard the land as theirs to sell or pass down to their heirs, formally handing over a straw from the land in the presence of one of the Lord's officials. This system was recognized in the Manx courts during the 16th century and confirmed by King James I in 1607, but in 1630 Strange sent commissioners to the Island with instructions to dismantle this arrangement and offer instead leases lasting for either three lives or twenty-one years. Based at Castle Rushen, the commissioners met with very strong resistance and achieved very little apart from creating the impression that Strange was keen to deprive the Manx of long-established rights. To his credit, however, it is on record that in 1631 he 'gave unto William Langley, son unto my servant Matthias Langley, Constable of my Castle of Rushen, the yearly pay or pension of six pounds towards his education in the University of Cambridge'.[37]

It seems that Strange visited the Island during the 1630s and stayed in Castle Rushen, which gave him the opportunity to become familiar with the buildings in Castletown and how they might be reorganized to the benefit of himself and the town. Roscow discovered that:

> The rent rolls show him take over the rent of Diall Hill at the south end of the Market Square and its associated gardens and workshop, from Thomas Teare. He bought the two garden plots for thirty-two shillings in 1638, reducing Teare's rent from eight pence to one penny and thereby enlarging the square to the benefit of the town market. Also within the Market Square the Lord paid the forty pence rent of the recently-built Governor's house. The Lord's stables and haggard, or stack yard, were off the north-west corner, near this house, and he took over a plot at four pence from Peter Robinson, in West Street, to provide an outlet from his

haggard.....In a different category was the Lord's acquisition of the property of William Faragher and Thomas Huddleston, rent six pence, as they were found guilty of highway robbery in England and sentenced to transportation. Being convicted felons the land fell into the Lord's hands under Manx law.[38]

These details would have been trifling to the Stanley coffers in financial terms but they do show that Strange and his officials were involved to some extent with the domestic buildings of the town though there seems to have been little attempt to impose any organized scheme for growth and development.

From 1640 onwards Strange was caught up in the growing political crisis in England which led to civil war. In August 1642 King Charles raised his standard at Nottingham against a Parliament determined to prevent him from ruling in future without consulting them. In October Strange's father died and he succeeded as the seventh Earl of Derby. Of about 130 members of the House of Lords some eighty supported the King and fifty supported Parliament and although James had disagreed with Charles' religious policy he had no hesitation in defending his royal rights and placed his own services and the wealth of the Stanleys at the disposal of the King. He raised a force of 5,000 men and contributed £40,000 – a colossal sum - towards the King's military expenses, and he was appointed one of the royalist commanders in the North-West. He was not, however, a natural military leader and he failed to capture Manchester or to prevent Preston and Lancaster falling to the enemy. He had no success in his attacks on Bolton and Lancaster in February 1643 and was soundly defeated at Whalley in April. The King and his advisers decided that he would be of more use defending the Isle of Man from possible Scottish attacks and he sailed to the Island in June 1643.

Probably to his great surprise he found that he was faced with serious critics of his own rule on the Island, led by Edward Christian of Maughold in whom he had placed great trust in the past. Christian was a successful naval commander who had won the support of the Duke of Buckingham, the favourite of Charles I, and Derby had appointed him Governor of the Island in 1628, a position which he held until he was dismissed, apparently for being considered too greedy, in 1639. In January 1643 Strange commissioned him to train all the able-bodied men in the Island but Christian seized upon this as an opportunity to create his own private militia with men who had been required to take an oath of loyalty to himself. One of his chief demands was that there should be an elected House of Keys to which the Lord should defer, a policy that revealed him to be a parliamentarian in the English style. John Greenhalghe, the Governor since 1640, was not able to deal with this situation and he also faced strong popular objections to the paying of tithes to the Church – a grievance which always reared its head at times of popular discontent. On his arrival Derby dealt with this crisis quite skilfully and he called a meeting of the Lord's Council and the Keys not at Castle Rushen, interestingly, but at Peel Castle, where he set up a Commission to inquire into grievances and managed subsequently to have Christian arrested, tried at Castle Rushen in December, fined a thousand marks and imprisoned.

In March 1644 Derby sailed back to England because he had left his wife and daughters at home at Lathom House, suitably fortified, but since February it had been under siege from enemy troops, and Countess Charlotte was bravely defending her position. Derby joined Prince Rupert and marched to relieve Lathom after a siege of eleven weeks. Rupert's troops, including Derby, captured Bolton on the 28th of March but massacred a thousand soldiers and civilian men – one of the worst atrocities of the war – and this made Derby a marked man in the eyes of Parliament. In July 1644 the royal forces, including Derby, were defeated at Marston Moor, Lathom was besieged again and by September 1644 Derby and his wife and family had retreated to the stronghold at Castle Rushen. In December they learnt of Lathom's fall and total destruction.

THE DERBYS AT CASTLE RUSHEN, 1644-1651

Charles I's defeat at Naseby in 1645 ended the first civil war, after which there were a series of complex moves leading to the outbreak of a second civil war, when Charles was supported by the Scots. Oliver Cromwell's defeat of the Scottish army at Preston in 1648 ended that adventure and he pressed ruthlessly for the trial of the King and his execution, which took place in January 1649. In England Parliament abolished the monarchy and the House of Lords and set up 'The Commonwealth' with a republican constitution. During all this time the Derbys were in residence in Castletown with their family, officials and retainers, constituting a small court. The existing accommodation in Castle Rushen was not suitable for them so in 1644 work began to enlarge the 'The Derby House', built in Earl Henry's time towards the end of the previous century, which was now provided with more spacious and elegant accommodation. Probably at the same time the outer defences of the Castle were strengthened by the construction of a new gun platform outside the castle gates, and in 1645 a second fort was built on St Michael's Island 'for the defence and safety of the harbour of Ronaldsway' and armed with 'one whole culvrain … and one demi-culvrain'.[39]

From 1644 until 1651 Earl James, Countess Charlotte and their family literally held court at Castle Rushen, doing their best to live in considerable style and putting on masques, balls and entertainments for the leaders of

Derby House, within the walls of Castle Rushen. (Author)

Manx society. In this way they maintained a little royalist outpost in the middle of the Irish Sea while all around them they saw only, in a saying popular at the time, 'the world turned upside down'. An account of one of the early entertainments put on by the Derbys at the castle runs:

> The Right Honourable James Earl of Derby and his Right Honourable Countess invited all the officers, temporal and spiritual, the clergy, the 24 Keys of the Isle, the coroners, with all their wives and likewise the best sort of inhabitants of the Isle, to a great masque, where the Right Honourable Charles, Lord Strange [Derby's eldest son and heir], with his train, the Right Honourable Ladies, with their attendance, were most gloriously decked with silver and gold, broidered works and mostly costly ornaments, bracelets on their hands, chains on their necks, jewels on their foreheads, earrings in their ears, and crowns on their heads; and after the masque to a feast which was most royal and plentiful....[40]

It is likely that James sponsored some horse racing on the Langness peninsula, imitating the fashionable races that had begun at Newmarket early in the century. Certainly his son Charles decreed after the Restoration in

Figure 1. The north-east corner of Castle Rushen, from a drawing by Daniel King, late 1640s. (Manx National Heritage)

1669 that 'It is my good will and pleasure that the two prizes formerly granted for horse racing and shooting shall continue as they did be run or shot for and so to continue during my good will and pleasure'. The course was probably about three furlongs and seems to have started and finished on the Castletown end of the peninsula.[41]

Among those who came to Castletown when the Derbys were in residence in the late 1640s was one Daniel King who amused himself by making several wash drawings of the castle and the town, from which simplified engravings were made. It is unlikely that he was a professional artist because the drawings are essentially 'primitives' which are inaccurate in some respects and certainly encounter problems with perspective. However, we must be grateful that we have them at all because they are not just the only contemporary illustrations of Castletown which survive from the sixteenth century, but also the earliest of all the illustrations of the Island. King's view of the north-east side of the castle (Figure 1) shows that no quays had yet been built on the river bank but does reveal the position of the new gun platform. Figure 2 shows the castle and glacis from modern Castle Street but King probably opted not to put in any of the houses round about in order to present an uninterrupted view. On the right can be seen the gable of the Derby House built for the Earl and Countess in 1644.

The remaining two drawings give us a glimpse into the Market Square. In Figure 3 there is what is probably a wooden gibbet standing on the right hand

Figure 2. The castle and glacis from modern Castle Street. (Manx National Heritage)

side, from which criminals would be hanged by the coroner, and next to it a diamond-topped stone which was the public whipping post. There is no sign in this drawing of the clock dial, which might have been somewhere inside the castle at this time. Two drag carts and one with wheels are pulled by rather small horses, and fashion apparently dictated that all individuals should wear hats. Figure 4 gives a more detailed view of the Square. Diall Hill has gone and the buildings on the left consist of three inns with the Governor's house in the far left corner, surrounded by a wall.[42]

While resident on the Island Earl James renewed his efforts to abolish the existing system of tenure in favour of leases which he offered for either 21 years or three lives and he appointed four commissioners who made considerable headway in introducing this new scheme, despite its unpopularity. Some tenants who accepted new leases assumed that they would no longer be subject to ancient 'feudal' obligations such as providing food for the Lord's garrisons and household but the situation remained unresolved, causing further discontent. An Act of Tynwald declared in 1645 that it was illegal to sell land without the Lord's permission and tighter restrictions were placed upon tenants who did not pay their rent. Rules introduced in 1429 concerning weights and measures were enforced with strict punishments for offenders.

When the bishopric fell vacant in 1644 Derby did not nominate a new bishop but fulfilled the bishop's secular responsibilities himself and also

Figure 3. The Market Square. (Manx National Heritage)

retained the bishop's lands and revenues – which were not particularly valuable, with rents worth only £116 in 1645. All these policies, designed to improve the Lord's financial position, do Derby little credit, though it does seem that he had some success in encouraging the manufacture of garments made of loaghtan wool and he wore woollen clothes himself. He considered establishing a university or place of higher learning on the Island but events overtook him before he was able to make any progress with this enlightened notion. The one positive gain was that Derby used some of the episcopal revenues to maintain four grammar schools, at Peel, Douglas and Ramsey as well as the one at Castletown.[43]

Largely as a result of his implication in the massacre at Bolton and also because he insisted on holding out for the royalist cause in the Isle of Man, Derby was not offered an amnesty by the Commonwealth and his offer to buy back his confiscated estates for £15,572 was refused. When the Commonwealth sent messages requiring the surrender of the Island in the summer of 1649 Derby replied, saying that if they made any more such demands he would burn the paper and hang the bearer. In Scotland Charles I's son had been recognized as King Charles II and Derby transferred his loyalty to him, inviting all royalist supporters over to the Island from where, he stated, 'we will unanimously employ our forces to the utter ruin of these unmatchable and rebellious regicides, and the final destruction of their interests both by land and sea'.[44] The Commonwealth's response to this was formally to divest Derby of the Lordship of Man and bestow it upon Lord Fairfax, previously the parliamentary commander-in-chief.

Though Derby's attitude might seem foolhardy he felt that he could rely on support from the Scottish royalists and during the years of his residence in Castletown he had built up significant military defences which included 288 cavalry of all ranks as well as infantry militia and garrisons in the castles and forts. He also had at his disposal a useful naval force whose main vessel was the frigate 'Elizabeth', under Captain Bartlett, supported by a number of long boats with 16 oars and 2 guns, and although one of these boats was captured by parliamentary forces in 1643 his 'Island navy' held off five enemy ships in 1644 and prevented an attack on the Calf of Man. Derby himself related an episode in 1650 when he was nearly killed in Derbyhaven harbour in what he considered was a possible assassination attempt:

> I escaped a great danger of being killed in a Manx boat coming from Captain Bartlett's ship at Derby Haven, a shot being fired from the said ship (whether by chance or no is doubtful). It was, as is pretended, a mistake of one piece for another but it was charged with musket bullets, pieces of iron, etc, which killed my dear friend Mr Richard Weston and a man that rowed and wounded Colonel Snead in a grievous manner, and I sitting in the midst of them escaped by the great goodness of Almighty God'.[45]

Figure 4. Another view of the Market Square. (Manx National Heritage)

39

A COUNTESS IN DISTRESS, 1651

In 1650 some of Derby's daughters who were still in England were imprisoned and the Commonwealth began to dispose of his estates. Charles II appointed him a knight of the Garter and gave him command of the royalist insurrection that was being planned in the north of England. In March 1651 Commonwealth ships attempted an attack on the Island but were repelled by Derby's naval force and in August he appointed his wife as regent and set sail for England in seven ships with a force of some 300 soldiers, many of them Manx. They landed on the banks of the river Wyre in Lancashire on August 15th but were crushed at Wigan on the 26th. Derby escaped and joined Charles II at Worcester where the royalist army was defeated by Cromwell on September 3rd. Soon afterwards Derby surrendered to parliamentary forces in return for a promise that his life would be spared, and he was imprisoned in Chester Castle. Oliver Cromwell was determined that he should die, however, and he was tried for high treason and, as an act of revenge, taken to Bolton where he was beheaded on October 15th 1651, aged 44.

Meanwhile, on the Isle of Man his wife the Countess Charlotte was faced with another rebellion, this time led by William Christian. A member of the family long established at Milntown near Ramsey, William had been a member of the Keys in 1637 and 1643 and his father, Deemster Ewan Christian, handed over to him the farm and estate at Ronaldsway in the latter year. Derby appointed him water-bailiff in 1644 and receiver-general in 1648, an important office which made him responsible for collecting all the Lord's rents and customs duties. When news reached the Island of the defeat of Charles II at Worcester many leading Manxmen, Christian among them, felt that to hold out against the Commonwealth any longer would be futile, especially as an expedition was assembling in North Wales under Colonel Robert Duckenfield, intent on invading the Island.

Christian and others felt that the sensible option would be to enter into negotiations with London but Countess Charlotte, without consultation, sent a letter to Duckenfield at Beaumaris offering to surrender the Island in return for her husband's life. Christian feared that a surrender of this kind would lead to a loss of all the special rights enjoyed by the Island for centuries and that it would simply be incorporated into the Commonwealth as a part of north-western Britain. Moreover he and many other Manxmen felt that Derby had governed the Island more in his own interests than those of the Manx, particularly in his determination to change the system of land tenure and his other money-raising schemes. Christian considered that the wisest thing to do was to co-operate with the British invading force and enter into peaceful negotiations. So he collected a force of about 800 men at his house at Ronaldsway on October 19th 1651 and they swore an oath of loyalty to him rather than to the Countess. He then secured most of the forts on the Island, though Peel Castle and Castle Rushen remained loyal to the Countess.

Duckenfield's invasion force arrived off Ramsey on October 25th and Christian sent a message saying that there would be no opposition to his landing, and accordingly the British soldiers were free to take up siege positions outside both Peel Castle and Castle Rushen. On the 29th Duckenfield sent a message to the Countess informing her of her husband's death ten days earlier and asking her to negotiate. No doubt in deep distress Charlotte did nothing and on the 31st her own soldiers inside Castle Rushen, probably Christian's men, opened the sally port which let the besiegers through the outer wall. At this point Charlotte capitulated and agreed to give up Castle Rushen and Peel Castle in return for being allowed to leave the Island unharmed, with her family and friends.

William Christian's role in all this has been much debated, with some considering him a traitor and others a patriot. He was certainly disloyal both to the Earl, whose official he was, and to the Countess, whose defeat he engineered. However, the result of his actions and the Countess' departure were that Castle Rushen and Castletown escaped the total destruction that would probably have followed their capture after a siege, while the Government in London, having already granted the Lordship of Man to Lord Fairfax, decided in the circumstances not to interfere with its unusual constitution, which was allowed to continue much as before. It is very unlikely that this would have happened if Duckenfield had been forced to conquer the Island after a tough campaign. As it was, the Keys, together with four men from each parish, convened at Castletown on 23rd February 1652 and formally proclaimed Fairfax as Lord of Man, though he was not present personally.

Fairfax had been the commander of the parliamentary forces from 1645 to 1650, during which time it is claimed that he never lost a single battle, siege or storm. But he resigned in 1650 rather than obey orders to attack the Scots, his former allies, and was replaced by Oliver Cromwell. He lived in retirement in Yorkshire and was free to take an interest in his Lordship of Man so it is perhaps surprising that he never visited the Island, probably because he suffered considerably from wounds gained in battle and from poor health. However, he took a close interest in the Island's affairs, especially in the details of the financial revenues due to him. After Countess Charlotte's surrender, Duckenfield stayed on at Castle Rushen as Fairfax's Governor until replaced by Matthew Cadwell. He remained in charge until 1656 when Fairfax took the rather risky step of appointing William Christian as Governor, bearing in mind the fact that he would have had both friends and enemies on the Island. Moreover Christian also continued to hold the office of receiver-general, which meant that he was responsible for the collection and administration of all the Lord's revenues and also those of the diocese, as there was still no bishop. For a while he was a very powerful man.

However, in 1658 Fairfax replaced Christian after only two years with his deputy James Chaloner, whom he instructed to undertake a comprehensive audit of the Island's financial affairs. This can only mean that Christian was suspected of corruption and indeed Chaloner's findings were that the accounts for the years 1650-1659 contained many irregularities and he accused Christian of embezzling about £1,000 and dismissed him from the office of receiver-general. Christian left the Island and lived on his estate in Lancashire, leaving his sons to pore over the financial details and attempt to rescue their father's reputation, which they did with some success.

Meanwhile events moved swiftly in England after the death of Oliver Cromwell in 1658. His son Richard abdicated from his inherited post of Lord Protector after a few months, opening the way for a power struggle between General Lambert and other rivals. Lambert prevailed upon Lieutenant John Hathorne, the officer in charge at Peel Castle, to arrest Chaloner and he was held captive in Peel Castle from November 22nd to December 27th. By then Lambert's bid for power had been thwarted in London and Parliament ordered the release of Chaloner, who promptly issued instructions that no ship should transport Hathorne from the Island and made preparations for his trial in 1660.

Observing the crisis in London, Fairfax emerged from retirement and threw his weight and influence behind General George Monck, the Commonwealth's commander in Scotland, who had decided that the best way out of the present problems was to restore the monarchy under Charles II. Tired of the Commonwealth and its short-lived expedients and experiments backed by a thinly disguised military regime, the people of London received the new king with rejoicing and acclamation and on the Island Chaloner went on a progress accompanied by the Keys, the Captains of the Parishes, the civil and spiritual officers and sixty cavalry, proclaiming Charles II King at the Cross in Peel on May 28th, at Castletown the next day, at the Cross in Douglas on the 30th and at Ramsey Cross on the 31st, each occasion being accompanied with 'shouting, shooting of muskets and ordnance, [and] drinking of beer, with great rejoicing'. Soon after this Chaloner died, as a result, so his son claimed, of his having taken 'a death sickness as the result of his imprisonment in Peel Castle'.[46]

Given that Castletown was at the centre of the more or less incessant political intrigues and manoeuvres between 1651 and 1660 with the siege of the Castle, the departure of the Stanleys, the new Lordship under Fairfax, the suspect administration of Governor William Christian, his denouncement by Governor Chaloner, Chaloner's own imprisonment and release and finally the restoration of the Stuart monarchy and the Stanley Lordship, life for the townspeople cannot have been entirely dull during these years and there were doubtless many days when they clustered in their houses round the Market Square, agog to discover what was going to happen next.

William Blundell, a member of the Lancashire gentry, came to live in the Island from 1648 to the mid-1650s and wrote about aspects of life there at the time. According to him three quarters of the people who lived in the four main towns were Manxmen and a quarter were 'foreigners'. He noticed a steady growth in the number of shopkeepers, who were the most prosperous citizens, often owning two or three properties, where many of them took in lodgers.[47] Blundell described Castletown as having 'one formal street' and 'a handsome piazza, which is the market place, with a cross in the middle'. Official records from 1648 and 1650 note that 'West Street' in Castletown was 'dirty and foul by reason of the unevenness thereof and that there is no passage for the conveying of the water thereout' and orders were given that the parishioners of Malew should come with horses, carts, spades and other implements to assist homeowners to repair the street'. Though it was probably a little larger than Douglas in the 1650s, Castletown was still a small place with fewer than 600 inhabitants.[48]

THE DEATH OF WILLIAM CHRISTIAN, 1663

While Charles II was restored to his throne in London, Charles Stanley, eighth Earl of Derby, resumed his father's Lordship in Man. Monck received a dukedom, riches and honours for the part he played in the Restoration, and Fairfax, who had also supported the return of the King, might also have sought great rewards. Instead he gave up his Lordship of Man quietly and retired again to Yorkshire where he died in 1671. In England Parliament passed an Act of Indemnity, which granted a general pardon to all anti-royalists except a small number of men still alive who had signed Charles I's death warrant. However, on the Isle of Man Lord Derby was determined to punish those who had rebelled against his parents in 1651 – possibly prompted by his mother, who was still alive. He declared a general amnesty in February 1662 but exempted William Christian as well as two members of the Keys, Ewan Curghey and Samuel Radcliffe, and John Caesar, Lieutenant of the Malew Militia. The last three were imprisoned but Christian was in London where he had spent several months in the Fleet Prison because he owed a debt of £20,000. After his release he played into Derby's hands by voluntarily returning to the Island in September 1662, assuming that the Act of Indemnity applied also to him.

Here lies

ILLIAM DHONE

WILLIAM CHRISTIAN
of RONALDSWAY

Shot to death at Hango Hill
2nd January 1663

A modern memorial to 'Illiam Dhone' by the Manx sculptor Bryan Kneale, in Malew Church. (Lily Publications)

On hearing this news Derby issued a warrant for Christian's arrest and he was imprisoned in Castle Rushen. In November he was indicted for treason by a six-man jury, though at his trial at the Court of General Gaol Delivery in Castle Rushen he refused to plead. The authorities consulted Deemster Norris who in turn consulted the Keys who, in their role as a High Court of Law, decided by a majority verdict that Christian's life and goods should be at the mercy of Derby. Looking for a unanimous verdict for the death sentence Derby dismissed seven members of the Keys, replaced them with more pliable men, and unanimity was achieved. Nowell, the Deputy Governor, then commuted the customary traitor's sentence of being hanged, drawn and quartered to being shot by a firing squad, and Christian's execution was carried out at Hango Hill on January 2nd, 1663. This was the site of an ancient burial-mound on the road to Derbyhaven, long used as a place of execution. Later the Stanleys built a small, castellated summerhouse nearby, of which the remains can still be seen opposite the present south entrance to King William's College. The records of Malew Church state that Christian 'died most penitently and most courageously, made a good end, prayed earnestly, made an excellent speech, and next day was buried in the Chancel of Kirk Malew'.[49]

While imprisoned in Castle Rushen Christian composed an appeal to the Privy Council in England, arguing that Derby's actions were in breach of the Act of Indemnity. The petition did not reach London until a week after his death but his case was pressed by his sons and in due course Derby, the two deemsters and three members of the Keys were summoned to London to hear the Council's decision that 'the Act of General Pardon and Indemnity did and ought to extend to the Isle of Man'.

The Council ordered that Christian's estate and possessions should be restored and the deemsters were for a time detained as prisoners in London. Whatever misdemeanours and acts of rebellion or corruption Christian might or might not have committed, this verdict of the Privy Council condemned his execution by Derby as illegal and increased the status on the Island of 'Illiam Dhone' ('Brown William', because of his hair colour) as a martyr to Manx nationalism.

Chapter Two

THE BARROW TRUSTS, 1663-1679

E arl Charles put an end to his father's policy of keeping the bishopric vacant by appointing his friend and former tutor, Archdeacon Samuel Rutter, to fill that role. He was installed as bishop in October 1661 but died six months later. Derby then appointed Dr Isaac Barrow, who was consecrated bishop in Westminster Abbey in July 1663 and also succeeded Roger Nowell as Governor in 1664. After 1660 the Governors abandoned the house formerly used by them in the Market Square and occupied the more splendid 'Derby House' within Castle Rushen, moving out to make way for the Lords when they made their comparatively rare visits to the Island. Although Barrow, as Bishop, was entitled to live at Bishopscourt it seems that he spent most of his time in residence in Derby House.[1] In these twin seats of authority he was a powerful man until his departure from the Island in 1669 and he made a lasting impression on Castletown and the Island at large through his educational foundations. A royalist and High Church follower of Archbishop Laud, Barrow was the son of an East Anglian squire and had been a Fellow of Peterhouse, Cambridge, and then chaplain at New College in Oxford. Considered one of the brightest of the rising generation he was nevertheless forced into retirement during the Civil War and did not again come to prominence until the Restoration, when he was appointed a Fellow of Eton College and Vicar of Downham.[2] A man with high standards in scholarship, he was not impressed with what he saw in his new diocese, as he made clear in a well-known diatribe:

> At my coming to the Island I found the people for the most part loose and vicious in their lives, rude and barbarous in their behaviour; and – which is I suppose the cause of this disorder – without any true sense of religion, and, indeed in a condition almost incapable of being bettered; for they had no means of instruction, or of being acquainted with the very principles of Christianity. Their ministers, it is true, took upon them to preach; but were themselves much fitter to be taught, being very ignorant and wholly illiterate; having had no other education than what the rude place afforded them: not many books among them, nor they intelligent of any but English books, which came very rarely thither. The poverty of the clergy gave no encouragement to such merchandise, their livings not amounting to above

five or six pounds per annum, which forced them to engage in all mechanical courses, even in keeping of ale-houses, to procure a livelihood; and this also, together with their ignorance, rendered them despicable to the people, who yet had no way of instruction but from their mouths (for there is nothing either written or printed in their language, which is peculiar to themselves; neither can they who speak it best write to one another in it, having no character or letter of it among them); whose manner of officiating in their churches was by an extemporary translation of the English Liturgy into the Manx language; and so likewise of the Holy Scriptures: which, how inconvenient for the people and injurious to the Scriptures it must needs be, we may easily judge, when done by such as do not perfectly understand the English, and much less the meaning of many Texts and Scripture. This being their condition, I suppose the best way of cure would be to acquaint the people with the English tongue, so that they might be in a capacity of reading Catechisms, and books of devotion: and for this purpose to set up an English school in every parish; and withal to fit the children for higher learning, in a Grammar School, which was also wanting. And, to vindicate the clergy from contemptible poverty, and free them from the necessity of base employments, an increase of their maintenance was necessary.[3]

It is probable that Barrow exaggerated the educational weakness of the clergy through having no knowledge himself of Manx. James Chaloner had found that 'considering the ministers are generally natives, and have had their whole education in the Isle, it is marvellous to hear what good preachers there be'[4] and when Governor he continued to use money from the bishop's estate to maintain the existing four grammar schools.[5] William Blundell felt the same, considering that 'Their ministers truly are not unlearned. I did not converse with anyone but that I found him both a scholar and discreet'.[6] Nor is it true that the Island was devoid of books because there had been a good many in Castle Rushen when it surrendered in 1651 and Lord Fairfax added considerably to their number. A century later Bishop Hildesley, still finding inadequacies among the clergy, decided that the answer was to provide Manx translations of the Bible and Prayer Book and Barrow might have achieved much by taking that course, but clearly he considered Manx a barbaric tongue and probably would not have entertained the idea. Instead he embarked energetically on a series of initiatives designed to achieve his new educational vision for the Island.

What he needed most was money and Charles II promised £100 a year from the King's Bounty to be paid out of excise revenue (though this proved to be far from a reliable source) and the rest Barrow managed to raise over a period of about five years through an Isle of Man Appeal to the great and the good in England for 'the erection of a free school in the said Island and of an English school in the several parishes thereof, and also for the augmentations of stipends to the poor livings of that Island'. The Dean of Gloucester gave a princely £100 as did Mrs Hall, the widow of the Bishop of Chester, and most bishops and deans made a contribution. By 1669 £916 had been raised and £1,041 in 1670, when the King's Bounty was paid three years in arrears. Lord Derby's contribution was to sell to Barrow, for £1,100 of the money raised, the tithes which had formerly belonged to the Island's monastic houses and which had found their way into Henry VIII's treasury in the 1540s: James I had honourably returned them to Earl William in 1609. Derby was not particularly generous in this deal: the sale was based on a 10,000 year lease which required Barrow's 'Impropriate Fund', as he called it, to pay back £62 a year and an additional £130 every thirty years.[7]

By 1669 Barrow had established the principle that the vicar of every parish should be responsible for setting up a school for the teaching of English in the parish, and in return he would benefit from an increased stipend. The Church laws required children to attend these 'petty' schools and in 1672 Earl Charles made it clear that:

> All farmers and other tenants in my Isle of Man of what degree and quality soever do and shall send their eldest sons and all other their children to such petty schools as they are capable wherein if any do fail or be remiss…[they] shall not only be fined severely but their children made incapable of bearing any office or place of trust … for want of such literature and education.[8]

The new parish school in the Castletown area was at Malew, though the town's own grammar school still existed. However, Barrow made no specific arrangements to fund this older Castletown school, or the other three grammar schools on the Island.

Indeed, it was his main intention that the new parochial schools should all be feeder schools for one new 'Free Grammar School' for the Island. He could have located this in Douglas, which had a similar population to Castletown by the late 1660s and was more centrally placed in an era of very poor roads, but he chose to establish it in Castletown. The master was to be paid £30 a year, a salary which ranked in the top ten of English grammar school stipends at the time, and the building chosen was St Mary's Chapel. Henry Lowcay was recorded as master in 1671 and he remained in post until succeeded by Gilbert Holt in 1686 and later by David Jenkins who was succeeded in 1695 by John Woods.[9] Whether the words 'Free Grammar

St Mary's Chapel, Castletown, converted into a Free Grammar School c.1670. (Lily Publications)

School' meant that the school was open to all children or that the tuition should be free remained unclear at the time and for many years to come.

Having thus established what we would now describe as a system of 'primary' and 'secondary' education, Barrow sought to set up a university college on the Island where the brightest pupils from the Free Grammar School could proceed to higher education. This college would be funded by two new trusts, the Academic Students' Fund and the Academic Master's Fund. In order to endow the Students' Fund Barrow acquired the farms of Ballagilley and Hangohill, just outside Castletown, and he leased them to John Norris, the Constable of Castle Rushen, stipulating that £20 a year should be used to send two students from the Free School at Castletown to the University in Dublin. Each student would receive a scholarship of £10 a year for five years, after which he would be obliged to return to serve the Island community.

Barrow's plan to make a university education accessible to able Manx students was thoroughly laudable but the farm of Hangohill was acquired entirely against the will of the sitting tenant, John Lace, who had been in dispute with the Lord about the precise nature of his lease since the time of Earl James. The Keys had judged this case on three occasions, finding in Lace's favour each time, and he had been firmly in possession of the farm since 1660. However, in 1667 Barrow decided to strike and as the land in question had formerly belonged to Rushen Abbey he held a secret session of the Abbey Court in Castle Rushen which dispossessed Lace of his farm. Archdeacon Stenning's account of what happened next is worth quoting at some length:

> Never before had an Abbey Court been held in Castle Rushen. No notice was served on Lace, who was not present. The Bishop sat as Governor, Bishop, Clerk of the Rolls and plaintiff! No consideration was given to the tenancy or ownership of Lace. No surrender of his claim was offered or referred to by the Court. No mention of compensation or alternative accommodation was made. No conveyance of any kind was drawn up. The proceedings of the Court were not entered into the book until a considerably later period, and then in the wrong place! The act was one of blatant confiscation. No time was lost. Lace was served with notice to quit. In fact he was away from home. His wife refused to go.
>
> The Bishop acted quickly. He appeared in person with his officials at the farmstead of Hangohill. The wife, staunch soul, refused to quit, and defied the Bishop. He sent to Castle Rushen to ask for Ensign Norris to bring a company of soldiers. They duly arrived, and proceeded to act with ruthless cruelty. Mrs Lace and her infant [son] at breast were sent to the dungeons of Castle Rushen. She had no food for four days. She and her infant suffered very seriously under the harsh treatment. At the end of the four days, the Bishop sent her four pennyworth of bread!
>
> At Hangohill the farmstead was unroofed, as also were the outhouses. The corn in store was destroyed by the weather. The cattle were driven to the shore and several calves killed by the soldiers. No protection was left against wind and weather. Lace himself returning in a few days was arrested and committed to the dungeons in Peel, and after eight days of ill treatment the wife and infant were released from Castle Rushen.[10]

Lace appealed for release and his case was heard by the Keys on December 4th and they found unanimously in his favour. So Barrow produced arguments casting further doubt on Lace's title to the farm, which a minority of the Keys accepted, though the majority still supported Lace. Barrow then turned for support to Earl Charles who summoned the compliant minority to Knowsley, and egged on by the Bishop, they persuaded him that the tenants of the Abbey lands were a threat to the authority of the Stanleys. Derby responded by informing the majority of the Keys that their attitude was 'rude and unjustifiable' and that if they did not agree to the transfer of the farm to the Bishop, their own land would be seized, among other penalties. Faced with this dire possibility, the Keys gave in and sanctioned the transfer on June 9th 1669. In Stenning's view, 'There is no more blatant case of the application of *force majeure* by the Lord in Manx history.'[11]

Barrow relented to some extent, releasing Lace and allowing him to graze two cows on Hangohill. Lace died soon afterwards but his infant son Henry grew to maturity and in 1698 unsuccessfully sued the Barrow trustees for restitution of the farm. Another appeal failed in 1704 but in 1708 the case was heard in the High Court where the trustees put their case in the hands of the then Academical Master, William Ross. The Court found for the Lace family and the trustees were ordered to give up Hangohill farm but Ross appealed in July and the verdict was overturned. The Laces might have appealed to the House of Lords but they could not possibly afford the expense. So the trustees remained in possession of the farm.[12]

In 1669 Barrow was appointed Bishop of St Asaph – hardly great advancement as it was a poor diocese in North Wales – but he continued to be Bishop of Sodor and Man in addition for one more year and he used all the profits from the Manx diocese (about £359) to set up The Academic Master's Fund which, together with other monies, was used to provide a salary for 'a public reader of logic, philosophy and history'. Trustees were appointed to administer this fund until such time as it was possible to erect a suitable school for higher learning. Here Barrow shows himself to have been more generous because he could no doubt have diverted the Manx diocese revenues into his own pocket had he so wished. The first 'reader' to be appointed was William Gostwicke, followed by John Shaw, but in 1681 a visitor to Castletown noted that though there was a school at one end of St Mary's Chapel, there was only one schoolmaster, receiving £60 a year, who taught the pupils in the Grammar School as well as 'reading logic and philosophy to four Academic Scholars, who are habited in black wide-sleeved gowns and square caps and have lodgings in the castle and a salary of £10 a piece ..'[13] So by the time of his death in 1679 Barrow's vision had not been fully realized, and though he had successfully set up three funds they were administered by different trustees who would often find themselves in disagreement over the coming years. Nevertheless, he left Castletown considerably more a centre of learning than it had been when he first took up his duties as Bishop and Governor.

A NEW CHAPEL AND LIBRARY 1698-1710

Meanwhile Castletown was expanding, though at a leisurely pace. Queen Street seems to owe its name to Catherine, the widow of Richard Quayle. The street had been extended westwards in 1577 after the enclosing of land from the quarterland farm at Knock Rushen and between 1675 and 1700 Catherine Quayle acquired three plots of land on the street. She built a small ale house on one and a brew house on another and according to Jim Roscow, 'local legend has it that in fine weather she sat outside her inn using as her chair an old Manx-style bee-hive made of wooden sallies and straw. This gave rise to her nickname of "The Queen of the Hive" and hence her house was shown in the rent roll as "Queen Hive House" and led to the eventual naming of the street as Queen Hive Street.' On a map of the town dated 1833 this had been reduced to plain Queen Street.[14]

The land across the river had been granted to Rushen Abbey by King Olaf in the mid-twelfth century and was in its possession until after the dissolution in 1540. At that point the Taubman family, who had been soldiers at Castle Rushen in the 1550s, acquired the former abbey lands at the Bowling Green, extending almost to the present-day airport, for which they were paying the considerable rent of 32 shillings and four pence by 1611. John Taubman, who lived in Bowling Green House, took up one of the new 21-year leases offered by Earl James in 1645 and extended this for another 21 years in 1666, though he paid less for it on account of the fact that he had suffered a big loss when his kiln, which had been full of corn, caught fire, and when the river constantly flooded a considerable part of his land – probably the area of the present Poulsom Park. Around 1666 the first bridge to span the Silverburn was erected outside the castle gates, roughly where the footbridge is now, and the Taubmans began to sell off plots of land on their side of the river. It is likely that by 1696 a stone quay had also been constructed.[15]

There is no record of Earl Charles having visited the Island but he died in 1672 and was succeeded by his son William, who was about seventeen. He came to the Island in 1686 and again in 1691, when he presided over Tynwald. Aware of continuing discontent over the question of leases, he appointed commissioners to resolve difficulties and came to Castletown a third time in 1699. Unlike many of the Stanley Lords he seems to have been genuinely interested in the Island and its affairs and in 1698 he compiled a list of improvements he hoped to make, which included the need to 'perfect Derbyhaven'. Unfortunately he died prematurely in 1702, leaving the Island to his younger brother James. Before his death, however, he appointed to the bishopric in 1698 a young man whose influence would be felt on the Island for the next fifty-seven years. This was Thomas Wilson, born the son of a Cheshire farmer in 1663, who had studied at Trinity College in Dublin and served as a priest in Ireland and Cheshire until becoming tutor to Earl William's family.

Within months of his arrival on the Island Wilson decided that the old Chapel of St Mary's, partly a school as we have seen, was inadequate for the religious needs of Castletown, and in any case, he disliked the use of religious buildings for secular purposes – especially as schools, whose pupils tended to be irreverent. He managed to raise some money to buy and demolish some of the cottages at the south end of Market Square, and Thomas Looney was contracted to build on this site a new chapel, partly furnished with items from the old one. The new St Mary's was built across the road to Knock Rushen and the piece of the road around it leading into Market Square was named Chapel Street. Several years later, in 1714, a steeple was built to embellish the front of the new building. The old St Mary's could now be re-organized purely for scholastic use and Thomas Looney was also engaged to make these alterations, eventually receiving £235 for all his work in 1704. A new wing was added so that the building could house both the petty school and the Grammar School but even so it was not big enough and the petty school returned to its former premises in 1708 . The official view was that, as the people of Castletown would benefit from the improvements to the Grammar School, they should pay for them, and it was ordered that:

> Whereas the Grammar School House of Castletown was, about two years ago, repaired, glassed and made much more commodious with a chimney in it for the use of the scholars that are or shall hereafter be educated at the school, and forasmuch as the voluntary contributions towards that work have not extended to discharge the expenses of it ... the churchwardens are ordered to collect an assessment from the inhabitants in and bordering the town to clear off the arrears due to the several workmen. [16]

Wilson also took a major step towards firmly establishing Barrow's ideal of a 'university level' of education by housing the Academic Master and his scholars separately from the Grammar School. Henry Bridgeman, bishop from 1671 to 1682 had attempted to move the 'university' to the derelict buildings of Rushen Abbey but this imaginative, if ambitious, scheme had foundered on financial grounds. Wilson's plan was to house the Academic Master in a new Library to be built in Castletown. When the castle was surrendered in 1651 the inventory included '265 great books, 54 gilded, and many small books beside', and these were augmented by a gift from Lord Fairfax of 217 books, mostly religious and in Latin. Since then there had been further donations of books by the Stanley family. In 1706 Wilson received permission from the Governor, Robert Mawdesley, 'to enclose and take in …a parcel of waste ground near the house of Arthur Halsall, porter…provided the Great Enquest of this sheading do first view the same and see that it be in no way prejudicial to any highway or water-course'. [17]

By April 1710 a two-storey building had been constructed on this site at a cost of £83, much of which Wilson funded himself. In 1709 the Keys, who up to this time had no designated meeting place other than in Castle Rushen, decided that a sum of £20 should be raised and employed 'towards the erecting or procuring of a convenient place in [Castletown] for the 24 Keys to meet in upon public business'. Wilson came to an agreement with the Keys by which in return for the £20 he offered them the use of the ground floor rooms in his new building 'to be the place of their sitting and meeting for ever'. The upper floor housed the Library, together with the Academic Master, William Ross, and his students. The precise size of this building is not known but it stood on the site of the present Old House of Keys and a woodcut illustration of 1790 shows that it had four 'Georgian' windows on the upper floor and two on the lower floor, with two doorways in addition.[18]

Wilson was very concerned about the education of the academic students and wanted the teaching of theology to be supplemented with logic, metaphysics and ethics as well as mathematics, geography, astronomy and natural philosophy, no doubt influenced by John Locke's 'Thoughts on Education', published in 1690. He also recommended to Ross that the students should read the Greek New Testament daily, translating a chapter at least every afternoon. Laziness was to be strongly avoided because, he wrote, 'A habit of trifling, not resisted, will insensibly grow upon you'. Later Wilson taught students himself in his residence at Bishopscourt, which in this respect became another branch of his little Manx 'university'.[19]

MAKING LITTLE PROGRESS, 1681-1726

Castletown's Market Place was often the scene at this time of the public punishment of individuals whose penalties would seem today to be barbaric. In 1686 Thomas Corlett had his ears cut off in the pillory and was fined twenty shillings for 'contemptuous expression against the Lord', while in 1691 John Quilliam was ordered to be 'set in the pillory upon Saturday next at Castletown, for the space of one hour, and have his ears nailed thereunto, and pay a fine of £20'. The town's main street had always been the one which led to Rushen Abbey via Ballasalla and after the dissolution it came to be known as Church Street because it also led to the parish church of St Lupus at Malew, where all burials took place. The second turn to the right up Church Street was by now called Mill Street because a small horizontal mill operated beside the river. A larger mill, owned by Thomas Moore, was fitted with an undershot waterwheel from 1644 onwards and was situated at Golden Meadow. Moore was obliged to grind the Lord's grain free, while the townspeople were required to provide straw thatch for both mills. By 1651 there was a postal service of sorts because the townspeople paid 20 shillings a

year as a contribution to the cost of paying a postman to walk to St John's
Chapel with letters. In 1703 the postman was Robert Corrin and it was
probably necessary to take letters for posting to his house in East Church
Street.[20]

However, these developments were not enough to preserve Castletown's
traditional position as the Island's largest and most prosperous town because
the well-informed traveller Thomas Denton wrote that by 1681 Douglas had
become 'the place of the greatest resort in the whole Island, because the
haven is commodious … unto which the Frenchmen and other foreigners are
used to repair'. The customs duties (to the nearest pound) for the four main
towns in 1690 reveal the situation clearly – Douglas came first with £31, Peel
second with £16, Ramsey third with £13 and Castletown well behind with
only £7. In 1721 Bishop Wilson described Douglas as 'much the richest town,
the best market, and most populous of any in the whole Island'. At the turn
of the century the townspeople complained to the Governor that 'this
metropolis, the place of your Honor's and the officers' residence scarcely
appears to be a market town, which exposes us to the contempt and ridicule
of all strangers'. A few years later they petitioned that farmers 'should be
compelled to come to their market instead of going to Douglas'.[21]

Unfortunately the situation was that the ports at Douglas and Peel were far
more safe and convenient than the primitive and risky facilities offered at
Derbyhaven and it was inevitable that trading ships would go elsewhere.
Ramsey had good facilities also but its development was seriously delayed by
a massive storm in 1630 which almost destroyed the existing town. So by
1700 Castletown, though still the Island's capital and administrative centre,
had been outstripped by Douglas in population and was the least prosperous
of the four main towns judged by the customs duties.

Castletown and the other main towns were by now under the control of a
captain in each town who was granted a commission giving him 'full power
and authority to command the peace, suppress riots, commit offenders, and,
either by himself, if occasion so require, or by the assistance of his
soldiers…to execute all civil actions, arrests, rules, orders, judgements,
processes, assistances and other proceedings of the several courts, both at law
and in equity'.[22] Clearly the towns were dirty places because in 1701 the
official record noted that the citizens did not keep their towns 'in that
decency and cleanliness they ought to do' and they were ordered to sweep
the streets thoroughly and forbidden to keep cows in the streets or allow pigs
to stray from their back yards. Soldiers from Castle Rushen, who filled the
role of police at this time, were instructed to make sure that these orders
were complied with. In 1713 the Keys decided that all pavements and streets
in market towns should be even and regularly paved by the citizens and began

to regulate this process. The generally insanitary conditions led to frequent visitations of serious diseases in all the towns, which claimed many victims and prevented a significant rise in the population. The first attempt at a census of the Island's population was made in 1726 and it came up with a figure of 14,426, of whom only 2,530 lived in the towns. According to this census 810 people lived in Douglas, 785 in Castletown, 475 in Peel and 460 in Ramsey. The accuracy of the census may be suspect but it does confirm that by then Castletown was not the largest town, though by only a slender margin, suggesting that both Denton and Bishop Wilson were exaggerating somewhat in their assessments of Douglas' superiority in 1690 and 1721.[23]

'THE FATHER OF HIS COUNTRY', 1704-1737

Earl William's government of the Island had been productive and enlightened but his death in 1702 without a male heir meant that he was succeeded as Earl of Derby and Lord of Man by his younger brother, James. He fought with distinction in the Duke of Marlborough's army and attained the rank of major-general but resigned in 1705 to marry and manage his estates. From the first he realized that the long-standing grievances concerning Manx tenure needed to be resolved and he asked Bishop Wilson to consult with the Keys and suggest some solutions. In 1704 he accepted most of Wilson's proposals, which became the basis of the Land Settlement Act of that year. In effect the 'straw tenure' system was retained – a victory for all those who had resisted the seventh earl's attempts to change it. In return for paying a fixed rent to the Lord, tenants would in future be able to bequeath or sell their land or property.

Having put that problem behind him, Earl James had next to deal with increasing unrest among members of the House of Keys. In 1688 the 'Glorious Revolution' in Britain had seen Parliament remove the Catholic James II from office and replace him with the Protestant William III, emphasizing the growing constitutional power of the Legislature. Under Earl William, Governor Sacheverell had accepted that the Keys were 'the representatives of the country' who 'in conjunction with the Governor and officers make the legislative power of the nation' and claims were made that no new laws could be enacted or customs introduced without the consent of the Keys and the deemsters.[24] However, Sacheverell's successor, Colonel Nicholas Sankey, took a less lenient view in 1697, ignored some of the constitutional claims of the Keys and even committed two members to prison for criticizing his policies. No wonder, then, that the Keys in 1710 were pleased to find a new home for themselves in Bishop Wilson's library, outside the castle walls.

Soon after his accession Earl James was asked by the Keys to agree to

Balladoole House, home of the Stevenson family for many generations. (Author)

legislation which would establish their right to be consulted on political and
financial issues concerning the Island, but he took no action. In 1715 the
Deputy Governor, Alexander Horne, acting on behalf of the titular Governor
the Hon. Charles Stanley, Earl James' brother, treated the Keys as though
they were merely a criminal jury and when they refused to act as such he
imprisoned all of them in Castle Rushen and also fined them 20 shillings
each. This was an outrage and it prompted a bold response from John
Stevenson, whose family had been established on the Balladoole estate near
Castletown for several generations. Born about 1655 he was the son of Major
Richard Stevenson of Balladoole, who has the distinction of being the first
Manx officer recorded in the British army, and he later served as deputy-
governor of the Island and receiver-general. His mother was Isabel, the
daughter of Deemster John Christian of Milntown in the north of the Island,
a member of another long-established family. John Stevenson is on record as
having been the leader of the Keys by 1704 and he had also served as an MP
at Westminster.[25] In 1714 he built a new 'Queen Anne' mansion at Balladoole,
a few hundred yards away from the original family home, and it has survived
reasonably intact as one of the Island's finest houses.

In 1719 the Keys asked Stevenson to take a petition to Earl James at
Knowsley Hall, making many complaints about the arbitrary nature of his
government and in particular the imprisonment of MHKs. As a result of this
a Tynwald Court met at Castle Rushen under Governor Horne's presidency
to seek an agreement, but none was reached. Stevenson then wrote to the

Earl making further complaints, as a result of which he was called before the Governor and Council and briefly imprisoned in Castle Rushen and then imprisoned again in 1722, this time for supporting Bishop Wilson in his suppression of a book entitled 'The Independent Whig' which advocated free-thinking principles.[26] In 1723 the Keys authorized Stevenson to appeal to the Privy Council for redress against Earl James and this prompted a response from Derby emphasizing that the Keys were a self-electing body with little substantial claim to represent the people.

Subsequently Governor Thomas Horton, who was appointed in 1725 and served until Earl James' death in 1736, successfully repressed the constitutional claims of the Keys and indeed dismissed eleven of them, replacing them with more compliant candidates. Clearly Stevenson had no time for Horton and he was accused in 1727 of saying that Horton forced labourers to weed his corn and of treating the Governor disrespectfully at the summoning of the Arbory militia, though the charges were not proved. Stevenson died in 1737 and his chief contemporary admirer was Bishop Wilson, who described him as 'the Father of his Country', while Wilson's biographer, John Keble, considered him 'an unflinching champion of popular rights and liberties'.[27] There is a memorial to him in the present House of Keys in the form of a stained glass medallion, which places him alongside a handful of the Island's most notable historical figures.

A BISHOP IN PRISON, 1722

Whereas Bishop Barrow lorded over Castle Rushen as Governor of the Island, Bishop Wilson found himself a prisoner in a dank cell there in 1722 on the orders of Governor Alexander Horne. Horne was Deputy Governor from 1713 to 1718 and Governor from 1718 to 1723 and he was under orders from Earl James to protect the ancient rights and prerogatives of the Lord. This had already brought him into conflict with the Keys and he had not flinched from imprisoning many of them as well as their Speaker, John Stevenson, as we have seen. Nor, when the occasion arose, did he flinch from imprisoning the Lord Bishop. The basic problem was that Wilson reduced the money fines levied by the ecclesiastical courts, replacing them with other punishments and penances which he was very zealous in imposing, taking the view that slackness was rife throughout the Island and immorality widespread. This irritated the Derby regime because the fines were paid into the Lord's treasury, which suffered from their reduction, while in his determination to impose Church discipline the Bishop was often considered to be interfering in matters which were outside his proper jurisdiction. In 1716 Wilson excommunicated a woman who had refused to do penance for an offence and she appealed to Derby, who summoned the Bishop to a hearing of the case. He refused to attend, considering that appeals should go to the Archbishop of York. For this Derby fined him £10, though this was later remitted.

In 1720 Horne refused to provide a military guard to take ecclesiastical offenders to court and in 1721 he imprisoned and fined the Bishop's registrar John Woods, who was the Vicar of Malew. Woods had already been imprisoned once, in 1719, for refusing to give up a document to the Governor until he had the Bishop's authority to do so. In 1721 Horne ordered that an appeal for charity to a starving family should be read out in all the southern churches but Woods refused to do this until he had consulted the Bishop and was promptly fined over three pounds and imprisoned for a week. Later Horne summoned Wilson and his two vicars-general to answer charges that the ecclesiastical courts were assuming powers that the law did not give them, and that Wilson called Convocation illegally. Wilson and his assistants refused to comply and the storm blew over for the moment. Then a soldier who was part of the garrison at Castle Rushen sinned and voluntarily offered to do the prescribed penance of the Church, but for doing this he was tried by a military court in Castle Rushen, imprisoned for fourteen days and drummed out of the garrison.

The final argument erupted in 1722, originating from a petty squabble between the Governor's wife and another lady, whom Mrs Horne accused of

Bishop Thomas Wilson. (Manx National Heritage).

making slanderous remarks about her. Wilson considered that Mrs Horne was at fault and when his Archdeacon, Robert Horrobin, supported her, he dismissed him. The Archdeacon was also the Governor's chaplain and Horne argued that the Bishop therefore had no jurisdiction over him, and, supported by the Council and the deemsters but not the Keys, he signed an order on June 25th which fined him £50 and the vicars-general £20 each. According to the historian A.W.Moore, who was also an experienced Island lawyer, 'this, being without the sanction of the House of Keys, was, of course, absolutely illegal'.[28] They all refused to pay the fines and Horne ordered the three of them to be imprisoned in Castle Rushen.

They stayed in prison for nine weeks and it seems that Wilson's cell was the small, dark and uncomfortable ground floor guardroom to the left of the entrance to the keep, while the vicars-general were held in the guard-room to the right. According to John Keble, 'the concern of the people was so great that they assembled in crowds, and it was with difficulty that they were restrained from pulling down the Governor's house, by the mild behaviour and persuasion of the Bishop, who was permitted to speak to them only through an open window, or address them from the walls of the castle'. Wilson's son later claimed that 'the horrors of the prison were aggravated by the unexampled severity of the Governor not permitting the Bishop's housekeeper …to see him, or any of his servants to attend him, during his whole confinement, nor was any friend admitted either to the Bishop or his vicars-general'.[29]

On the advice of the Archbishop of York the prisoners appealed to the Privy Council, which eventually ordered their release. Wilson, despite his strictness, was very popular among the Manx people because of his personal humility, generosity and gifts as a preacher and public speaker. People came from all over the Island to kneel at the window of his cell and receive his blessing, and at the news of his release there was, according to Keble, great jubilation throughout the Island and 'never were there more sincere congratulations than were expressed on this occasion. Old and young, rich and poor, broke forth into acclamations of joy, and formed such a procession as had never before been witnessed'.[30]

Upon his release Wilson prepared a case against Derby, Horne and other officials, which was considered by members of the Privy Council. They decided in July 1724 that the order of June 25th 1722, which did not have the sanction of the Keys, was therefore not a legal order of the Tynwald Court and that the Governor had acted beyond his proper authority. Moreover they agreed with Wilson that Horne had been in contempt of the royal authority because of his reluctance to obey their Orders in Council and they ordered his arrest. However he had either resigned or been dismissed from his post as Governor in 1723 and probably escaped punishment. He must certainly be considered as one of the most unsatisfactory Governors in the Island's history but Earl James was not prepared to give in to Wilson, and Governor Thomas Horton after 1725 not only took a tough line against the Keys but he also declared that the Island's separate spiritual laws had been abolished when it became part of the province of York in 1542. Wilson appealed again to the Privy Council but this time he received little support and up to his death in office at the age of 93 in 1755 he gradually lost his battle to increase the power of the ecclesiastical courts on the Island.

TWO JAMES MURRAYS, 1736-1761

James, Earl of Derby, who, though he never visited the Island must be considered one of the most repressive of the Stanley Lords of Man, died in February 1736, aged 71, leaving no children. This brought the long rule of the House of Stanley to an end because, though the earldom passed to a distant cousin by male descent, the Lordship of Man, by the terms of the grant made by James I to Earl William in 1609, passed to the heirs of his son Earl James and Countess Charlotte, and through the female line if necessary. One of their daughters married the Marquess of Atholl and their grandson James Murray, the second Duke of Atholl was, according to these rules, declared the rightful heir to Man. The new Earl of Derby contested this decision in 1738 but the Court of Chancery, which worked notoriously slowly, eventually dismissed his claim, though not until 1751.

In fact it was in the interests of the British Government that the Murrays should replace the Stanleys because since 1660 the Manx had come to see that there was a lot of money to be made in 'the running trade' (i.e. smuggling) by which tobacco, tea, brandy, spirits and wines were bought in France, Spain, Portugal, Norway and Sweden and shipped to the Island where the Lord's low customs duties were paid. Then they were re-shipped to destinations on the west coast of England where they were sold secretly to individuals and organizations who thereby avoided the very high rate of customs duties (about 10%) imposed in the UK. Earl James had allowed this trade to prosper because he gained a lot of revenue from the Manx customs duties but the UK Treasury gradually realized that they were losing vast sums as a result and Prime Minister Robert Walpole made an agreement with Atholl in 1733 that he would not oppose his succession to the Lordship of Man if Atholl would agree to sell his sovereign rights (including the customs but not his estates) within seven years of becoming Lord. So in theory Atholl became Lord of Man in 1736 only for seven years, but during this time Britain became involved in a major war with France, Walpole went out of office and the issue was shelved for the time being.

Derby had been very unpopular in the Island and for that reason few tears were shed for either his passing or that of the House of Stanley. The Duke of Atholl, as the new Lord, dismissed the ruthless Governor Horton and appointed as Governor his namesake James Murray, a former soldier in the clan regiment and the heir to a baronetcy, who worked in the British Treasury. Having arrived on the Island Murray required the Keys and principal officers to meet him in Castletown four days later and at this meeting his Commission from Atholl was read out and he said that he would be sworn in as Governor that afternoon and that he would confirm in office all those who were prepared to acknowledge the Duke as the rightful Lord. All did so promptly except the Comptroller, Quayle, who took a couple of hours to think about it before agreeing.

Murray took his oath standing on a white stone and holding a white wand of office, and five guns fired a salute. Then he led a procession of dignitaries, accompanied by thirty soldiers, to the Town Cross in Market Square where beer and punch were distributed to all, and cannon and muskets were fired in celebration. Then Murray repaired to the castle where toasts were drunk for the next four hours. 'Lord, what a terrible thing it is to be great man', he reported to Atholl, 'I have swallowed more wine in a week than would serve most men for a year'. Soon enough he was giving orders that he should be served only coloured water. Neil Mathieson, who has researched this period in the relevant Atholl papers discovered that:

> The drinks provided were certainly of a type to test the strongest head. For the most important guests there was a hot one known as 'shrub', which, while potent, was simple, being nothing more than neat brandy flavoured with sugar and lemon. For less exalted but just as thirsty individuals there was 'bumbo' which was composed of rum, water, sugar and nutmeg – a mixture by no means to be despised. And of course there was plenty of ale, brewed in the castle brewhouse by a woman who was paid two shillings for acting as brewer and dealing faithfully with the malt and hops purchased locally.[31]

Given that the Atholl succession was to some extent contested it was important that the new regime should make itself popular with the Manx as quickly as possible. The Duke himself visited in 1736 and was accompanied to Tynwald with a regiment of foot-militia described as being 'well-armed'.[32] Subsequently Murray got down to work efficiently but tactfully and gave several parties for the leaders of Island society in Castle Rushen, where endless local women kept him on his feet dancing until well after 3am. He did not much enjoy presiding over the sheading courts where he had to sit for eight hours as a 'mere cypher' while the proceedings were conducted in (to him) incomprehensible Manx, and he found that getting money out of the Treasury was complicated because the door had four locks, all held by different men who had to be present to open it.

Murray's views of the Manx in general were that they were all in poverty and full of complaints, though deeply religious, and they adored Bishop Wilson. The Island's lead mines were no longer being worked and needed to be reinvigorated, he thought. He visited Peel Castle and found that, though the cathedral had no roof, the vault beneath it was 'as dismal, dark and damp as the Spiritual Court could wish' though the Porter's House was in good condition and he suggested that the Duke would find it an agreeable place to spend a summer, though Peel itself was not to be compared with either Castletown or Douglas. The Sword of State, he felt, was very shabby and he advised the Duke to 'order another one....never mind what it is made of as long as it glitters'. He obviously found his first winter (1736-37) a trial, because he confessed that he 'passed lonely hours by his fireside, brooding on dismal apprehensions' while the sea wind howled round the castle walls and the rain cascaded from the roofs.[33]

However, Murray became used to the Island as the years passed and he governed it quietly and without major incident, establishing far better relations with the Church and the House of Keys. Indeed, soon after his appointment the Keys in 1737 gained important recognition of their legal right to give or withhold consent to customs legislation. When Britain went to war with France in 1740 Murray felt that the Island was very poorly defended, having not thirty firelocks fit for service, leaving it a prey to enemy ships or privateers. However, no invasions took place and he left the Island in 1744 and returned to a post at the British Treasury.

Murray was replaced by Patrick Lindesay who came from a well-established family in Fife and had been an army officer as well as Lord Provost of Edinburgh, and he was married to a daughter of the Earl of Crawford, which brought an aristocratic flavour to life in Castletown. As with all Governors of this period he found that communicating with the Duke was extremely difficult because letters came by ship from Liverpool where they could wait for months for a suitable vessel bound for the Island. Sometimes a letter could be sent to Scotland in the small boats that plied between Ramsey and Galloway. In 1745 the Jacobite rebellion took place in Britain and Lindesay was worried that rebels might attempt to land on the Island, where he considered the militia to be loyal but ill-armed and of poor spirit; but no threat materialised. In 1751 Lindesay resigned because of ill health and he was followed by Basil Cochrane, a son of the Laird of Ochiltree in Ayrshire and a brother of the Earl of Dundonald, and his salary as Governor was £200.

In 1753 he suffered from a severe attack of scurvy which threatened his eyesight and caused him to lose the use of his hands and feet so that he had to leave the Island for several months until he found a cure in Edinburgh.[34]

An impression of Castletown about this time was given by George Waldron, an Englishman who was effectively a customs spy, probably living in Ballasalla and 'residing in the Island on a watching brief for the British Crown, gathering intelligence on the running trade'.[35] He arrived around 1723 and wrote a few years later:

> It is the metropolis of the Island and the place where most of the persons of any note choose to have their residence, because the Governor keeps his Court in it. The castle is a fine, ancient building and has been honoured with the presence of several of the Lords of Man.…Just at the entrance of the castle there is a great stone chair for the Governor and two lesser for the deemsters; here they try all causes, except ecclesiastic, which are entirely under the decision of the Bishop. When you are past this little Court you enter a long, winding passage between two high walls.…The extremity of it brings you to a room where the Keys sit: they are twenty-four in number: they call them the Parliament, but in my opinion they more resemble our juries in England because the business of their meeting is to adjust differences between the common people, and [they] are locked in until they have given their verdict. They may be said in this sense, indeed, to be supreme judges because from them there is no appeal but to the Lord himself.[36]

COCHRANE V STEVENSON, 1759

Unlike the diplomatic James Murray, Basil Cochrane seems to have been capable of high-handed actions in his role of Governor, forcing the Keys on one occasion to deliver a verdict by confining them in Castletown for three days. In particular he had a long-standing row with a Castletown lawyer, John Stevenson, probably a nephew of the celebrated John Stevenson of Balladoole. It is likely that in 1756 Stevenson had represented the Revd Paul Crebbin, Vicar of Kirk Santan, who had lost a case over a right of way adjudicated by Deemster John Taubman and had publicly described Taubman's conduct as 'an innovation and an open and notorious violation and breach of the Constitution never before attempted by any magistrate in this Isle'. As a punishment for this outburst he was fined and sent to prison for a month, 'for his malicious, scandalous, false and insolent libel against Deemster Taubman …and ordered publicly to own his offence at the bar of this Court and on his knees to ask pardon of the said Deemster'.[37] The fact that Stevenson represented Crebbin on this occasion and supported his criticisms of

Taubman would not have recommended him to the Castletown Establishment.

Basil Cochrane pursued a policy of encouraging foreign merchants to settle in the Island in order to stimulate trade, and some of these were Irish Catholics. This provoked a hostile response from a number of Protestant residents who complained to the Bishop and the Keys, though the Governor's reaction was that those who complained 'deserved to be drawn alive by wild horses as for an act of high treason..' The residents turned to John Stevenson who took the advice of lawyers in England and may have advised the Keys, who in 1757 sent a petition to the Duke of Atholl, complaining of the Governor's naturalization policy. This made Stevenson a marked man as far as Cochrane was concerned.

Some time after this Stevenson represented two juries which had 'been fined in twenty-six shillings and eightpence each juror, for giving verdicts in a matter of view, according to their consciences' and Cochrane threatened to have Stevenson's petition on their behalf burnt by the common hangman. Calling Stevenson before him in the Court of Chancery in March 1759 the Governor asserted before a crowded audience 'that Mr Stevenson undertook all villainous appeals; that he knew no villainous or rascally case in Court but what Mr Stevenson was concerned [with] or had a hand in; that Mr Stevenson was a nuisance to the country' etc. Stevenson asked the Governor not to take such liberties with his character, but Cochrane replied that he had 'not the least pretention to a character', to which Stevenson rejoined that 'he was as honest a man and had as good a character as His Honour had'. Next, according to Stevenson's account, the row got completely out of hand:

Then the Governor threatened Mr Stevenson with being hindered from practising in the Court as an attorney. Mr Stevenson saying 'he apprehended he was not impeached of any crime in the way of his profession to merit such a treatment', the Governor quitted his bench, violently assaulted Mr Stevenson, and with his own hands forcibly turned him by the shoulders out of the bar and declared he should never be allowed to plead or practise as an attorney in the same Court while he presided therein. He then ran out of the Court in a great passion and called for soldiers to commit Mr Stevenson for impertinence: but returning soon after and a soldier being arrived for that purpose, the Governor thereupon gave verbal orders for imprisoning Mr Stevenson in the castle.[38]

Stevenson spent a night in a 'cold, dark, damp and loathsome' cell with two narrow windows about six inches wide, an earthen floor with a 'canopy of cobwebs' and rain dripping in. There was no furniture except some filthy straw in a corner and he was allowed no fire and no candle. The next day he was brought before the Governor again, sitting in the Court of Exchequer with the Comptroller, John Quayle, Deemster John Taubman, and the Attorney-General, John Frissell, and 'without any charge being made against him, or any evidence heard, or a single question being asked him, they proceeded (upon his coming into the room)' to fine him ten pounds for his 'insolent behaviour' in the Court of Chancery the previous day and commit him to prison for one month.

Stevenson served his sentence and paid his fine and then began a campaign to achieve redress, starting with a 'petition of doleance' to Atholl asking for a commission to be appointed to review his complaints and demanding considerable damages from the Governor. He also received testimonials of good character from fifteen members of the Keys and four clergymen. The Commission was convened but three of its members, the two vicars-general and the Vicar of Malew, were 'dependent upon the Governor for lettings of tithes and for livings in the Church …. The fact is they browbeat Mr Stevenson's witnesses'. Cochrane then took exception to remarks in Stevenson's letter to Atholl stating that 'public clamour and discontent circulated through all classes of people in the Island' and sued him for criminal libel. These cases were put before the Duke of Atholl's Commissioner of Appeals in London and Stevenson travelled there in June 1760 to await the hearings.

He was still waiting when early in 1761 Cochrane was appointed one of the Commissioners of Excise for Scotland and announced his resignation as Governor. On this news Stevenson instructed a Manx attorney, William Makon, probably a son of James Makon, who had been a master in Castletown Grammar School, to claim colossal damages from Cochrane of £3,000. The Governor replied by putting Makon in prison for 22 hours while he produced £50 bail. On his release Makon then additionally sued the Governor for a further £2,000 for excluding Stevenson from the bar and brought a suit in Chancery for the seizure of the Governor's property until he stood trial. Deemster Taubman and Daniel Mylrea, the Receiver-General, saw to it that the first claim for damages was rejected with £5 costs and the second with £10 costs. This no doubt satisfied Cochrane who had announced that both claims were brought 'purposely to asperse, traduce, and bring an odium and reflection upon the defendant's administration as Governor, and also unjustly to injure him by having his effects publicly arrested, and an indignity to his public character as Governor'.[39]

With all this in the air, Cochrane left the Island and the Duke of Atholl thanked him warmly for his services as Governor and consulted him subsequently about the Island's affairs, so he must have retained confidence in him. However, the legal wrangle between Cochrane and Stevenson in London was not yet completed. In January 1762 the Duke's Commissioner of Appeals held five different sessions on the matter, attended by eminent counsel on each side, and finally in May 1762 he decided that Stevenson had no right to damages from the Duke but that he could pursue his case in the courts of the Isle of Man if he wished. He also dismissed Cochrane's plea of criminal libel and ordered that Stevenson should be allowed to continue in practice as an attorney, but he did not award him costs. The battle was not yet over because Stevenson then appealed to the Duke's Commissioner against the costs of £15 awarded by the Manx Courts in 1761 and this appeal was dismissed in February 1763.

With Cochrane gone and the installation of a more reasonable Governor, John Wood, Stevenson felt able to calm down and resume his interrupted career as an attorney, and he died at some time between 1768 and 1770. As most of the evidence upon which this account is drawn comes from a document probably compiled by Stevenson, which was presented to the Manx Museum Library in the 1930s by Surgeon General H. W. Stevenson of Balladoole, it may be biased to some extent in his own favour. The document is entitled 'The case of John Stevenson, showing the grievous hardships which he laboured under in the Isle of Man, in the year 1759, from the arbitrary proceedings of the late Governor and his officers, and the different methods that have been taken to shut the doors of justice against him; humbly submitted to all lovers of liberty in the Kingdom of Great Britain'. However irritating Stevenson might have been, it does seem that Cochrane's reactions were entirely unfitting to his position as Governor and that he was surrounded by a clique of official cronies who were too scared of him to urge restraint. Clearly, whoever you were, you had to watch what you said and what you did in Cochrane's Castletown.

JOHN WOOD, 1761-1777

John Wood was the fourth Scot to be appointed Governor by the Duke of Atholl and he came from Carse, near Dumfries. A captain in the army, he was recommended to Atholl by the Duke of Argyll and he resigned his commission to take up his appointment on the Isle of Man in 1761. He does seem to have been a contrast to Cochrane in many ways, lacking his aristocratic connections and being aware of the need to build bridges with certain sections of the Manx community. Wood took up his office in wartime because in 1756 Britain had begun the 'Seven Years War' with France and there was always the possibility of a naval attack. Indeed, in February 1760 three British ships had fought a sharp engagement with three French ships off the Ballaugh coast, resulting in the capture of all the enemy vessels. This proved to be the only significant involvement of the Island in the war, but during this period Castle Rushen and Peel Castle were fully garrisoned, and British redcoats would have been a common sight in the streets of Castletown which in 1757 was recorded as having 878 inhabitants, 412 male and 466 female, while the total population of the Island in 1765 was about 20,000.[40]

James, Duke of Atholl, died in 1764, aged 74, and his death gave the British Government the opportunity it had long been waiting for. As we have seen, the Duke had agreed to sell his sovereign rights to the Island within seven years of his succession to it in 1736 but this had not happened, partly because the British Government was pre-occupied with other matters. Island merchants had continued to make fortunes from the 'running-trade', which the UK estimated in 1764 to be mostly centred on shipping tea from Sweden, tobacco to and from the UK and rum and coffee from the West Indies, all at a loss to the British Treasury of something between £200,000 and £350,000.

John Murray, the new Duke of Atholl, was in a weak position for several reasons. First, the late Duke had left no sons, so his daughter Charlotte had in fact succeeded to the Lordship of Man while he, as Duke James' nephew, had succeeded to the dukedom. However, these first cousins had married, so Duke John technically held the Lordship of Man in right of his wife. Second, his father had fought on the rebel side in the 1745 Jacobite rising and had been declared a traitor by Act of Parliament and it was only with the support of the Government that he was allowed to succeed his uncle. The third weakness was that neither John nor Charlotte had ever visited the Island and they knew very little about it.

The Prime Minister, George Grenville, therefore informed the Duke that the Government wished to buy the sovereign rights to the Island and hinted that if he was not prepared to sell, stronger measures might be used. In 1765 Atholl offered to sell all his rights and properties in the Island for £299,773 but Grenville unwisely went for a cheaper option and offered £46,000 for the sovereign rights and £26,000 for the customs duties, leaving the Duke in possession of most of the Island's land, the right of patronage to the bishopric and church benefices, and manorial rights. He therefore remained very powerful, but the new Lord of Man was King George III of Great Britain.

Governor Wood was kept completely in the dark while all these negotiations were going on, and the 'Act of Revestment' had been passed in May 1765 before he received word from London about his own future. In fact Whitehall decided that he had been doing a good job and was the right man to preserve a sense of continuity, so he was confirmed in office and on July 11th he presided in Castletown over a ceremony to celebrate the accession of the new Lord of Man. The Manx flag was lowered from the battlements of Castle Rushen and replaced with the Union Jack while the 42nd regiment of the Black Watch fired three volleys. Wood made a carefully tactful speech and afterwards entertained the leading members of Island society to dinner in the castle, at the same time making sure that there was plenty of beer available for the soldiers to drink the health of King George. Outside there were 'bonfires, illuminations and other demonstrations of joy'.[41]

Wood was given firm orders to stop the running trade and official British reports showed that under him it was very much curtailed, thereby seriously affecting the prosperity of many Manx merchants and traders. He also reduced the number of members of the Lord's Council from twelve to five and in future Englishmen rather than Manxmen were appointed to senior positions, such as Sir Wadsworth Busk, who was appointed Attorney General in 1774. This meant that Castletown society began to take on an even more English flavour. No firm guidance came from London on how the Manx constitution should develop and lawyers and politicians had to work through a web of 'grey areas' concerning whether jurisdiction lay with the Island authorities or with the Home Office, which assumed responsibility for Manx affairs.

When Wood died in 1777 the 'Cumberland Pacquet' newspaper reported that 'so universally respected was the late Governor of the Isle of Man that on Sunday ….the sermons in several churches turned principally on the important subject of death and called to mind, in an appropriate manner, the virtues of the deceased'.[42] He was replaced by Colonel Edward Smith, an able professional soldier who held the office until 1793 and was promoted major-general during this period. However, he was frequently absent from the Island attending to military duties elsewhere and therefore the role of Lieutenant Governor, held by Major Richard Dawson, became more significant. Wood, Smith and Dawson all seem to have been popular with the Manx and with the people of Castletown, which was just as well because their determination to reduce the running trade, and the British Government's policy of channelling Manx revenues back into the British Treasury was not in the best interests of the Island's prosperity or that of many Manx people.

ATHOLL V SMELT, 1774-1830

In 1774 the third Duke of Atholl died in his mid-forties and he was succeeded by his son John, who was barely twenty. The new Duke was convinced that his father had died from remorse at having agreed to sell the Lordship of the Island, though a more credible cause was the fact that he drowned after suffering an apoplectic fit. For the next 56 years the affairs of the Island were dominated by the determination of the Duke to regain power and influence and also to seek compensation for financial losses which had resulted from Revestment. First of all he claimed manorial dues, which had not been paid since 1765, and then in 1781 he introduced a Bill in Parliament to amend the terms of the Revestment Act on the grounds that his father had not been paid enough. Sir George Moore, Speaker of the Keys, travelled to London to argue against this and was so successful that the Bill was dropped. In 1791 Atholl persuaded the Crown to set up a Royal Commission to inquire into his grievances and this tended to agree with him that his father had been paid too little for the Lordship, and also that manorial dues had not been properly paid since 1765. Atholl then made the unusual demand that he should be appointed Governor of the Island when the post next became vacant, and when General Smith died in 1793 the British Government, no doubt hoping that the gesture would keep Atholl quiet, appointed him Governor, a decision officials at Westminster and Castletown came to regret over the next thirty-seven years.

Clearly a salary of around £300 a year was of no consequence to Atholl, who owned vast estates in Scotland, centred on Blair Castle in Perthshire, and who has easily been the richest and most socially prestigious individual to have held the post of Governor in all the Island's history. However, he hoped to use the position of Governor to ensure that the entitlements which remained to him as owner of most of the land on the Island were fully paid. It should be said that he also had a genuine desire to improve the Island's economy, though largely because this would ultimately result in more revenue for himself. Although throughout his long tenure of the post he was essentially an absentee Governor and visited the Island very rarely, he decided at once that the Governor's accommodation in Castle Rushen was totally inadequate for his needs, and eventually decided to build a small palace, which he called Castle Mona, on the shore in Douglas Bay. Costing an incredible £36,000 – half what his father had been paid for the Lordship and customs duties – the Duke's new home, designed by George Steuart with attractive 'Adam-style' furnishings, was opened in 1804. However, Castle Mona was a considerable distance from Castletown, especially on the very poor roads of the time, and the Duke fully expected to be provided with accommodation in the Derby House in Castle Rushen when he visited the capital to preside over the law courts or meetings of Tynwald.

Unfortunately Atholl's expectation that he would be able to make use of the comforts of Derby House brought him into sharp conflict with his deputy. Although many Governors in the past had appointed deputies from time to time to cover their absence from the Island, the official post of

Lieutenant Governor seems to have been created in 1773 for Henry Hope, who was succeeded two years later by Richard Dawson. His popularity and success in deputizing for the frequently absent Governor Smith gave prestige to the role and this was continued under Alexander Shaw (1790-1804). Because the Duke of Atholl was essentially an absentee Governor, Shaw lived in Derby House and this meant that when Atholl occasionally visited Castletown he had nowhere to stay without returning to Douglas. On the retirement of Shaw in 1804 Atholl appointed his brother Lord Henry Murray to the post of Lieutenant Governor but was told firmly by the Home Office that the appointment lay with them and not with him. So Henry Murray had to go and instead the Home Office in 1805 appointed Colonel Cornelius Smelt, aged 57, an experienced professional soldier, on a salary of £400 a year, plus expenses. Married, with two daughters, he reckoned that he had to spend £300 of his salary on the requirements of his job, and he remained Atholl's deputy for 25 years. As the Duke only visited the Island a handful of times during this period, it was essentially Smelt who carried out the day-to-day duties of the Governor and who was responsible for routine administration, leaving strategic decisions to Atholl, who kept in touch by letter. Hence the Atholl papers in the Manx Heritage Library are a rich source of detailed information for this period.

Smelt was a gentleman of the old school and he became extremely popular in Castletown and with the Manx people in general, carrying out his duties with efficiency but also charm. Indeed he got on well with everyone except Atholl. Within a few days of his appointment Atholl requested the Home Office to give Smelt a housing allowance so that he could live somewhere other than in Derby House, and demanded that Smelt should not have the power to summon the Keys on his own authority or preside over trials when Atholl was himself on the Island. The Home Office did nothing and four years later Atholl was objecting to official communications between the Home Office and Smelt without reference to himself. In 1813 he repeated his request for Smelt to move out of Derby House. Having recently visited the Island and presided over the law courts in Castletown, he found that after a six-hour day it was impossible to travel back to Castle Mona because of the bad roads and he complained to the Home Secretary that he had been 'put to the inconvenience and disgruntled appearance of retiring to a paltry inn or lodging and wading through the dirty streets and the gaol-yard to take my seat as His Majesty's Governor'. The Home Office again did nothing and Smelt stayed in Derby House, increasing Atholl's irritation with his deputy and fuelling his suspicions that British officials preferred to operate through Smelt rather than himself, which was true enough.[43]

THE CASTLE RUSHEN GAOL, 1765-1827

In 1798 John Feltham, having toured the Island, found that Castletown was 'an airy, pleasant town, smaller than Douglas, containing about 500 houses, but more spacious and regular. The town is divided by a small creek which opens into a rocky and dangerous bay. The difficulty of entering its harbour in some degree injures its commerce'. He also thought that the town's generally clean appearance, its society, the military, the vicinity, the pleasant walks to Ronaldsway, Scarlett and Stack, together with its closeness to the other towns 'all conspire to render Castletown a very agreeable place'. He also reported that there was a market on Saturdays and a fair in July, but that there were no regular butchers' shops. However, Castle Rushen he found to be in a dilapidated state and thought that 'the meetings of the legislature are held in places ill-suited to the dignity of their functions; the Keys assemble in a mean, small building [Bishop Wilson's Library]; the Courts of Chancery and Common law are held in an indifferent apartment in Castle Rushen. The place in the castle used as a gaol has but one apartment to receive all persons committed for debt, and any offence less than capital; this is small, dark, without any divisions and altogether unfit for its purpose'.[44]

One of the results of Revestment was uncertainty about who should pay for the upkeep of the castle. Governor Wood described the situation in 1765 as being that:

> The castle of Rushen is the principal gaol for debtors and felons; the castle of Peel is a temporary gaol for all debtors and felons until they are transferred to Castle Rushen....the forts at Douglas and Ramsey are also adapted as temporary gaols for the immediate commitment of debtors and felons until they are likewise sent to Castle Rushen; in all of which cases one or more of the soldiers belonging to the garrison and forts attend to see the person delivered to the constable of Castle Rushen and lodged there; and the constables of Castle Rushen, Peel Castle and the commanders of the forts at Douglas and Ramsey are liable for the debts of the prisoners in case they escape; on which account men of some property have always been appointed to these offices.

As for the general condition of the castle, Wood wrote that there were 'on the outward walls houses containing court-rooms and seven other rooms and two kitchens, all out of repair. The apartments of the Earl of Derby [are] the only place to quarter soldiers. No accommodation in the inner castle save ruinous dungeons – the common gaol of felons'. The Derby apartments he refers to here would be the main rooms of the castle, not the Governor's

Castle Rushen and the harbour, by George Pickering, 1832. (Manx National Heritage)

House (Derby House) where Wood himself lived. The Home Office turned deaf ears to Wood's requests for improvements to be made to the castle and in the last months of his life, in 1777, he complained that the gaol 'is at present in such a state of ruin and decay that the same affords but one small apartment for the reception and security of prisoners, in which apartment (though the state thereof is shocking to humanity) persons of all descriptions and the different sexes are indiscriminately confined together'.[45]

The Home Office still did nothing, so in 1781 Governor Smith appealed to the Keys, pointing out that 'the gaol is in so miserable a state as to let water through down to the very lowest apartment, thereby endangering the prisoners' lives and bringing upon them pains and illness they may never recover from, which is surely adding torments to the necessary severity of the law, and inflicting miseries on the unhappy sufferers never permitted in civilised nations.' The Keys produced a detailed reply showing that before 1765 the Lord had met the expenses of Castle Rushen out of various revenues which were now under the control of the Home Office and the Governor should take the matter up with them. Writing to British officials Smith complained of starving prisoners and lack of funds and said that much damage had been done to the gaol as a result of repeated attempts of prisoners to break out, which they would have done had he not been able to call upon the garrison of Manx Fencibles. Eventually, in 1787, Smith persuaded the Keys to introduce a Bill which would have charged Island revenues for the repair of the public offices, court-room and gaol in Castle Rushen, as well as the maintenance of prisoners. However, the young Duke of Atholl objected to this because the money would have come out of his manorial revenues and he made sure the Bill did not receive the Royal Assent. When he became Governor himself he did eventually manage to persuade the Home Office to accept responsibility for the repair and upkeep of Castle Rushen, but not until well after the turn of the century.

In 1811, John Stapleton, Inspector-General of the UK's Ordnance Department, produced a report on the castle which found that there were 22 prisoners, most of them debtors, and it seems that by this time convicted felons were housed in the derelict keep and that all other prisoners, male or female, and including debtors, individuals guilty of misdemeanours and those awaiting trial, were held in the three lower rooms of the outer gatehouse, with crude facilities for cooking and few comforts. Atholl's own view in 1813 was that 'at present the old castle is in a progressive state of decay and dilapidation' and he urged the British Government to take responsibility for it.[46]

At last the Home office was prompted to take action, probably because they were persuaded that the castle's ruinous state was a security risk at a time when Britain was still locked in the war with Napoleonic France. Between 1814 and 1827 the castle was thoroughly renovated, the alterations at first under the control of Captain Holloway of the Royal Engineers. The keep was fully restored and equipped as a prison for felons, and its fine state of repair today is largely the result of this work. The upper floor of the gatehouse was converted into a courtroom, a range of buildings was constructed next to it in limestone ashlar and exercise yards were laid out between the walls.[47] These alterations were the work of Thomas Brine, who also produced many drawings of the castle at this time. Before 1817 the death penalty was generally imposed for thefts of sixpence or more but new rules introduced in 1817 replaced this with imprisonment or transportation for thefts of ten shillings or more. This liberalization of the law, together with an increase in the population, led to a growth in the number of prisoners, and though the prison itself had been much improved as a building, many inadequacies remained, especially in the careless way prisoners were often treated.

In 1823, for instance, William McChain, a young Irish fisherman, was involved in a Friday night brawl in Peel between local men and several of his shipmates, all of them drunk, as a result of which seven Irishmen, including McChain, were locked up in Peel Castle for the night. Here, apparently, McChain stripped off his clothes in a state of excessive intoxication, which resulted in him developing a fever. On Saturday he and his shipmates were transferred to Castle Rushen where McChain complained of feeling ill. The prisoners received no food until Sunday and no doctor came to see McChain until Monday, by which time he was delirious. By Tuesday, he was dead. The authorities attempted to hush up this scandal by delivering the corpse to McChain's shipmates without further ado but they were forced to hold an inquiry, which fairly recorded the regrettable circumstances of his death and ordered that any deaths in prison in future should automatically be the subject of an immediate inquiry.[48]

EDUCATION, 1710-1824

By 1710 the schools in Castletown consisted of the Academic Scholars under 'Professor' Alexander Ross, who were taught on the upper floor of Bishop Wilson's new library, the boys of the Grammar School who were taught in the old St Mary's Chapel by James Makon, and the pupils of the 'petty school' in the town. Makon also held the post of government chaplain, in charge of the new St Mary's Chapel. Both Ross and Makon had to defend themselves against charges of 'popery' and they also became entangled in the row between Bishop Wilson, Archdeacon Horrobin and Governor Horne. Far worse, however, was the fact that the succession of the Duke of Atholl to the Lordship in 1736 had a disastrous effect on Bishop Barrow's Impropriate Fund. For complicated legal reasons the deal negotiated between Barrow and Derby over the tithes which financed the Fund did not apply to the Duke of Atholl who reclaimed the tithes and so impoverished the Fund, affecting the stipends of Makon and Ross as well as many clergy and teachers in the petty schools. Barrow had apparently foreseen this possibility and had arranged alternative funding, should the situation arise, from two manors in Lancashire belonging to the Stanleys, but the new Earl of Derby was reluctant to surrender revenue from these. Accordingly the case went to the Court of Chancery and it took twenty years before the Court required the Stanleys to make good the unpaid revenues. This effectively meant that for all this time the payment of many salaries from the Impropriate Fund was drastically reduced.

In fact Makon, who had been in charge of between twenty and thirty boys, soon resigned and Ross was asked by Castletown parents to take over responsibility for the Grammar school as well. He reluctantly agreed to 'undertake this drudgery' with the help of three of his brightest Academic pupils, but he was getting older and he drank too much. Even in 1731 Wilson had reprimanded him for 'drinking to an unbecoming excess'. In these unpromising circumstances Ross remained in charge of both establishments but by 1743 Wilson had to recognize that 'the public school house of Castletown is falling into ruins to the great concern of all such as have any regard to learning' and he encouraged the vicars of Malew and Santan to raise money for it, though to little avail. Ross was allowed to stagger on and when Wilson made a serious attempt to dismiss him in 1751 Governor Cochrane leapt to the schoolmaster's defence, regarding it as 'a cruel and barbarous case as the poor man is in all probability fair dropping into his grave, and as he has lived with a fair and good character, it is hard to disturb him'. Clearly the welfare and education of Ross's pupils was not a high priority. In his last years Ross's daughter wrote that 'for three years before his death [he] grew very feeble and helpless and was obliged to pay an usher for taking care of the school'.[49]

Ross died in 1754 and for four years a Mr Wills and then John Quayle, the Vicar of Malew, held the fort until a permanent appointment could be made. This was the Revd Thomas Castley, MA, a Senior Wrangler (top of the first class in mathematics) of Cambridge University, where he was a Fellow of Trinity College. He was appointed both Academic Master and Schoolmaster, against the spirit of Barrow's intentions, and also chaplain of St Mary's. The will of Catherine Halsall in 1758 provided for the building of a house for the Grammar School Master, so in this respect he was well off. However, he found the Grammar School at a very low point and his solution to its financial problems was to charge fees. This was extremely unpopular and Vicar-General Wilks, who had praised him at first for being a man of good morals and learning, soon berated him for abandoning the principle of a 'Free' Grammar School. A public petition in Castletown drew attention to this and, to weaken his credibility further, also accused him of seriously mistreating pupils. According to one account:

> In an age when severe physical punishment was the accepted norm, Castley shocked his contemporaries by his ferocity and cruelty, which made thoughts of his school 'odious to his scholars' and himself 'not a fit person to be entrusted with the care of youth'. Among his novel punishments was the coiling of a cord in a serpentine manner, called by him a colt, with which he struck the pupil on the temple with such force as to level him to the ground with one stroke, while another consisted of forcing pupils to hold up finger and thumb, and then strike them on the points of the fingers with a plank. The unfortunate dunce or 'booby' found his hair was pulled out, and then he himself forced to put it on the fire.[50]

The petition described Castley as a 'Public Nuisance and Grievance' and alleged that there were only a handful of boys in the school. The House of Keys appointed a committee to look into the matter, but Castley survived and indeed began a long campaign to have his salary raised. He had been appointed on £100 a year but after Chancery judgements in 1751 and 1757 concerning the tithes issue at last found in favour of the Manx clergy, more funds became available and Castley wanted a share of them. So did Ross's daughter Grissel, who claimed that nearly £1,000 was owed to her late father's estate.

In a blizzard of claims, counter-claims, petitions and long lists of expenditure real and imaginary, Castley managed to emerge with more pay for himself and more funding for his school, which was gradually repaired and restored to a respectable state. He also secured the appointment of an assistant master to teach writing. This was because the standard of education in the 'petty' schools was by now so poor that many pupils could not even read or write, a situation that some historians lie at the door of Bishop Wilson. He had made the fundamental mistake of forbidding clergy to teach in the petty schools on the grounds that they had more important responsibilitie, but the result was that elementary education was left to low-paid and ill-educated teachers.[51] With one assistant master and probably a few Academic Scholars as additional helpers, Castley now had some claim to the title of Headmaster.

By 1764 he was on good terms with the third Duke of Atholl who asked him to go to Cambridge and cast his vote for Lord Sandwich as Chancellor of the University, and in 1774 he was angling to be appointed Vicar of Malew in addition to being headmaster of the Grammar School, though Bishop Richmond, in refusing, pointed out that Castley's post at the school was 'far more lucrative than the vicarage of Malew'. He had managed to restore the number of boys in the school – drawn from all parts of the Island - to between twenty and thirty, about the same as the number under Makon in the first half of the century, so he cannot be credited with any great increase in numbers. On the other hand he made a good impression on some of his pupils, who spoke highly of him later. One was Robert Brown, later Vicar of Braddan and father of Thomas Edward and Hugh Stowell Brown, who wrote in 1835 that the Island had not seen Castley's equal and 'in all probability we will not see the like again'.[52] An intriguing petition to Castley from his pupils has survived, unfortunately without a date, which begs 'that you would be pleased to grant us this day's play upon account of the Fair held at Ballasalla, particularly as there is a man to be flogged there, an uncommon sight, which therefore raises our curiosity to see it. The granting of which shall infinitely oblige your dutiful and loving scholars.'[53]

Castley's teaching of the Academic Students, who by now wore wigs and gowns, seems to have brought out the best in him. Joseph Stowell, who became an Academic Student in 1786 claimed that the teaching of Greek and

Latin under Castley was far better than he had experienced previously at the Grammar School in Douglas, and Colonel Mark Wilks, the Governor of St Helena when Napoleon was a prisoner there, claimed that he had never had a better teacher of natural philosophy than Castley. We are therefore left with a somewhat contradictory impression of this man who remained in his posts for fifty years, eventually resigning in 1808. Was he indeed an outrageous sadist, or was this an exaggerated accusation brought by his critics to speed his dismissal? Was he really an outstanding teacher? If so, why did he not manage to increase the number of pupils in his school? His undoubted strong point was his success in putting the finances of the school back onto a firm footing, thereby increasing his own emoluments as well as the scholarships awarded to Academical Scholars.

Perhaps the most significant comment on Castley is the rapid failure of the man chosen to succeed him, the Revd Joseph Brown, a Scotsman who had a Master's degree from Glasgow. Within a short time it was clear that he could not control the pupils, even with the help of a young 'old boy', the Robert Brown already mentioned, who was an assistant at the school from 1809 to 1816, going on to become Master of the Douglas Grammar School before he moved to Braddan. Joseph Brown was swiftly moved out to be Vicar of Kirk Michael and in 1818 the Revd Thomas Thimbleby was appointed in his place as Academic Master, Grammar School Headmaster, and Chaplain of St Mary's. However, a disastrous tactical error was made by the Barrow Trustees who, in order to encourage the separate identity of the Academic Students, paid Thimbleby a handsome £220 a year to teach them and stipulated that he could 'provide himself with a residence and hold or keep the Academy in the town of Castletown, or within a mile thereof…'. As Chaplain of St Mary's Thimbleby also earned nearly £80 a year but his salary as Headmaster of the Grammar School was only £60 a year. Shocking to relate, his reaction to this was to close down the Grammar School building and open an expensive boarding school, which was free for the three Academic Scholars, though everyone else had to pay. A ten year-old day boy, for instance, was charged ten guineas a year and a sixteen year-old boarder had to pay an astonishing £60.[54]

The House of Keys regarded this situation as totally unacceptable and complained to the Home Office that Barrow's Fund was being seriously mismanaged in this and in other ways. Thimbleby resigned as Headmaster and the post, still at £60 p.a., went to the Revd George Parsons, (often referred to in all seriousness as Parson Parsons), who re-opened the school. In 1822 the Castletown architect Thomas Brine was commissioned to repair the roof but in 1829 his opinion was that the building 'was in as bad a state as before' and he renewed the timbers and provided new desks, tables and floors. Brine presented a bill for this work of £110 but ten years later he had not been paid, because 'funds were very low'.[55] By this time the Keys, the Bishop and the Lieutenant-Governor had all come to the conclusion that Barrow's three tier system was not working and had set up King William's College to replace it.

Bishop Barrow's Fund had provided education for boys in the Academic and Grammar School, but not for girls. The will of Catherine Halsall arranged for the endowment in 1758 of 'a free school to be built in Castletown for the education of girls only' and it was constructed about 1761 near the Old Grammar School. Three of the headmistresses shared the same name – the first Mrs Finigan retired in 1803, Isabella Finigan was in charge from 1811-1832, and Harriot Finigan is noted in 1837. In 1831 there were forty pupils and twenty poor pupils in the school, but no record of it exists after 1837.[56] Another endowed school in Castletown was founded for boys as a result of provisions of the will of John and Esther Taubman in 1799, who entrusted their son (also John) with revenues of £25 to provide 'for the support of a Free School in Castletown, for the education of twenty-five poor boys'. Twenty pounds was to be for the master's salary – which compares favourably with the Clothworker's School in Peel – and £5 for books, ink and paper. In 1847 the school was still in existence, one of only two in the Island to possess a globe as a teaching aid.[57]

The drive towards educating the poor in Britain, many of them workers in the new factories, began to influence the Island after 1800. The idea that senior pupils, or 'monitors' could be used to impart elementary information under the control of experienced teachers was widely adopted and resulted in the development of schools with large numbers of pupils. In 1810 a projected 'monitorial' school in Castletown came to nothing but in 1820 a committee was formed, with Thomas Thimbleby as its secretary, to raise subscriptions for the establishment of a 'National School' in the town. In August 1822, 128 boys and girls gathered in a converted Castletown warehouse under their newly-appointed teacher Thomas Kewley. By March the following year there were 132 boys and 101 girls as well as a mistress, Ann Stowell, who lost no time in becoming Mrs Kewley in 1824.[58]

METHODISTS

Methodism first came to the Isle of Man with the preacher John Murlin who visited Ramsey in 1758 by mistake, having apparently boarded the wrong boat. He left after a week, considering the Island an unpromising prospect for conversion, and it was not until 1775 that another evangelist, John Crook, was sent to the Island by Methodists in Liverpool, and he visited again the following year, having met with some success. John Wesley himself, then aged 74, sailed from Whitehaven and arrived in Douglas on 31st May 1777. On his landing, early in the morning, he was met by Methodist converts who conveyed him in a chaise to Castletown, where he preached at an open air service near the castle at 6pm, mentioning in his sermon that Castletown reminded him of Galway, in Ireland. After this he spent some time with the widow of Governor John Wood, whose husband had died very recently, and then stayed the night with two enthusiastic Methodists, Charles Clague and his wife. Clague was the master of a small boat which brought coal from Whitehaven to Castletown, where it was sold on the Quay, and he lived at No 47, the oldest house in Arbory Street, built of clay rather than mortar.

An early riser, Wesley preached again at 6.00 am in the Clague's house and then left for Peel, though entreated to stay longer. There, as in Castletown, he preached out of doors, because Bishop Richmond had forbidden his clergy to permit Wesley to preach in their churches or any Methodist preacher to take communion there. Wesley had a clear view of the illegality of this: 'Is any clergyman obliged, either in law or conscience, to obey such a prohibition? By no means. The will even of the King does not bind any English subject unless it be seconded by express law. How much less the will of the Bishop? But do you take an oath to obey him? No, nor any clergyman in the three kingdoms. This is a mere vulgar error. Shame that it should prevail almost universally'.[59] No wonder that Wesley and the Methodists were regarded as dangerous radicals by the Church Establishment. By 1778 the number of Methodists in the Island had reached about 600 and it was designated as a separate Methodist circuit. The number of adherents grew quickly, reaching some 1,597 in 1781.

Wesley returned to the Island for his second and last visit on June 1st in 1781 and rode to Castletown the next day, preaching in the Market Square at 6pm on the text 'One thing is needful'. The following day was Whit Sunday and he held another service in the Market Square at 9am, taking as his text 'I am not ashamed of the gospel of Christ'. By 4pm he had ridden to South Barrule to preach again and between 6pm and 7pm he preached to a congregation said to have been the largest ever seen on the Island, on the sea shore at Peel.[60] Based upon what he had seen of the Island, including Castletown, Wesley found it 'shut up from the world and having little trade … visited by scarce any strangers', while the Manx were 'a plain, artless simple people, unpolished, that is unpolluted; few of them are rich or genteel; the far greater part moderately poor; and most of the strangers that settle among them are men that have seen affliction. The local preachers are men of faith and love, knit together in one mind and judgement. They speak either Manx or English, and follow a regular plan'. He had a poor opinion of

the Manx language, considering that 'we should do everything in our power
to abolish it from the earth and persuade every member of our Society to
learn and talk English'.[61]

From 1781 Castletown Methodists met in a number of properties until
1801 when a chapel was built in Arbory Street. In 1833 a second chapel was
constructed alongside and described as 'neat and commodious' by Island
journalists. John Bowers, a noted preacher from Stockport, took the opening
service and preached 'one of the most luminous sermons ever heard in that
town'. Sermons were also given in the first few days by John Stamp from
Liverpool and Robert Aitken from Crosby. The new chapel cost £900 to build
and could accommodate three times the number of the old one, which was
leased to Whitehead, a corn merchant. In 1865 it was brought into use again
by the Methodists as a hall and schoolroom and probably provided with a new
façade and traceried window at this time. In 1890 substantial alterations were
made to the main chapel, with the addition of a chancel and the decoration of
the pews by members of the congregation who were joiners. Apparently they
took panels home to be worked on in the evenings in their spare time, for
which they received three or four shillings and sixpence per panel.[62]

The 'Primitive Methodists', who broke away from the main Wesleyan
movement, were founded in England in 1810 and in 1822 John Butcher, from
Bolton, was given the task of recruiting adherents in the Isle of Man. He
preached at Castletown and elsewhere and had 360 followers within twelve
months. The first Castletown Primitive Methodist meeting place was the
Freemason's Hall in Hope Street, followed by a new church and Sunday
school in Malew Street built on the site of Big Tree House. The two
Methodist chapels continued in friendly rivalry until 1972 when economic
circumstances and decisions made by the governing bodies of Methodism in
the UK led to the closure of the Primitive Methodist chapel in Malew Street
and its union with the Arbory Street congregation.

Chapter Three

A NEW HOUSE OF KEYS, 1821

In 1710 the Keys had been pleased enough to move into the upper floor of Bishop Wilson's Library for their debates. Unfortunately the accommodation was cramped and unimpressive and in 1734 money gained from the fees from public house licences had to be spent on repairs and improvements. In 1792 a UK official reported that 'the Keys assemble in a mean and decayed building little more than sufficient to contain the number of which they consist'. The Duke of Atholl commissioned some designs for a new House of Keys from George Steuart in 1797 but they went no further than the drawing-board. In 1813 Atholl put before a Tynwald Court held in Castle Rushen on July 13th a number of plans for the improvement of public buildings in the Island, including designs and estimates for a new House of Keys from the Castletown architect Thomas Brine.[1]

Brine was born about 1767 but details of his early life are not known except that by 1808 he was working for the UK government as a surveyor in the Barrack Office, at work on the new barracks being built at Chester to the designs of Thomas Harrison, an experienced architect whose ideas influenced Brine's own work. In 1811 he was sent by the UK to Castletown to assist with the construction of new barracks at Castle Rushen, acting as Clerk of Works under Captain Holloway. George Steuart had died in 1804 and the Duke of Atholl was sufficiently impressed with Brine to commission him to produce designs for several buildings on the Island. In 1812 he married, as his second wife, Anne Kelly, whose father Robert was Castletown's most prominent mason, holding the contract for the maintenance of the castle. His wife's family was numerous and well-connected in Castletown and when summoned by his employers to return to work in the UK Brine decided to resign and stay in Castletown. In addition to undertaking a lot of work as an architect, he was also employed as an agent for Lloyd's.[2]

Although, as we have seen, Atholl was able to convince the Home Office of the need for repairs to Castle Rushen in 1813, he made no progress in receiving money for a new House of Keys. In 1817 the Keys considered that conditions in the Library were so poor that they held a meeting in the George Inn, recording at the same time that they considered it 'highly improper for any Court of Justice and particularly so for one of so much importance in this Island as the House of Keys'. In England their cause was

Brine's House of Keys, after recent restoration. (Lily Publications)

taken up by John Christian Curwen, who had first become an MHK in 1777 before moving to England, where he was elected an MP. He brought the problem to the notice of Lord Sidmouth, the Home Secretary, and this initiative was backed up with correspondence from Cornelius Smelt, the Lieutenant Governor. Brine's first scheme had a price tag of about £1,300 but the Home Office asked for a smaller-scale building at a lower cost so Brine produced another design estimated at just over £1,000. Even this was too much and the Home Office haggled with the Keys over how the money should be raised until they reached a compromise in 1819, agreeing to meet a substantial part of the cost of Brine's design if the Keys paid the rest.[3]

By this time Brine had been responsible for a number of prominent buildings on the Island, in addition to his role in the restoration of Castle Rushen. He built St Paul's Church in Ramsey (1814-1822) and extensively re-modelled and enlarged Bishopscourt for George Murray, Atholl's nephew, who had been appointed Bishop in 1814. In Castletown Brine built Beach House for Deemster Crellin soon after 1812, a house that has been described as 'possibly the first low-built Regency villa on the Island'.[4] Work on the new House of Keys began with the demolition of Bishop Wilson's Library, probably late in 1818, and the new building was finished by February 1821. One of Brine's draft designs is for a much larger and more elegant building than the modest one he constructed, presumably because of financial restrictions, and it did not impress an anonymous visitor who wrote in a local paper in January 1822 that:

> ...the most glaring defects in a public edifice are perceptible in the House of Keys; neither the exterior nor interior of the building giving any idea of its being the Senate House of a respectable body of Representatives, or rather the Parliament House of the Isle of Man. ...there is neither order nor consistency preserved in it; - the portico light and trifling and the windows small and numerous; the external appearance more like that of a small country villa, or village jail, than a Senate House. On examining the interior I was alike displeased and disgusted; the Speaker's Chair is a little elevated, but 'crammed in a space I blush to own' – the recess of one of the windows where the Speaker is obliged to have the lower half of the window-shutter closed to screen him from the gaze of passengers in the street. Around the walls and under the ceiling, where a bold and appropriate cornice ought to have been placed, is a light and delicate moulding 'fit only for a lady's bedchamber', and instead of some suitable ornament or flower on that part of the ceiling from which its chandelier can be suspended, is a thing with a few circular mouldings, or rather scratchings, upon it, resembling both in dimensions and appearance, a turned pot lid. The designer of this building has committed an outrage on all the admitted principles of architectural beauty.[5]

It is difficult not to agree with this assessment. Brine's new building, much the same as the present structure from the outside, was small and unimpressive and did him little credit, even though he had limited funds for it. Perhaps the Home Office did not want the Manx Parliament to get too big for its boots, agreeing (for once) with the Duke of Atholl who famously told the Keys in a Tynwald Court held in 1822, soon after their new home was completed, that they were 'a self-elected body, in the choice of which the people of the Island have not the smallest share' and that 'they were no more Representatives of the people of Man than of the people of Peru.'[6] Six of the Keys in 1798 were Castletown men, John Taubman, the Speaker, George Quayle and Richard Symons, both merchants, Norris Moore and James Kelly, both lawyers, and Thomas Kirwan, 'Esquire'. They were not, of course, elected to the office. When a member of the Keys died or resigned, the remaining members recommended two names to the Lord or the Governor, who made the choice. They were therefore an oligarchy of the most notable and wealthy men on the Island, a fact which would cause increasing resentment during the century as the UK Parliament introduced a series of Acts which increased the number of individuals eligible to vote in Britain.

A NEW ST MARY'S CHAPEL, 1824

Brine made a more impressive job of his next important Castletown commission, which was to rebuild St Mary's Chapel. Bishop Wilson's 'neat and elegant' building had seen a number of crises during the previous century, most of them connected with the imperious Governor Alexander Horne, who found the preaching of James Makon, the first chaplain, so unacceptable to him that he prevailed upon Wilson to replace him in 1719 with Robert Horrobin, who later became Archdeacon and quite a friend and supporter of the Governor. In 1722 Wilson suspended Horrobin for supporting the Governor in his dispute with him and he appointed the schoolmaster, William Ross, to do his work as chaplain. Horne responded to this by locking the chapel and refusing to give Ross the keys, and it remained locked for three and a half years, until re-opened by Governor Horton. Ross was confirmed as chaplain from 1727 until he died, aged 86, in 1754. The post remained vacant until Thomas Castley was appointed both schoolmaster and chaplain in 1758, posts he retained until 1807 when he was replaced by Joseph Brown. An organ was installed in 1811, played from 1815 to 1863 by the official organist, Philip Caley.[7]

By the 1820s the chapel was no longer large enough to accommodate the growing population of the town which had reached 1,423 in 1792 and 2,036

The Market Square about 1900, dominated by St Mary's Chapel and its tower, taken down in 1912. (Manx National Heritage)

in 1821. The Island's population as a whole increased steadily from about 20,000 in 1765 to about 52,000 in 1866 despite checks such as cholera outbreaks, and this was partly because between 1736 and 1814 the Island was a haven for debtors from the UK and elsewhere, who were not fully liable for debts incurred outside the Island. Tynwald closed this loophole in 1814 but from about 1820 debtors were replaced by British officers, who, after the conclusion of the Napoleonic Wars in 1815, were pensioned off on half-pay. They found the cost of living much lower on the Island and came over in considerable numbers. Most of them settled in Douglas, but several came to Castletown. Moreover, by 1820 the Island had begun what was to be a long career as a holiday resort, and many visitors made their way to it in the summer months. Hence there was quite a building boom in Douglas and Castletown and many of the most impressive 'Georgian' houses and public buildings date from this period.

Joseph Brown moved to Kirk Michael in 1818 and he was replaced at St Mary's by Thomas Thimbleby, during whose term of office the chapel was completely rebuilt. The initiative for this came from Bishop George Murray, who wrote to his uncle the Duke of Atholl in June 1817 pointing out that the chapel was not big enough for the growing population of Castletown and suggesting the building of another aisle on the town side. If this were not done, he argued, worshippers might defect to the Methodists! After much discussion and delay a vestry meeting confirmed in June 1822 that the entire existing structure should be demolished because the walls were 'ruinous and dangerous'. Thomas Brine was commissioned to produce designs for a new chapel, to cost about £1,675, and the funds were raised partly by a Tynwald grant of a third of the cost, and partly by the sale of pews. On Easter Monday 1824 the foundation stone was laid by Cornelius Smelt and the chapel was consecrated by Bishop Murray on June 11th, 1826.

Designed in the 'Gothick' style, the new St Mary's was much larger than the first chapel on the site, and it was rectangular in plan with an apsidal west end. There was also an impressive tower with an octagonal lantern, reminiscent of the famous Lincolnshire 'Boston Stump', which had to be taken down in 1912. It could seat some 900 people, about half on the ground floor, which had square pews occupied by officers from the castle garrison and their families. Above was a gallery which normally seated other military personnel as well as members of the civilian congregation.[8]

There were also a small number of Roman Catholics in Castletown. Father Johnstone, a Benedictine monk from Whitehaven, reckoned that there were about 29 on the whole Island in 1779 and in 1789 Father Louis, a priest fleeing from the French Revolution, lived in Castle Rushen and said Mass in a barn at Scarlett belonging to a Catholic family. The Irish rebellion of 1798 prompted over a hundred Irish Catholics to move to the Island and Father Collins, chaplain to the Fagan family, may well have ministered to the Castletown fishing community until his death in 1811. In 1823 the Irish Jesuit College sent over Father Gahan as a resident priest in 1823 and he opened a small chapel, also dedicated to St Mary, in Castletown.

In 1821 Thomas Brine received a commission from Atholl to re-build the George Hotel (formerly the Governor's House in the Market Square) which had fallen into a ruinous state. Why Atholl did not build a house there for himself or for Colonel Smelt, and thus end the problem of who should reside in Derby House, is an interesting question. Possibly, as he was forced to stay in a hotel when in Castletown, he preferred to be its owner. It was later converted into barracks and then offices and it should not be confused with the present hotel of the same name, which was built nearby in the early 1830s by a consortium of prominent local men and designed by John Welch. Between 1829 and 1831 Thomas Brine constructed the battlemented Market House (now Barclays Bank), which had arched openings on the ground floor and a newspaper reading room above, and he also repaired and refurbished the Grammar School building. It was in or around the 1820s that the Georgian houses of the Parade were constructed and the Red House as well as numbers two and three have features often found in Brine's work. The Parade Stores, built for the trustees of Catherine Halsall's charity, and Stanley House as well as the National School (later St Mary's on the Harbour) have also been linked with him, as has Lorne House.[9]

A GROWING TOWN, c1750-1850

Thomas Brine certainly left his mark upon Castletown, which when he died in 1840, aged 72, could be considered a more handsome place than before, with many attractive public and domestic buildings. Coffee houses seem to have been established in Oxford about 1650 and in London about 1659 and the Receiver's accounts indicate that five shillings was paid 'towards a coffee house sign to be set up in Castletown' in 1698, though there is no indication of its location.[10] In 1822 there were 422 public houses in the Island, 28 of them in Castletown, and a contemporary noted that between 1825 and 1840 'most Manxmen got drunk with great regularity' and that the Hollantide Fair, held in Athol Street in Douglas, 'was a scene of drunkenness so great that you could scarcely see a sober man on the ground'.[11] A temperance movement was founded in 1830 but the situation did not significantly improve until the passing of Tynwald's Taverns Act in 1857. This closed public houses on Sundays and substantially raised the fees for licences, with the effect that the total number of public houses on the Island had been reduced to 248 in 1862, at a time when the population was larger. Famous pubs in Castletown by then included one known as The Queen's Arms in 1845 which had changed its name to The Castle by 1853, though it is now better known as The Gluepot. Another was The Union, at the end of Arbory Street, whose owner, Mrs Eyre, did not blush at advertising it in 1853 as 'immediately contiguous to a beach where there is the finest sea bathing in the world'. [12]

Although it is possible to identify buildings connected with Thomas Brine, many other, more anonymous, local builders constructed impressive houses in the town during this period. Bridge House was built for the Quayle family in the late 18th century, just across the small bridge from the castle, and Lorne House was completed in 1827 for Robert Cuninghame, who probably employed Thomas Brine as architect for at least some of the work. 'Westham', in Arbory Road, was built for Captain James Wilks, a collector of customs, and bears a plaque dated 1814. It features chimney stacks in a Dutch style and indoors there are fine rooms with fireplaces of black Poyllvaish marble. Balcony House, in the Parade, was constructed in the late eighteenth century and embellished with a fine ironwork balcony and an elegant fanlight over the front door. Behind the House of Keys there is an early eighteenth century building, formerly the Royal Oak Inn, which has steps and railings leading up to the front door, and fine interiors with an Adam-style chimney piece. The handsome Scarlett House, south of the town, was built about 1800 with stone from the nearby quarry, which had become operational a decade or so before. 13

Castletown social life was given a good deal of style and glamour by the presence of the garrison. The first corps of Manx Fencibles, a paid militia, was founded by Lieutenant Governor Richard Dawson and they lasted from 1779 until 1783, with their headquarters in the castle, and many well-known Castletown names such as Taubman, Quayle, Cuninghame and Geneste appearing on the list of their officers. A second corps was raised in 1793 by the Duke of Atholl and disbanded in 1802, though other corps continued until 1811, with detachments quartered in Castletown as well as the other main towns. In 1808 the South Manx Volunteers are recorded as performing garrison duty at the castle and in 1810 they were commanded by John Taubman, with William Cuninghame serving as a major. [14] A theatre opened in the town in 1814, presumably patronized by soldiers and their ladies, but after the war ended in 1815 there was a drastic change in the military establishment, which was reduced to half a company from an English line regiment, though they were still stationed in Castletown. Dorothy Wordsworth, visiting the town in 1826, likened it to a foreign place, with 'draw-bridge, handsome, strong fortress, soldiers pacing sentinel, officers and music, groups of women in white caps listening, very like a town in French Flanders'.[15]

By 1851 there was only one officer (a lieutenant), one colour sergeant, three sergeants and 46 privates, accommodated in permanent barracks in what later became the Town Hall, and they were accustomed to holding a firing party in the Market Square each year on the occasion of Queen Victoria's birthday.[16] There were several unsatisfactory features of life in Castletown at this time, and one was the lack of an effective police force. Before Revestment military forces had maintained order in the towns, under the command of their Captains. After 1765 they were replaced by police constables but there were only a handful of them and they were for the most part very elderly and badly paid. Worse still, they did not work at night, when many townspeople considered it unsafe to go out alone. In 1777 the post of Captain in the main towns was abolished and replaced with that of High Bailiff, who was responsible for law and order, as well as an increasing range of other civil and legal duties, but he had to work with resources that were overstretched.[17]

The second main problem was public health. The population of the town had risen sharply from the 878 recorded in 1757, swelled by the arrival of debtors and then half-pay officers and by immigration from the countryside. By 1830 there were some 2,000 inhabitants but the provision of fresh water and of sewage and sanitary arrangements was inadequate. Smallpox was a regular killer and there were island-wide epidemics of it in 1765, 1772, 1780 and 1799 as well as in 1839, 1851 and even between 1864 and 1866. This seems largely to have resulted from the practice of inoculating individuals against the disease, resulting in their developing it. Typhoid fever killed many on the Island in 1837 and there were serious outbreaks of cholera in 1832, 1849 and 1853. For Castletown the worst calamity was the cholera epidemic of 1832 which killed 90 out of the population of 2,000.[18] A temporary hospital was set up on the Claddagh and one of the last to die was Dr Jones, who had devoted himself to treating other victims.[19]

QUILLIAMS, QUAYLES AND TAUBMANS

One of the occupants of Balcony House was Captain John Quilliam, who gained fame and hero status for his role in the battle of Trafalgar in 1805. Born in 1771, a farmer's son from Marown, he was either press-ganged or volunteered for the Navy and quickly made his way from the lowest rank to a commission. By 1799 he was a lieutenant on the frigate HMS 'Ethalion' which had the good luck to capture the 'Thetis', a Spanish treasure ship, in October that year, making young Quilliam a rich man with no less than £5,000 as his share of the prize money. At the Battle of Copenhagen in 1801

Captain John Quilliam, from a contemporary portrait. (Manx National Heritage)

he was left in command of the 'Amazon' when it came under heavy fire and all his senior officers were killed. Admiral Nelson was impressed with his performance and gave Quilliam rapid promotion as 'first lieutenant' (confusingly, only the most junior of five lieutenants), aboard HMS 'Victory', a post he held for four-and-a-half years. As 'Victory' bore down upon the enemy at Trafalgar in 1805 the wheel was badly damaged by cannon fire and it fell to Quilliam to rig up an alternative steering mechanism and thus keep Nelson's flagship on course.

After the battle Quilliam was rewarded for his enterprise and courage with a command of his own, the bomb-ketch 'Etna' and later the 'Ildefonso',a former Spanish warship captured at Trafalgar. He returned to the Island in 1806 and he was hailed as a Manx hero for his part in Trafalgar and for the trust placed in him by Nelson. He was appointed to the Keys in 1807 but then returned to service and commanded four successive warships until the war ended in 1815. Back home again, he was re-appointed to the Keys and in 1817 he married Margaret, the daughter of Richard Stevenson of Balladoole. By this time Quilliam owned a number of properties on the Island and after marriage he and his wife divided their time between Ballakeighen, in the country, and Balcony House, where they lived in the winter.

In 1827 Quilliam was an influential member of a Tynwald inquiry into the reasons for the decline of the herring trade, which recommended that smaller, Cornish-style fishing craft should be used. He owned an undecked fishing smack called the 'Davis', which he kept at Derbyhaven and he had it rebuilt along the lines recommended by the inquiry, thus encouraging Manx fishermen to cast aside their traditions and follow suit – with excellent results for the herring industry. At the same time Quilliam was keen to improve the facilities of Derbyhaven and urged the building of a breakwater, though this was not achieved until 1840, eleven years after his death. Also, according to one of his friends:

> Captain Quilliam entertained the project of opening a canal from Derbyhaven Bay into Castletown Bay for the purpose of allowing the dozens of Dublin coal brigs to proceed on their voyage. Sometimes these brigs would be detained many weeks by easterly winds and there was no tug to take them to the offing. Out of his own pocket he employed several men with long iron bars probing the soil according to his directions. Failing health, however, caused him to abandon his plans.

He died in 1829 and was buried in Arbory parish church, where a memorial with a long inscription marks his resting place.[20]

The Quayle family had lived on the Bridge House site since the early eighteenth century and they succeeded in making the important office of Clerk of the Rolls peculiarly their own. John Quayle I was Clerk from 1736 to 1755, his son John Quayle II from 1755 to 1797, and his son Mark Hildesley Quayle I from 1797 to 1804. The Clerk was responsible for all legal records and proceedings, and before 1765 he was also in charge of the Lord's household. Retaining a position of this importance for nearly seventy years made the Quayles one of the most influential families in Castletown, respected for their professional skills and their public spirit. John II's elder son George was born in 1751 and he joined the first corps of Manx Fencibles in 1777, rising to be a captain, and then raised his own corps of yeomanry which he commanded until 1802. He was also a member of the House of Keys from 1784 until his death over fifty years later.

In 1802 he and his younger brother Mark Hildesley Quayle I joined with John Taubman and James Kelly to launch 'The Isle of Man Bank Company', the first bank on the Isle of Man, each of the partners contributing 500 guineas. George Quayle was managing director, and part of Bridge House was used as the bank's headquarters. A drawing of the building appeared on the bank notes, issued in denominations of one guinea and five guineas, with in addition penny and half penny tokens. In due course 'Quayle's notes' were said to be as safe as the Bank of England and the bank became very popular with gentry and merchants in the Island. In 1804 Mark died at the age of 34, in 1805 James Kelly was bought out and the partnership with John Taubman was dissolved in 1807. George ran the business on his own until 1810 when he entered into a new partnership with Patrick Lightfoot and Edward Cotteen. This remained in place until Cotteen withdrew in 1816, after which the bank got into serious difficulties. The reason for this, it would seem, was the simple one that has sent banks to the wall ever since – Quayle's bank lent more money than it had on deposit. George conscientiously sold a number of his personal assets, including the barony of St Trinian's, so that he could pay off his depositors, and the bank closed in 1818.[21]

In addition to his occupation as a soldier and banker, George Quayle was something of an inventor and Bridge House was equipped with a lathe, a working bench and an astronomical telescope. He was credited with a number of mechanical inventions, winning a gold medal from the Royal Society of Arts and Sciences in London. A lifelong bachelor, he was a member of Britain's 'Ancient and Noble Order of Bucks', a branch of which was founded in Douglas in 1764, and he entertained fellow members, who came from the leading Island families such as the Drinkwaters and Heywoods, and hosted meetings in a room he designed at Bridge House which resembled the cabin of a ship. This survives today, painted in the elegant duck-egg blue which is thought to be the original colour.[22]

Another survival is the 'Peggy', a schooner-rigged, clinker-built yacht 26 feet 5 inches long which George kept in a boat cellar below the house, with access to the harbour. He frequently sailed her in Manx waters and probably made several crossings to England. She was a very fast craft and in 1796 George took her to a regatta on Lake Windermere where she won races and was much admired. Sailing her home George encountered rough weather and was thankful for the sliding keels, which he seems to have invented and which soon became standard equipment on sailing boats of this size. '...The quarter cloths', he wrote later, 'were of very great protection: without them I believe we had gone to Davy Jones' locker, and without the sliding keels we could not have carried sail enough'.[23] George also travelled widely in Europe and explored Turkey. He died, aged 84, in 1835.

As we have seen, one of George's younger brothers, Mark Hildesley Quayle I died at the age of 34 in 1804, having succeeded his father as a very young Clerk of the Rolls in 1797. Another brother, Basil, who lived at the Creggan's farm near Castletown, was a pioneer of new agricultural methods and produced an influential pamphlet suggesting various ways in which the Island's productivity could be improved – including the desirability of commuting tithes for money payments. Mark's son, Mark Hildesley Quayle II, lived at Bridge House and also at 'Crogga', a baronial-style house at Santon. He trained as a lawyer and was a member of the Keys from 1842 to 1847 when he was appointed – no surprise – Clerk of the Rolls, and he was acting Governor in 1860 and 1863 on the resignation of one incumbent and the death of another. He was respected both as a lawyer and a judge as well as an antiquarian and philanthropist and he was responsible for introducing a system of voluntary poor relief to Castletown.[24]

If the Quayles had something of a monopoly on the office of Clerk of the Rolls, the Castletown Taubmans produced four Speakers of the House of Keys who served as such for a total of 77 years between them. Established in Bowling Green House since the second half of the sixteenth century, the Taubmans – who had the confusing tradition of calling their eldest sons John for many generations – produced their first Speaker in John Taubman (1780-1799), followed by his son John (1799-1823). He broke the family's immediate connection with Castletown in 1773 when he ceased to live in Bowling Green House and moved to the more prestigious estate of the Nunnery in Douglas, previously owned by the Heywood family for generations. Bowling Green House gradually fell into disuse and was subsequently demolished.

A document in the Atholl papers lists the names of MHKs around 1800 and no less than twelve were related to the elder John Taubman, while a further four were linked to him through business.[25] Not only did his son John become Speaker, but his grand-daughter Isabella Taubman married General Alexander Goldie, another Speaker (1831-1844), and their son John Goldie-Taubman held the office from 1844 to 1847 and his son Sir John Goldie-Taubman from 1867 to 1898.

RIOT AND REVOLT, 1825

From early times the Church had claimed a 'tithe', or a tenth of the produce of the people, which as far as country folk were concerned, traditionally involved surrendering a proportion of their corn. Money raised from this was used to pay the parish clergy, who, poor enough in any case, would have been destitute without it. During the eighteenth century a revolution in agricultural methods had led to the planting of potatoes and turnips instead of wheat and the Church had attempted to tax these, as well as introducing a 'fish tithe' on herring. All these demands had been met with

Bridge House, home of the Quayle family for many generations. (Author)

strong resistance and despite the fact that Orders in Council from the UK
recognized the legality of the fish tithe in 1769, Manx fishermen had refused
to pay it and the Church backed down. Soon after Atholl's nephew George
Murray was appointed Bishop he decided to sort out the issue, well aware
that clergy stipends had dwindled. First he asked for troops from England to
be sent in 1818 to enforce collection of the fish tithe, but received no
support. Then in 1819 and 1821 the Manx Court of the Exchequer upheld
the Bishop's claim to be able to levy tithes on potatoes and turnips on farms
belonging to Robert Farrant of Ballamoar, Jurby, and Caesar Tobin of
Ballamiddle. Tobin and Farrant's son, William, appealed to the Privy Council
and Lord Mansfield eventually rejected their appeals in June 1825.[26]

Murray announced in July that tithes on turnips and potatoes would be
levied from November and there was an immediate outcry in the Manx
countryside, partly because there had been a fall in prices since the end of the
French Wars in 1815 and many poorer farmers and crofters were unable to
pay. William Farrant from Jurby. who was Captain of the Parish, led a
movement of protest and encouraged his followers to sign a pledge, or
'bond', promising that they would not pay. A similar pledge was signed by
inhabitants of Ballaugh and Kirk Michael with the support of their Captains
of the Parish, and other villages prepared to take the same action – which had
been declared illegal in England some years before. In the absence of his

uncle the Governor, Murray appealed to his deputy, Colonel Smelt, who held an inquiry and delivered a mild reprimand to William Farrant, John Hughes and John Caine, the Captains of the Parishes of Jurby, Ballaugh and Kirk Michael, stating that they had no doubt acted 'from error rather than wilful intention'.[27]

Murray's chief agent (or 'proctor') for the collection of tithes was James McCrone, a tough Scot who had been accused of perjury some years before in a tithe case: he was acquitted and held a grievance thereafter. It was announced at each parish church that a tithe of twelve shillings per acre would be levied on potatoes – a very high rate considering that in Ireland the charge was three shillings and in the North of England two shillings and six pence. On top of this the potato crop in 1825 had been poor and the herring fishing a complete failure. The first attempts to collect the money were made in the parishes of Kirk Arbory and Kirk Christ Rushen by two men well-known to be of bad character, who set off with three assistants and three carts on Friday October 28th when most farmers were away from their farms attending local fairs. The two collectors behaved aggressively and infuriated several labourers who set upon them at Kentraugh and knocked them down. Edward Gawne, the owner, did not come to their assistance, so they fled to Port St Mary and hid in some houses which were surrounded and had their windows smashed. Meanwhile the collectors carts were broken up and the horses driven into the sea.

The news of this reached Castletown the next day and the High Bailiff rode to Port St Mary and arrested alleged offenders, but attempts to arrest the ringleaders on October 31st were thwarted when the constables were driven off by demonstrators. The next day McCrone sent the Bishop's gardener, Cobb, armed with a horse pistol, but he too was beaten up and the constables were stoned. The High Bailiff then called in troops from Douglas to bolster the handful of soldiers in Castletown and they spent the next couple of days in a fruitless search for the law-breakers. On November 3rd a crowd of men said to number about a thousand marched from Port St Mary towards Castletown carrying a red flag. The Council and High Bailiff sent Archibald Cregeen, the Coroner of Rushen (and famous Manx lexicographer), to negotiate with them and they dispersed, having made clear that 'it is unreasonable to expect to be able to get the potato tithe paid this year when there is not half a crop in the Isle, but we are ready to deliver all other tithes and dues or pay a fair value for them'.[28] This would be done in return for the release of those already arrested and a free pardon to everyone else.

Agitated farmers and labourers, waving the red flag, piled into the Market Square the following morning to see how the Bishop would respond to this request and Colonel Smelt ordered the castle gates to be shut, with soldiers visible on the battlements. The Bishop demanded that martial law be declared but Smelt had pointed out that this would be difficult with only seventy regular troops at his disposal. Relying on his popularity with the Manx people Smelt went among them and ordered them to disperse, and many began to leave the town. Some of these were met by Edward Gawne of Kentraugh 'who asked them where the Devil they were going. They replied in Manx that they were going home, for the Governor had given them a slap in the face'.[29] A deputation was allowed into the castle where Murray reluctantly told them that he had decided to remit the tithe for that year and the crowd went home. Murray attributed the need for this climb-down to the vacillation and weakness of Smelt, who, he thought, was too old for the strong action that was needed.

Yet Smelt's moderation prevented in Castletown some of the excesses which were committed elsewhere on the Island. On the same day a mob considerably the worse for drink marched to the vicarage at Kirk Michael and burnt the storehouse, where tithe potatoes were kept, and the tithe cart. After more drink at an inn, about a hundred men moved on to Knockaloe, the home of an unpopular tithe collector. His house was attacked and windows, doors and furniture destroyed, then seventeen stacks of hay, corn and peas were set on fire. The next day, armed with sticks, the mob moved on towards Bishopscourt, determined to set it ablaze, but they were confronted by the High Bailiff of Peel who persuaded them to disperse by promising that he would ask the Bishop on their behalf to cancel the tithe for that year. At the same time 23 members of the Castletown garrison rode to Bishopscourt and conveyed the Bishop's family to the relative safety of Castle Mona. Faced with the possibility of continued unrest, Murray gave in and made it known that he would abandon his plan to raise tithes from potatoes on the Island for that year.

The Home Office were critical of Smelt's handling of the situation, considering that he had been too lenient, and he responded by a swoop on the agitators. On November 21st, in the dead of night, the High Bailiffs of Castletown, Douglas and Peel, together with a contingent of soldiers and constables arrested eight men in Glenfaba, two of whom were tried in December, charged under an Act of 1817 which prescribed the death penalty for arson. Seeking to spare the accused, the jury insisted that the Act specified that burned stacks had to be 'adjoining' the house and in this case they were not, so the accused were instead transported for life to Australia. Meanwhile this experience of popular disturbance soon led to the setting up of justices of the peace on the Island.

These events dealt a considerable blow to the popularity of the Anglican

Church on the Island, and increasing numbers defected to the Methodists. Bishop Murray, badly shaken by his experiences, managed to obtain for himself the more desirable see of Rochester and left in 1827. His successor, William Ward, worked for many years on a scheme which would commute tithes to the satisfaction of all parties, while the British Government used a blatant bribe to make sure it was enforced. In 1836 an Act was passed at Westminster stating that the Manx see would be merged with Carlisle at the end of Ward's episcopate, which caused outrage in Tynwald. When Ward died in 1838 Tynwald was informed by Westminster that 'supposing the Legislature of the Isle of Man should pass a law carrying into effect the scheme in regard to tithes …the advisers of the Crown would be disposed to entertain favourably the proposition to retain the Bishopric of Sodor and Man upon the scale proposed'. Tynwald duly passed an Act for the Commutation of Tithes in 1839, the bishopric survived and the tithe controversy ebbed away.[30]

SMELT'S COLUMN

The tithe revolt got rid of Bishop George Murray and probably also persuaded his uncle the Duke of Atholl – whose son and heir sadly had mental health problems – that after a lifetime of disputes with the Manx and also the British Government, his dream of a restored Atholl lordship could not be realized. He therefore offered to sell the British Government all his remaining rights, lands and properties on the Island for the hefty sum of £417,144. This was in addition to £70,000 he had already received by the terms of an annuity granted in 1805. A further reason why he was prepared to sell was that he had unwisely demolished one of his Scottish properties, Dunkeld House, and his rebuilding programme proved to be cripplingly expensive. So in 1829 the deal was done and the UK became the proud owner of the Isle of Man in its entirety. A high price was paid and the UK intended to get some of the money back in the future by diverting Manx revenues to the Treasury and reducing investment in the Island to a minimum. So it has to be said that while the Duke of Atholl largely achieved his aim of gaining greater financial compensation for his father's sale of the sovereign rights in 1765, this was at the expense of the Island and its economic development.

Despite the fact that Atholl had long considered his deputy Cornelius Smelt to be too old to do his job properly, Smelt was still very much alive when Atholl died in Scotland at the age of 74 in 1830, having not visited the Island for four years. Smelt was 83 but the Home Office ministers decided to bide their time before appointing another Governor and left the Island in his hands as Lieutenant Governor. This disappointed the old man, who wrote begging to be appointed to the higher post, with its larger salary, because he claimed that he was so poor that he would have to sell his personal effects to provide for his funeral. However, he was able to enjoy two years in charge without Atholl breathing down his neck. During this time he had the satisfaction of seeing Caesar Bacon, the husband of his daughter Frances, become one of the co-owners of Castle Mona. Bacon and four others bought the mansion and its 179-acre estate in 1831 and opened it as a hotel on Easter Monday, 1832, with a glittering dinner for 80 in the Grand Saloon. On the same day the foundation stone was laid of the Tower of Refuge in Douglas Bay.

Smelt died a few months later, in November, aged 85. Always popular with the Manx, his funeral at St Mary's was attended by a great crowd and a brass six-pound cannon fired eighty-five rounds between mid-day and two o'clock to mark each year of his life. His coffin was made with fir, lead and Castle Rushen oak and covered with purple velvet, and he was buried in the chancel of the chapel. The Revd Hugh Stowell, in his eulogy, stressed that Smelt had 'identified himself with the people over whom he was called to preside. He regarded their interests as his interests, and their welfare as his welfare.' He had, he said, generously patronized charities and educational provision and had loved the Manx nation.

A public subscription in 1826 had already collected about £52 for a portrait of Smelt by Thomas Barber. In 1835 Sir William Hillary, one of Smelt's chief admirers, led a movement to raise £200 for a public monument and the design was entrusted to the architect John Welch, the designer of the Tower of Refuge, who submitted two plans – one for a plain Doric column and one for an obelisk. The Doric column was chosen and erected on the Parade, facing Castle Rushen, where it remains at the heart of Castletown today, the only monument raised by the Manx to one of their British Governors.[31]

KING WILLIAM'S COLLEGE, 1833-1865

The House of Keys, supported strongly by Cornelius Smelt, had been so outraged by the temporary closure of the Grammar School under Thimbleby that after the departure of Bishop Murray they determined somehow to take control of the Barrow Trust monies and make sure that they were used properly. In 1811 Lord Derby made a final settlement of £16,000 to meet any claims of the Trust on his estate and by 1828 the income from the farms at Hango Hill and Ballagilley was far more than was needed to maintain three Academic Scholars, so money was available to fuel the idea of building a grand new boarding school. Whose idea that was and why they thought it would work are interesting questions because, as it turned out, the college was the first of all the new nineteenth century boarding 'public schools'.

John Welch's monument to Lieutenant-Governor Cornelius Smelt, late 1830s. (Lily Publications)

King William's College and Chapel. (Lily Publications)

Bishop Ward was very reluctant to abandon the idea of a theological college that would train future Manx clergy but he was outmanouvered by the determination of Smelt and the Keys who succeeded, after many months of legal disputation, in having Barrow's various trusts amalgamated into one 'Bishop Barrow's Charity' under the control of predominantly secular trustees chaired by the Lieutenant Governor.

After meetings in Castle Rushen the trustees decided that a college should be built on the Hango Hill estate and the foundation stone was laid by Smelt on St George's Day, 1830, the annual celebration of King William's birthday, before a huge crowd of 5,000 people, two and a half times the size of Castletown's population. Smelt was impressively kitted out in Windsor uniform, dress sword and cocked hat, and on his arrival the crowd gave him three hearty cheers and the band played 'See the Conquering Hero Comes'. In his speech Smelt voiced the hope that the college would be 'a blessing to this Island to all generations' and that the great benevolence of Bishop Barrow would never be forgotten. Bishop Ward, accepting gracefully the train of events, threw his weight behind the scheme and laid the foundation of the college chapel of St Thomas on the same day.

The architects entrusted with the project were the firm of Hansom and Welch, and the brothers Edward and John Welch were responsible for the basic design in collegiate Gothic style. The initial scheme proposed a pinnacled, octagonal tower but the simple, solid sentinel that eventually loomed above the college and the whole area around was a last-minute change made by John Welch. From the start there were financial problems because, although the Barrow funds were quite buoyant, the new college was conceived on a grand scale: indeed, it was one of the largest buildings so far contemplated on the Island. The first estimate for it was £3,000, though many feared it would cost more, and hopes were raised that if there was a shortfall, the endowment might perhaps be increased by public subscription or royal benevolence. For this reason the projected name was changed from King's College to King William's College, but King William gave little more than his permission for the name.

Bishop Ward very nearly pulled off a move which would have guaranteed the college a steady revenue and transformed its fortunes. He suggested that some of the revenue from tithes should be diverted to the college and the Crown agreed to this: but then it was discovered that they were not entirely in the Crown's gift and the scheme fell through. The college opened on August 1st, 1833, despite the fact that the building was unfinished, with the Revd Edward Wilson as principal, the Revd Robert Dixon as vice-principal, the Revd John Stowell, who was Manx, as third master and bursar, and six assistant masters. Wilson was a Fellow of St John's College, Cambridge and very much a 'scholar and a gentleman'. He had a salary of £200 a year plus £30 a year as dean of the school chapel, which was to be open for public worship, especially for Derbyhaven residents. The first pupils numbered 43, with three 'senior students' – who were the old Academic Scholars, to be prepared by Wilson for ordination. Tuition fees ranged from about £1-£2 a quarter, with boarding fees from £25 to £30 a year.

The financial aspects, however, did not go well. The total cost of the building came in at £6,572, more than double the estimate, and the builder went bankrupt. The Barrow fund provided £2,071, public subscription £1,692 and Bishop Ward's Manx Churches Fund £1,000, leaving a shortfall of £1,809. The trustees were therefore obliged to mortgage the estate, thus saddling the college with a heavy debt from the start. The best answer to this was to attract as many pupils as possible and charge them suitable fees. By 1834 the pupils numbered 70 English boys, 50 Irish, 30 Manx, 10 Scots and a few sons of Indian missionaries. It may seem surprising that a remote boarding school, close to a town where there had recently been a deadly cholera outbreak, should have appealed to so many parents in England and Ireland. The answer is that education in general and boarding schools in particular were becoming very fashionable among the increasingly wealthy middle classes; the earnest, evangelical tone of the college was popular, and though fees were charged, they were comparatively low.

Despite attracting a good number of pupils and establishing a workable framework at the college Wilson did not have an easy time, with very little money for completing an unfinished building, a carriage accident that left him with the loss of his left arm, and few cultural opportunities in Castletown. After five years he thankfully accepted a parish in Somerset and handed over to the Revd Alfred Phillips, the Headmaster of Crewkerne Grammar School, who did so well that after three years he was offered the post of Principal of Cheltenham College. To maintain stability the trustees then appointed Robert Dixon as principal, with Joseph Cumming, a noted geologist, replacing him as vice-principal. Dixon had to face a rising tide of criticism on the Island, fuelled by the Vicar of Braddan, Robert Brown, formerly a teacher at Castletown Grammar School and Headmaster of Douglas Grammar School. In a letter to a Manx newspaper in 1836 he complained that the Barrow funds had been squandered on building a school which was far too large, had only 30 Manx pupils and was not providing free instruction to prospective clergymen.

To meet these objections the trustees made some attempts to provide suitable scholarships but at 2am on the morning of 14 January, 1844, the college caught fire and a strong wind fanned the flames. Soldiers rushed out from Castletown but the nearest fire engine was at Douglas and it did not arrive until about 7.30am. By 10am the fire was out but most of the building had been destroyed, including the Academic Library with its fine collection of rare books, and many Castletown property deeds which had been kept there temporarily. The estimate for rebuilding was £3,791 but the insurance only covered half of that amount. A public subscription came to the rescue with £1,871 and most of the college was again in action by May, 1845, rebuilt by John Timperley, a civil engineer from Castletown, who made his new construction as fireproof as possible.

In 1847 Mrs Margaret Quilliam (the widow of Captain John Quilliam) left her Castletown estate at Orrisdale to the trustees and by 1850 Deemster Heywood endowed the first Barrow scholarships of £10 a year and the trustees provided 20 foundation scholarships for Manx boys. The 1850s brought further financial problems, especially after the collapse of Holme's Bank in 1854 with £500 of college money, but in 1860 Tynwald passed the Bishop Barrow's Charity Act, which permitted funds from the endowment to be used for new buildings. Flaxney Stowell of Castletown designed a new cloister and yard as well as a dining hall and other amenities and by the time Dixon retired in 1865, after 24 years as principal, the college was fully established as a significant factor in Island life. Many of its early pupils became notable later on, such as George Hills, a bishop in Canada, Frederick Farrar, Dean of Canterbury, Thomas Fowler, Vice-Chancellor of Oxford, and Field Marshal Sir George White, VC. Manx boys included the lawyer Sir James Gell, the Manx National Poet, T. E. Brown, and Daniel Cregeen, who

The interior of the second King William's College Chapel, opened in 1879. (Lily Publications)

built London's Blackfriars Bridge. Despite criticisms that it did not do enough for the Manx, there was a real sense in which King William's College put Castletown 'on the map' through being an educational institution increasingly well-known and respected throughout Britain and beyond.[32]

THE LORNE HOUSE ERA, 1832-1860

After the death of Lieutenant Governor Cornelius Smelt, the Home Office decided that the full title of Governor would not be resurrected, and his successor was appointed with the same title of Lieutenant Governor, probably because within Britain's growing Empire Governors ruled larger territories than the Isle of Man. The choice fell upon Colonel John Ready, aged 60, who had been a very popular and successful Lieutenant Governor of Prince Edward Island, in Canada, since 1824. He was a widower, but his daughter Mary Jane kept house for him. He arrived in Castletown in December 1832, where he was met near the four mile bridge on the Douglas road by a party of the gentlemen of the town and neighbourhood on horseback, and they escorted him to his residence at the castle. At 2.00 the ceremony of inauguration was performed in the Court House by the Clerk of the Rolls and the High Bailiff read a long and florid address of welcome.[33]

Ready was not destined to live in Castle Rushen for very long. The growing administrative needs of the Island, together with the inadequacies and discomforts of Derby House, made it seem sensible to convert the former Governor's residence into a Court House and offices for the Clerk of the Rolls and the Water Bailiff, and Ready was granted an allowance of £150 a year as rent for a suitable 'Government House'. This came at a time when the perfect house was available in Castletown. Lorne House (spelt 'Lorn' until the 1930s) was built during 1826/1827 for Robert Cuninghame, whose father William, a Scottish aristocrat, and mother (born Christian Taubman) had lived in a more modest house close to Bridge House on the harbour. According to the most recent historian of Lorne House, William 'had a spat with his neighbour George Quayle, who, in return, extended and raised the height of Bridge House to block Cuninghame's view of the harbour. Cuninghame's riposte was to plan the demolition of [his own] house and build the much grander house on the hill'. He was in the process of buying a large plot for this purpose when he died in 1825, so his son Robert completed the purchase and went ahead with the construction of an attractive Regency-style mansion, possibly designed to some extent by Thomas Brine.

On February 18th, 1828 Robert and his wife hosted a celebration party, described in the 'Manx Sun' by a correspondent who considered that 'Great taste was displayed in the decoration of the elegantly colonnaded hall: the

Lorne House soon after its completion in 1827. (Manx National Heritage)

grand staircase was peculiarly striking, from the singular and beautiful effects
produced by the neatly entwined wreaths of evergreens which encircled the
light fluted columns of this princely mansion'. Tragically, both Robert
Cuninghame and his wife died at an early age soon after this, leaving five
children to be brought up by relatives. From 1830 the house was
uninhabited, the contents were auctioned, and it was available to rent. Ready
negotiated a thirteen-year lease with his allowance of £150 a year, and moved
in during 1834. Two years later he married as his second wife Sarah, the
daughter of Sir John Tobin of Liverpool, and a daughter was born to them in
1837.[34]

A charming and popular man, promoted to the rank of major-general in
1841, Ready presided over an elegant and happy establishment at Lorne
House, where he hosted many parties and entertainments for Castletown and
Island society. Politically, the main issues that confronted him were a growing
demand for an elected House of Keys, prompted by Britain's parliamentary
reforms of 1832, and resistance by the Manx to attempts by the Home Office
to increase Island customs duties, in order to bring them into line with those
of the UK. Ready steered a diplomatic course through these problems until a
tragic mistake cut short his life in July1845. He had been seriously ill for
several months and was receiving medication. Two bottles were placed by his
side, one containing morphine, which was relatively harmless, and the other
atrophine, which was a deadly poison suitable for external application only.
Neither bottle was marked, and he took a draught of atrophine and died
almost immediately. The coroner recommended that, in future, all medicines
on the Island should be clearly labelled.[35]

Ready's successor was the Hon. Charles Hope, aged only 37, a son of the Earl of Hopetoun, who had been MP for Linlithgowshire since 1838. In 1841 he married Lady Isabella Douglas, a daughter of the Earl of Selkirk, and they had begun to raise a family. The lease on Lorne House had two years to run when Hope was appointed and he renewed it in 1847 for a further thirteen years. In September that year he suffered a severe embarrassment when the Royal Yacht, with Queen Victoria and Prince Albert aboard, dropped anchor in Ramsey Bay and Prince Albert went ashore for an exploratory walk. Hope had not been forewarned and though he hastened from Castletown to Ramsey the poor roads slowed his progress and by the time he reached Ramsey the Royal Yacht had moved on. The reforming party in particular enjoyed giving voice to the popular ditty which resulted:

> Hey! Charley Hope, where are you now?
> The mob are kicking up a row –
> The very dogs do bark bow wow
> To welcome the Queen to Mona.[36]

A more enjoyable occasion for him was the official opening in September 1854 of the impressive waterwheel built to drain the Laxey mines. He turned a small handle which let water onto the wheel so that it began to turn and Mrs Dumbell, wife of the Chairman of the Mining Company, smashed a bottle of champagne ornamented with lace against the structure and named it 'Lady Isabella' in honour of Hope's wife.

In 1848 there were serious disturbances in many European capitals, with crowds agitating for more democratic forms of government. The Chartist movement in England, which demanded a wider electorate, among other things, gave new life to the movement in the Island for an elected House of Keys. Hope resisted this on the grounds that, with a popular mandate, the Keys would prove too troublesome: already they were seeking control over expenditure on the Island, especially regarding the development of harbours. He negotiated a compromise over this by which their demands were partially conceded in return for an increase in the customs duties to parity with the UK – which incidentally put a stop to the last vestiges of 'smuggling'. Hope was also able to negotiate a compromise over the UK's decision to enclose parts of the 26,000 acres of land which had been bought from the Duke of Atholl in 1829, thus depriving many Manx people of long-established commons rights.

T.E.Brown, who attended King William's College as a boy and was vice-principal there from 1855 to 1861, gave a lecture in Peel in 1893 in which he described Castletown during Ready and Hope's time in his own very droll style which had his audience in fits of laughter. 'I am not a native of Castletown', he said:

> but it was to me for many years a very delightful home, and I have innumerable recollections of that town. I should like to give you some idea of its social aspects and constituents. It was the most aristocratic place that was ever known. Oh, you have no idea. It was tremendous – the various circles, the inner, outer, first outer, second-outer, fourth-outer, fifth-outer. All these circles were as much like – well, the planetary system as anything else, or perhaps like a large, round Portugal onion…Now round (the Governor) was what I may call the inner circle. Dr Dixon, I suppose, the Principal of the College, and the Clerk of the Rolls, and Mr Mark Quayle, would be considered the principal members of that circle. It was a very difficult position. It was a very difficult society, but a society of extreme inflexibility and extreme touchiness. There was a very serious difficulty connected with that society. It was this. The great problem that Dr Dixon and the Governor had to solve was the management of the loose class of English that came to settle in Castletown. The inner circle undoubtedly consisted of most respectable men, half-pay colonels, majors, captains, good and excellent men, most pious men, men who would have been an ornament to any society. Well, the test of such men as was visible to us youngsters was their being invited to Government House, so that you see, the Governor, by excluding or admitting these gentlemen to his dinner table, and to his At Homes, gave, as it were, a tone to the society of the place…[37]

The thirteen-year lease on Lorne House was due to end in 1860 and when it became clear that the owners would not renew it, Hope recommended that the UK should finance the building of a new Government House in Castletown. The Office of Works estimated the cost at £7,000 and quickly suggested that the Manx Government should foot the bill, promising Hope only his £150 a year rental allowance. This prompted Hope to come to the conclusion that, after a tenure of fifteen years, it would be a good time to resign, especially as his wife was heiress to her childless brother the Earl of Selkirk, who owned great estates and property in Scotland. Although reformers in the Island were probably glad to see him go, his resignation was doubtless a blow to members of Castletown's high society, who had found him a congenial figure socially, with his pleasant manner, scholarly tastes and aristocratic status. Moreover, the unwelcome possibility loomed that the next Lieutenant Governor might rent a house somewhere else in the Island, thus diminishing the prestige of the capital.

Chapter Four

ABANDONED, 1860

The departure of Hope and the prospect of a new Governor prompted some of the leading citizens of Douglas to begin a subtle campaign to persuade the new man to take up residence there. According to the census of 1861 the population of Castletown, at 2,373, had remained more or less static for the last 40 years, while that of Douglas had forged ahead to 12,511. The main reasons for this were that the natural harbour facilities in Douglas were far better than those in Castletown, while with its spectacular bay and beach Douglas was considered a more attractive location by many of the half-pay officers who had flocked to the Island after 1815, and by the increasing number of visitors who came for a holiday. Perhaps most importantly, there was an entrepreneurial spirit among the 'self-made' citizens of Douglas which was lacking in Castletown, dominated as it was by the 'Castletown clique' of officials and 'dignitaries' who thought along traditional and conservative lines.

At a time when it must have been clear to many people that the future of the Island lay with the visiting trade, little was done to develop Derbyhaven as a holiday resort and it remained just a picturesque cluster of cottages and former red herring-houses. These had been built soon after 1771 by John Woodhouse, who introduced the Yarmouth method of curing herring to the Island, and it involved stacking the fish for several days in layers, with salt between, to purify them. After this they were washed in brine, drained and threaded on rods through their mouths and smoked for several days over a fire. Then they were packed for sale at home or for export. But the herring fishing declined and by the middle of the nineteenth century the buildings had been converted for farm use.[1] Though a stone jetty was built at Derbyhaven around 1842 to give more shelter to the anchorage, no-one seemed prepared to make use of the potential of the beach for development as a seaside resort. This may have seemed a good thing to some people both at the time and even now, but the result was that the initiative passed to the more dynamic Douglas.

Towards the end of 1860 it was announced that the new Lieutenant Governor would be Francis Stainsby-Conant-Pigott, who had been MP for Reading for thirteen years. In his late fifties he arrived on the Island on November 10th with his wife and army officer son, and with no official accommodation at his disposal, he stayed at the Castle Mona Hotel. On the 11th he came to Castletown where he took the oath administered to him in Castle Rushen Court House by the Clerk of the Rolls and Deputy Governor, Mark Hildesley Quayle. Ten days after his arrival he wrote to the Home Office informing them that despite making every possible effort to find a house or building site in Castletown, he had found nothing and had instead rented Marina Lodge, an elegant Regency house by the sea in Douglas, for £250. The allowance of £150, he pointed out, was inadequate, as rents in the Isle of Man were high.[2]

This was a fantastic coup for the businessman Samuel Harris who was both the owner of the house and the chairman of Douglas Town Commissioners, and when Pigott and his family returned to take up residence formally in February 1861 he made sure that the town put on a massive celebration as a welcome. Pigott's arrival in Douglas aboard the 'Tynwald' was commemorated with a picture published in the influential 'London Illustrated News', emphasizing that what happened in the Isle of Man had begun to be of interest to the British public. Once settled behind his desk, Pigott announced, no doubt influenced by Samuel Harris and other Douglas businessmen, that it was his policy in due course to move both the law courts and Tynwald to Douglas. Fate intervened to prevent this because Pigott suddenly died in December 1862, probably from cancer, while visiting his English home in Hampshire. Mark Hildesley Quayle was again appointed Deputy Governor and, being a loyal Castletown man, he announced on his own authority that for the time being, at any rate, the law courts would stay where they were.

Pigott's successor was Henry Loch, aged 36, destined to be the Island's most creative and dynamic Governor. The 'Castletown clique' brought to his notice the availability of a suitable house in the town called 'Paradise' but Loch was clear in his own mind that, like Pigott, he would live in Douglas. He and his beautiful young wife Elizabeth rejected Marina Lodge but chose instead 'Bemahague', a larger house in Onchan which has served as Government House ever since. It could be argued that the Lieutenant Governor's decision to live in Douglas was not in itself a body blow to Castletown: after all, the Duke of Atholl had built Castle Mona near Douglas. But Atholl had been an essentially absentee Governor and the day-to-day administration was carried on during his time in Castletown by his deputies who were based at Castle Rushen. Loch saw no reason to reverse his predecessor's stated intention to move the law courts to Douglas and in 1864 he announced that the courts would be held alternately in both towns until new and more spacious accommodation could be provided in Douglas.

The members of the Keys, only a handful of whom were Castletown men, had long been dissatisfied with their cramped and increasingly insanitary premises. As early as 1840 there had been a disaster when a cesspool burst and flooded the floor of the debating chamber, and the plumbing arrangements of the building had been deeply suspect ever since. Hope had been requested to provide more suitable premises in 1859 after Robert Cain, a local builder, had produced a survey which found that the building was in a state of disrepair and the interior accommodation was inconveniently arranged. Also, the debating chamber was small and 'in consequence of the offensive sewers and other nuisances in the immediate neighbourhoods, the atmosphere of that apartment is rendered so impure and tainted as to be almost intolerable [and] exceedingly injurious to health'.[3]

The Keys made a serious blunder in 1864 when they took the drastic step of imprisoning James Brown, the editor of the 'Isle of Man Times', who had published scathingly critical articles about their rejection of a Bill to increase the powers of the Douglas Town Commissioners. Brown spent seven weeks and three days in Castle Rushen before his release was ordered by the British Courts in response to a writ of *habeas corpus*. Brown then sued the Keys and won damages of £519 with costs. This, together with the arguments of the long-established reform movement, helped Loch to make up his mind that the Keys should become an elected body, and he cleverly acquired their agreement to this by promising them in return control over any surplus Island revenues. On December 20th 1866 the Keys passed an Act creating ten electoral districts, which were to be the towns of Castletown, Peel and Ramsey with one member each, Douglas with three members and the sheadings of Glenfaba, Michael, Ayre, Garff, Middle and Rushen with three members each. The first Manx general election took place in April 1867, with 13 of the previous 24 members being returned, and one of their first priorities was to petition Loch to move the House of Keys to Douglas. Another of the immediate effects of the change was that whereas in the past there had usually been three or four members of the Keys who were Castletown men, now there was only one.

The elected House met very seldom in Castletown, preferring to use the Douglas Court House, and they had estimates prepared for a new building in Douglas and held a competition for possible architectural designs, none of which found favour. Their last sitting in Castletown took place on November 26th 1874 when they minuted that the repairs to their building that had been undertaken without reference to them had been 'simply a waste of public money'.[4] The building was acquired by Dumbell's Bank and after extensive renovations it opened as their Castletown branch in January 1878. The following year the former Bank of Mona premises in Douglas became vacant and the Keys moved in there and a purpose-built chamber for Tynwald was constructed next door in 1894. So by 1874 the Lieutenant Governor, the law courts and the House of Keys had all abandoned Castletown, which could claim to be the Island's capital no longer.

CASTLETOWN'S FIRST MHK, 1867-1882

Castletown's single seat was vigorously contested, in the first parliamentary election ever held in the town, by R.T. Quayle and J.M. Jeffcott, who had been a member of the old House of Keys since 1855 and High Bailiff of Castletown since 1865. Jeffcott won and he was re-elected in 1874 and 1881, resigning in 1882, though retaining the office of High Bailiff until a few years before his death in 1892. As he was one of the most influential figures in 'post reform' Castletown, it is worth looking at his career in some detail for the insights it gives into aspects of life at the time. He left a brief manuscript memoir of his early years, recounting his birth in July 1816, the son of John William Jeffcott, 'a member of an old and reputable family in the county of Kerry, Ireland', who was a surgeon in the Royal Navy. His mother was the daughter of John Moore, the Vicar of Braddan, but she was widowed in 1824 after twelve years of marriage, when her husband died of typhus fever, aged 64. With her son and two daughters Mrs Jeffcott moved to Ballaclague, Arbory, and John was at first educated privately by a number of local clergymen and then in 1828 the family moved back to Castletown. John was by now twelve and his experiences of schools in Castletown were very mixed:

> The Revd William Gell then had opened a private boarding and day school for boys at the Green in that town – though there was at the time another school in the town kept by the Revd George Parsons [i.e. the Grammar School] and which had long flourished under the name of 'Academy'. Mr Gell was selected as my master and to him I was sent. With him I remained for two years and during that time was compelled to tolerate within school hours the society of some of the blackest young villains I ever saw. After bearing, as well as I could, the torments I had to endure in this pandemonium for two years, I was removed to the Academy of Mr Parsons. Here I met with genial companions and learned as much in three months as I had done in the whole of the previous two years. I remained with Mr Parsons' school until I went to King William's College [aged 17] on its opening in the autumn of 1833. At that time the Revd Edward Wilson was Principal. He was a correct and elegant scholar and was so genial and good that he won the respect and affection of his colleagues and pupils.....I am deeply indebted to Mr Wilson for the love which I have always borne to literary pursuits and much of the enjoyment

which I have experienced in life has been derived from my literary hobbies. Soon after the opening of the college a literary debating society was established at Castletown which was kept up for some time with much spirit and ability. The meetings were held in the old Grammar School, [and] the value of such institutions is unquestionable.[5]

Unfortunately this brief scrap of autobiography ends at this point but a lengthy obituary notice in the 'Isle of Man Times' provides information about his later career. From KWC he studied law at the Rolls office and was called to the Manx Bar in 1839. In due course he married Lucy, the daughter of John Christian Corrin, and raised with her one son and five daughters. He spent 26 years building up his practice and reputation as a lawyer so that 'for a considerable number of years he possessed the largest legal practice in the south of the Island and earned the reputation of being a sound and trustworthy lawyer'. During this period he was also elected to the Keys in 1855. Then:

> In 1865, on the retirement of Mr James Gell from the chief magistracy to be Attorney General, Mr Jeffcott was appointed by Governor Loch High Bailiff of the ancient capital. Some people were surprised that he should give up an excellent practice for the modest emoluments of the bailiwick. As High Bailiff his conduct upon the bench was distinguished by the utmost impartiality; and whilst he administered justice with an even hand, his gentle and benign disposition led him to mingle with his decisions that mercy which has been described as the better half of justice. As chief magistrate of the town he had a watchful eye over its interests and was always ready to take the lead in any movement started for the advantage of the quiet little town in which he had been born and bred.[6]

Next came the excitement of the 1867 election and fifteen years in the reformed House of Keys. Clearly he was a man of conservative tastes, while his 'modesty and reticence, which were leading traits in his character, rather prevented him taking that prominent position in insular politics which his character and attainments would have entitled him to'. Indeed, the obituary admitted that his 'standing in the House of Keys was useful rather than brilliant. His tastes were not at all in the direction of an enthusiastic partisanship in stormy debates..' He was a member of the Highway Board and the Harbour Board for many years and influenced the provision of improved harbour facilities in Douglas and Port Erin, though not, it must be said, in Castletown. He retired from the Keys in 1882 because of ill health, though he 'efficiently discharged the not over-onerous duties of High Bailiff' until his death. He was an excellent shot and a good painter, considered to be 'the best brush on the Island', with pictures exhibited in Liverpool's Walker Art Gallery. He was also an enthusiastic naturalist, botanist, antiquarian and archaeologist, and the author of most of the report on the Island issued by the Archaeological Association, of which he was chairman, in 1878. He died peacefully in May, 1892, in his 76th year.

Clearly Jeffcott was an admirable man, widely respected for his many civilized qualities. But he was not the sort of dynamic politician who might have felt it his duty to fight Castletown's corner at a time when it had already been eclipsed by the go-ahead entrepreneurs of Douglas. As the century neared its end, Castletown quietly marked time: in Douglas the number of houses grew from 2,057 in 1871 to 3,119 in 1901, while in Ramsey it grew from 685 to 1,012. The increase in Castletown was just eleven - from 439 to 450.[7]

COMMISSIONERS AND MHKS

One of Governor Loch's many achievements was the establishment of a single-track narrow gauge steam railway network round the Island, thanks to the investment of his friend the Duke of Sutherland, an immensely rich railway enthusiast. The first line, from Douglas to Peel, opened in 1873 and a much more ambitious line from Douglas to Port Erin via Castletown was finished in 1874. The effects of this railway on both Port St Mary and Port

The railway arrived in Castletown in 1874, making it easier to go to the shops in Douglas! (Lily Publications)

Erin were very considerable because it encouraged their development as holiday resorts, but Castletown and Derbyhaven were content to remain much as they were, perhaps because of a lack of local leadership. If anything, the commercial effect on Castletown was adverse because many locals could now go by train to the shops and market in Douglas instead.

In 1883 Castletown officially expanded in size when by Act of Tynwald the town boundary was extended to the east and to the north-west, increasing its area by just over a third.[8] Then in March, 1884, Tynwald's Castletown Town Act created five elected Town Commissioners who would be responsible for setting rates and running the government and administration of the newly-extended town. Ten years later the number of commissioners was raised to seven. The first chairman was local grocer James Mylchreest, who served again in 1886 and 1887. In 1891 he defeated one of the Stevensons of Balladoole in the election to become Castletown's third MHK in succession to Thomas Vondy, who had taken over from John Jeffcott. Mylchreest remained MHK until 1903 and in his twelve years in office his voice was frequently heard in Tynwald urging three successive Lieutenant Governors (Spencer Walpole, Sir West Ridgeway and Lord Henniker) to take more notice of Castletown's needs. The long and brilliant career of Sir Henry Loch as Governor (1863-1882) had done wonders for the Island in general and Douglas in particular, but Loch did not pay much attention to Castletown.

Mylchreest made it his main priority to agitate for improvements to be made to Castletown's harbour facilities, which had languished far behind the other Island towns. By the 1830s the harbour had silted up to some extent and a road was built between it and the castle, while a short pier and dry basin were constructed around 1844. Beyond that, little had been done. In 1889, when Thomas Vondy was the town's MHK, a Tynwald committee was appointed, chaired by Spencer Walpole, which looked at the possibility of making provision for a low-water landing in the outer harbour and 'they were of the opinion that the landing-place might be improved by removing the boulder-stones, etc. along the lines of the old jetty and by repairing its surface, carefully avoiding the raising of such a jetty above the height of the adjoining ground but making a small channel alongside'. The cost was estimated at £400, which Tynwald approved. In 1887 an important advance was made when the stone arches which separated the inner harbour from the 'duckpond' were replaced with an ingenious swing bridge, the first of its kind on the Island, which could easily be turned by one man in less than ninety seconds. This made it possible for quite large ships to be moored in the 'duckpond' until a fixed bridge was built in the 1960s.[9]

In May 1895 James Mylchreest expressed the hope in Tynwald that a vote for the improvement of Castletown's harbour would be provided for in the

The harbour entrance, early 20th century. (Ron Ronan collection)

next year's estimates. The lack of deep water in the harbour was a great loss to the town, he said, and he hoped plans for carrying out the necessary work would receive every consideration.[10] The harbour made news again when in the following year Mylchreest asked the Governor in Tynwald; 'May I ask what steps, if any, have been taken with regard to the widening of the opening through the Castletown harbour bridgeway, a small Norwegian schooner being all but wrecked on the 8th instant, in consequence of the opening being too narrow to get her through into safety'. Lord Henniker replied that estimates for the work had been much higher than expected, but that 'the matter shall not escape my attention'. Mylchreest told him in reply that 'the loss of that [vessel] would have been a serious matter, if she had not been got into a place of safety'.[11]

Two years later Mylchreest again demanded to know when the necessary improvements to the harbour would be made but Henniker, who had a growing reputation for putting things off, replied simply that the question would not be overlooked. Clearly it was, because the next year Mylchreest was on the attack once more: 'over and over again I have said that we are losing £500 a year by extra freight or goods imported into Castletown from want of a few extra feet of water. We have had promises now from three successive Governors that something would be done, so, I hope before anything is done in building harbours elsewhere [i.e. Port Erin] that the requirements of Castletown will be considered.'[12] This tirade produced some results because by 1900 the outer swing bridge had been repaved with creosoted wood and the bed of the harbour had been thoroughly cleared out, and in the next two years the upper harbour was cleaned out at considerable expense. Unfortunately, a steamer crashed into the bridge, causing serious damage, and another Mylchreest campaign resulted in Tynwald voting £1,300 in February 1903 'for defraying the cost of a widening of the harbour at Castletown at the outer swing bridge, by setting back the eastern abutment of the bridge six feet and providing a new foot swing bridge.'[13] Later that year the official view was that Castletown's harbour was by then 'in fair order'.[14]

Another contentious issue was the provision of water to the town. In 1891 the Castletown Water Bill was passed, its preamble stating that its purpose was 'to extend the powers of the [Waterworks] company, obtained under two previous Acts, so that they could take water from the Whallag stream at all times and from the Cringle stream for 36 hours a week, from Saturday night to Sunday morning'. This plan had worried local mill owners as well as landowners, who all feared that they would be deprived of adequate water as a result, but a long campaign of persuasion as well as 'incentives' from the Waterworks Company had won them round.[15]

In the early months of 1896 the UK withdrew the last of its troops stationed in Castletown and in May Mylchreest attempted to put pressure on Lord Henniker in Tynwald either to get them re-instated or to claim compensation from the UK for the £10,000 paid by Tynwald for the defence of the Island. Henniker said that it was true that by an agreement made in 1866 the UK was obliged to protect the Island by land and by sea, but the Manx government was not entitled to tell the UK how to do this. The short service system recently introduced into the British Army had made it undesirable for men to be away from the colours for long periods, and a fast cruiser would be just as effective for defence as soldiers.[16] Hence the military, so long a feature of Castletown life, disappeared from the scene and the unoccupied barracks in Market Square were eventually bought by the Town Commissioners for £600 in 1911 and converted into public conveniences and offices for themselves. When they later moved to the Old House of Keys the building was converted into an office complex known as Mannanan House.[17]

Though the troops left town in 1896, that year saw the great benefit of the opening of Poulsom's Park. According to an article in the 'Mona's Herald and Fargher's Advertiser', dated July 8th, 1896, Castletown people had 'from time immemorial' enjoyed

> .... the right of ramblage and recreation on the extensive turf tracts called the Claddagh and the Racecourse. The former of these places, as the name suggests, adjoins the town river, the Silverburn. The other stretched along the shore front from the point queerly named the Big

Cellar on to Langness itself. But the ownership in these properties recently changed hands, and by way of asserting untrammelled proprietory rights, the new owners granted leases and made uses of the Claddagh and the Racecourse which the Castletownians looked upon as an infringement of their immemorial rights of use …The claiming owners were persistent and the champions of the public rights were equally so. A veritable state of war prevailed, culminating in a grand night march of the [townspeople] to the Racecourse with brass band and torchlight accompaniment, in order to assert their enjoyment of recreative rights over the ground from time immemorial and their determination to maintain it for all time to come. Nothing was allowed to bar the progress of the crowd on the ground. One of the new owners who thought by his presence to inspire terror was hustled aside, and newly placed fences were torn up to allow of the unimpeded passage of the public-righters on to the debateable ground. The result of the night's work was an appeal on the part of the new owners to the arbitrament of the law. The champions of the people's rights were made the defendants in the case which in due course came to a hearing and ended in a verdict in favour of the new owners of the land and against all right of ramblage and recreation claimed by the public.[18]

A Castletown woman, Mrs William Poulsom, whose husband had once been Mayor of Bootle, came to the rescue and bought seven acres of land at the Claddagh, next to the river, which were levelled and walled in and then presented to the Town Commissioners as a public park. On July 2nd 1896 local schoolchildren accompanied by horse-drawn carriages and led by the Castletown and Foxdale brass bands processed from the Town Square to the new 'Poulsom Park' which the benefactress opened with a gold key presented to her by the Commissioners. She also received an illuminated address, ornamented with the Manx arms and local views, which had been crafted by Flaxney Stowell, a well known Castletown character and accomplished artist. The address was signed by James Gell, the High Bailiff, Edward Crellin, the Chairman of the Commissioners, and James Mylchreest.

It was also in Mylchreest's time that Deemster Sir James Gell, the High Bailiff's father and one who frequently used his influence to the benefit of the town, proposed in Tynwald in January 1899 the construction of a new police station to replace the existing one, which he considered 'a most wretched one and not fit to take prisoners in, and it will not hold more than two at a time'. He recalled an occasion when there was a riot in the town 'and ten or eleven people were arrested and the constable had to put them inside the gaol to keep them in custody until they were brought before the magistrates.

Sir James Gell, 1823-1905. (Manx National Heritage)

It is a damp place, except where the policemen sit'. He recommended a new building on a plot of land just outside the castle walls, costing about £500, and Tynwald voted the money accordingly. The new station was completed in 1901, one of the last works on the Island of the well-known architect Baillie Scott.[19]

When James Mylchreest made way in 1903 for Colonel George Moore as MHK he could reasonably feel that he had personally done a fair amount to improve several aspects of life in Castletown, but it still lagged behind all the other towns in economic development. The rateable value of Douglas in 1887 was £85,773 and in 1899 £138,720. Ramsey increased from £16,591 to £23,217 and even Peel from £7,654 to £10,794 while Castletown only managed to grow from £5,876 to £7,340 in the same period. Moreover, while the populations of all the other towns, especially Douglas, rose between 1871 and 1891, the population of Castletown actually fell from 2,320 to 2,178, despite the increase of its boundary by a third in 1883.[20]

Whereas Douglas had forged ahead with a diversity of commercial enterprises run by exceptionally able entrepreneurs such as Henry Bloom Noble and Samuel Harris, Castletown made very little progress as a centre of commerce during the nineteenth century. Quayle's Bank had foundered after a few years and another local enterprise, the Castletown brewery, only made slow progress. As we have seen, Castletown had for centuries supported a domestic brewing trade in individual houses but in the 1780s a number of more formal businesses began to take shape on the north of the river. Thomas Faulder and his family ran a brewery there from 1823 onwards and between 1824 and 1852 the Quayle family operated another near the bridge. However, there was little enthusiasm to invest in brewing and the ale produced was of poor quality. When the Quayles gave up their brewery in 1852 it was run successively by John Bell, Thomas Usher, and Theodore Sherlock in partnership with Edward Tooker. Sherlock's death in the late 1880s prompted an offer to purchase the brewery from a group of Castletown business people led by Richard Cain, a young man whose ability and enthusiasm would eventually succeed in making Castletown brewery a force to be reckoned with – but only in the next century.[21]

The second most significant industry in nineteenth-century Castletown was boatbuilding, and by the 1850s there were four boat yards round the harbour, though they were relatively small. Joseph Qualtrough moved to Castletown from Port St Mary, where he had learnt the boat-building trade as an apprentice to his father, and he went into partnership with his sister's husband James Coole. Together they ran a prosperous boat-building business, also importing coal and other materials, which lasted for over a hundred years. After Coole's death in 1891 'J. Qualtrough and Co' was run by Joseph and two of his sons, and they also operated a fishing fleet based at Peel.[22] Unfortunately, both brewing and boatbuilding were comparatively small industries and their contribution to the prosperity of Castletown during this period was modest.

THE VICARS OF MALEW

Little is known about the early vicars of Castletown's parish church except some of their names and dates. The nave was built in the early fourteenth century and there were at first no windows on the north side, as was typical of old Manx churches. The parish of Malew included Castle Rushen, Rushen Abbey and Castletown itself, so it was arguably the most important parish in the diocese until Castletown ceased to be the capital. The parish registers were started in 1649, 'Illiam Dhone' was buried in the churchyard after his execution in 1663 and Earl William presented a bell to the church in 1677. John Woods, who as we have seen was twice imprisoned by Governor Horne, was succeeded as vicar by John Quayle in 1739 and John Gill in 1758, though he soon moved to Lezayre in 1761. His successor Daniel Gelling had to face the ecclesiastical courts to tell them why he did not live in the vicarage at Malew, but he explained that it was in ruins and that he would very happily live in a habitable vicarage if he were provided with one. Gelling was succeeded by William Clucas in 1778 and during his time the church was considerably enlarged when in 1781 the north transept and chancel were added, partly to accommodate the Castle Rushen garrison. Clucas left in 1783 and there followed the long incumbency of David Harrison until 1817. As there was still no habitable vicarage at Malew he lived in Castletown in Big Tree House, a fine early Georgian building in Malew Street.

Harrison's successor was William Christian, who was quite clearly an unsuitable appointment because there were many complaints about his failure to perform his duties and about his personal characteristics. Christian was suspended for three years in 1827 by Bishop Murray after a court hearing, and ultimately he was defrocked as a priest, but the legal fees involved amounted to over £40, which the parishioners of Malew refused to pay. Fortunately an exceptional successor was found to replace him in 1830. This was William Gill, who remained at Malew until his death in 1871, and it has been said of him that 'on any count he was one of the outstanding Manx clegymen of the century'.[23] The first matter he tackled was the lack of a vicarage and he managed to drain the glebe lands at Malew, which had become a bog, and he raised the considerable sum of £500 to build a new vicarage and also rebuilt the parish schoolhouse.

Unusually among the Manx clergy, Gill was a High Churchman and his installation of a stained glass east window in his church was not approved by some of his congregation. He married Anne Stowell of Ballaugh and raised with her a family of five sons and four daughters, all of whom he maintained on his stipend of £200 a year, sending four of his sons to university and one to qualify at the Bar. He had a special interest in education and served as a Diocesan Inspector of Schools while also working hard for his parish day school and Sunday school. One of his friends was the well-known academic John Keble, a leading light of the 'Oxford Movement' and the biographer of Bishop Wilson, who stayed with him on several occasions at Malew Vicarage. Gill was himself a gifted Manx scholar and he edited 'Kelly's Manx Grammar' in 1859 and acted as part-editor and reviser of 'Kelly's Manx Dictionary' in 1866. He was also the official translator into Manx of the laws promulgated on Tynwald Day, and as these were read out in full, the task was a formidable one.

A tall, strong man with a shock of white hair, usually reserved and quiet, though with a lively sense of humour, Gill was above all a much loved and

Malew Church. The nave dates from the early 14th century and it was the parish church of Castletown until 1922 despite its considerable distance from the town centre. (Lily Publications)

respected parish priest whose good judgement and fairness were widely appreciated, especially by the poor, whom he visited frequently, usually on foot. Hardly ever ill, he set his parishioners a fine example by avoiding luxury or self-indulgence, rising early, eating the simplest food, never smoking and abstaining totally from alcohol. On weekdays the Evensong service at Malew was held in the afternoon and in the evening Gill and his family would sing hymns. After lunch on a Saturday the Vicar would spend the rest of the time until the first service on Sunday alone in his study in prayer and meditation.[24]

Gill died in the winter of 1871, a few days after suffering a stroke while presiding over a wedding. His death on Tuesday the 17th of October was followed by the closure of many of the shops in Castletown and round about until the following Monday and he is remembered by a memorial window in Malew Church presented by his widow. His son Hugh Gill, the Vicar of Rushen, succeeded him, partly to be near his mother, who moved to Castletown, and partly so that his sons could attend the Grammar School there. In 1874 the church was re-decorated and a pulpit and reading-desk were placed on the south side while the following year several rooms were added to the vicarage to accommodate the Vicar's growing family. Apparently Hugh Gill had no trouble keeping order in public meetings because he had large eyes and bushy eyebrows and could look very fierce, though he was very fond of children and could tell interesting stories, often in Manx dialect. He rode about in a one-horse trap, driving recklessly and not always punctually. In 1879 he was appointed Rural Dean of Castletown and in 1891 Proctor in Convocation for the Manx clergy, being by then 'probably the best loved and respected clergyman in the diocese'.[25] In 1895 he was appointed Archdeacon of Man and moved to Andreas accordingly. He received a purse of gold worth £143 and an illuminated address by way of thanks as well as a marble clock from the church choir.

Hugh Gill was succeeded by John Spicer, a vigorous evangelical who was very much in demand as a preacher. Shortly after he arrived, the churchyard was extended westwards, at a cost of £400, which was raised on a twenty-year loan. Inside the church a new vestry was constructed and the font was moved to the west end while the organ was rebuilt and enlarged and the door in the south wall was closed up and a new one opened. During the course of 1897 some bad feeling was caused when six Methodists were elected as churchwardens because of the large number of Methodists in the congregation, but their election was found to be irregular and they were replaced by Anglicans. In 1898 a lectern was installed in memory of Illiam Dhone and paid for by public subscription. Spicer, who was kind, genial and hard-working, died aged 69 in 1919.[26] In 1922 Malew ceased to be the parish church of Castletown on the creation of a new parish based at St Mary's, with R.W. Carter as its first Vicar.

A CASTLE FOR TOURISTS

In 1827 Castle Rushen was still at the centre of Island life. It was a stronghold defended by a garrison, and it was the home of Lieutenant Governor Smelt and his administrative offices. It also housed the law courts as well as being the Island's gaol. As we have seen, the Lieutenant Governor moved to Lorne House in 1834 and his former residence was converted into court offices and the Rolls Office, while some of the law courts began to be held in Douglas after 1864. In 1844 a four-man commission of enquiry was appointed to report on conditions in the gaol and it was very critical of its facilities. It made several recommendations, in particular that convicted felons and 'dangerous lunatics' should be kept well apart from less serious offenders. Apparently prisoners did not have separate beds and the bedclothing was often filthy. The commissioners' report prompted the Home Office to build twelve new cells and fund additional prison staff. In 1849 Tynwald empowered the Governor to make use of parts of Castle Rushen as an asylum for the insane and as a result of this regrettable decision a number of mentally ill individuals were added to the existing prison population without suitable accommodation or care until 1864, when they were moved to Oatlands, in Santon. Executions in the castle were rare during the nineteenth century and the last prisoner to be hanged there was John Kewish in 1872, but the prison population gradually grew, largely because of the general increase in the Island's population.[27]

Even when the castle was a fully-functioning and busy prison it was open to visitors, and in 1874 13,084 adults and 797 children were shown round the walls and battlements by the overworked staff. In 1885 Sir Edward du Cane, the Chairman of the UK's prison department, came to the Island to review the situation at Castle Rushen and reported to the Home Office that:

> Castle Rushen is an ancient building of great interest and its appropriation as a prison is in accordance with a practice which has ceased in England for very many years, for such buildings are entirely inappropriate... Castle Rushen is incurably defective, except in regard of one small block of eleven cells in three storeys built not very long ago. The remainder of the prison accommodation is in rooms in the old castle. These rooms occupy four floors, which are reached by narrow, winding stairs, and the rooms either communicate with one another or are reached by narrow, dark and tortuous passages.[28]

His main recommendation was that either a new prison should be built or that prisoners should be sent to the UK, and that to replace the present lax regime and poor discipline, there should be rigid separation of the different offenders and sexes, with hard labour, hard beds and hard fare. Tynwald was reluctant to spend money on a new prison and Spencer Walpole told the Home Office in 1886 that discipline had been tightened up and that hard labour and plank beds had been introduced. Tynwald also commissioned plans for improving the gaol but the Home Office stood by du Cane's verdict that Castle Rushen was 'incurably defective' as a prison and Tynwald eventually agreed to commission a new prison in Victoria Road in Douglas, which was opened in 1891. All prisoners were transferred there from Castletown and Castle Rushen faced a new future. The Home Office agreed to it remaining in the custody of the Manx government as long as they did not contemplate 'letting it, say, as a tea garden for the benefit of the Island revenue, or treating it other than as an interesting historical monument'.[29]

When the British soldiers were withdrawn a few years later, in 1896, the castle had little function as an administrative centre except that it housed one law court, and it remained, and still remains, the location for the ceremonial swearing-in of new lieutenant governors. It was, however, without doubt a major asset as a tourist attraction at a time when the Island's holiday industry was increasing year by year as a result of the development of Douglas, **123**

Ramsey, Port St Mary and Port Erin as seaside resorts. During the 1887 season some 347,968 people stepped off the Steam Packet's ships onto Douglas pier and by 1913 the number reached 634,512. Clearly, Castle Rushen, which, though small, was one of the best preserved examples of a mediaeval castle in the British Isles, could bring in a good deal of revenue if properly marketed.

Lord Raglan, who was appointed Governor in 1902, was keenly interested in the Island's history and antiquities and also an enthusiastic patron of its Natural History and Antiquarian Society, founded in 1879. He liked Castle Rushen and used it as the background for social functions such as the one held on Friday October 26th 1906, when he and his wife gave an 'At Home' to mark the fourth anniversary of his inauguration as Lieutenant Governor. Guests were invited to board a special train from Douglas to Castletown where from 12.30 to 4.00 they were treated to a picnic lunch and to lectures on the castle's history from the architect Armitage Rigby and the antiquarian Philip Kermode. Raglan could see that the appeal of Castle Rushen as a tourist attraction would be greatly enhanced by demolishing many of its ugly later additions, such as the offices and prison accommodation, and restoring it as much as possible to its late mediaeval state. It was largely through his drive and initiative that funds were made available for this and he entrusted the work to Armitage Rigby, who was a Manx-based architect, born in Cheshire in 1864. He trained as an architect in England, married a Manx girl and settled on the Island soon after 1889. He designed many prominent Manx buildings, some of them in a style he christened 'new antique', and he surveyed and produced plans of archaeological sites. He advised on the 'restoration' of Castle Rushen between 1905 and 1912 and this led him to visit many castles in the UK and to become an expert on mediaeval structures.[30]

After Rigby's work on the castle was completed the exterior looked essentially the same as it appears today. Stripped of ungainly structures, it began its new life as a money-spinning tourist destination and also as a museum until the opening of the Manx Museum in Douglas in 1922. Unfortunately, as it was in the care of the Manx government, any surplus money after maintenance costs had been paid went into the Island treasury and not to the Castletown Commissioners, though local shops, restaurants and inns profited from the daily influx of visitors. Between 1914 and 1918 revenue from holidaymakers virtually ceased and the castle's maintenance account fell seriously into deficit, though matters improved after the war and the UK formally handed over full ownership of the castle to Tynwald in 1929.[31]

T.E.Brown, from a portrait by Sir William Richmond, R.A., commissioned by Clifton College. (Author's collection)

MEMORIES

A number of Castletown characters have left memories and stories – some of them no doubt not entirely accurate – of life in Old Castletown. The Manx National Poet, T.E.Brown, attended King William's College, aged 15, in 1845 after the premature death of his father, the Vicar of Braddan, caused his widowed mother to move to a small house in Bowling Green Road. At King William's his exceptional intellectual abilities were quickly recognized and he became an 'Academic Scholar' there. In 1847 he won a scholarship to Oxford where he gained first class degrees in two courses, read concurrently. After this triumph, he was elected a Fellow of Oriel College and took deacon's orders but soon decided that the life of an Oxford don was not for him, partly because he missed the Isle of Man, partly because he wished to marry his Manx cousin, Amelia Stowell, and partly, no doubt, because as a former Academic Scholar of King William's he had a duty of service to the Island.

In 1855, at the age of 25, Brown was appointed vice-principal at King William's and he set up home with his new wife in a cottage in Derbyhaven. He brought a powerful mind and new teaching methods to the school and delighted residents of Castletown with lectures on various aspects of Manx life and culture. It was a good time for him: 'In Castletown', he wrote later, 'I spent the brightest and happiest part of my life'. He left in 1861 to take up a headmastership in Gloucester and moved to Clifton College in Bristol in

Shipping in the 'Duckpond', from an early 20th century drawing. Note the swing bridge, installed in 1887 and replaced in the 1960s by a fixed road bridge. (Manx National Heritage)

1863 where he was second master, head of the modern side and a housemaster until 1892, when he retired to Ramsey until his death in 1897. During the Bristol years he wrote his 'Fo'c's'le Yarns', a series of dialect poems about ordinary Manx folk, which were highly acclaimed by the British literary establishment and brought Brown international recognition. He was proclaimed the Manx National Poet on the centenary of his birth in 1930.[32]

Although Brown refused the offer of the Archdeaconry of Man he stood in as a 'locum' for several clergymen during his retirement in the 1890s and he gave many lectures on Manx subjects. He also wrote a little pamphlet as a guide book to Castletown, even though he hated 'trippers' and the baneful effect he felt they had on Manx culture. 'Castletown', he wrote in the pamphlet,

> is situated on a nearly land-locked bay, of which the converging points are Langness and Scarlett. The town is charmingly grouped round the castle, which is close to the harbour. Though standing on a limestone flat, the town looks up to the schistose mountains of South Barrule and Cronk-ny-irey-laa, from the slopes of which it obtains its excellent water supply....The town is quiet, the houses well and substantially built, and within easy reach of the shops and other places of business. The whole effect is cosy, compact, clean and cheerful. Lovely distant views haunt every turn of this charming retreat, which is, in itself, so quaint and

beautiful. The population counts many fine sailors and fishermen, who have not yet lost the stamp of real old Manx character. The chief object of interest is, of course, the castle ..[which]... looks as fresh as if it had been built yesterday, a marvel of masonry, adamantine, and of a singularly noble aspect. From the clock tower there is a magnificent panoramic view, quite beyond what might be expected from so small an elevation; the whole southern half of the Island, with the mountains of the north, rises like an orchestra to the stroke of some unseen baton'.[33]

Charles 'Charlie' Watterson was born in 1869 'alongside the Quay and in the shadow of Castle Rushen' in a house in which he was still living when after being Town Clerk for many years he wrote a few memoirs about the Castletown of his youth in the 1870s and 1880s. 'I have listened', he began, 'to the poet T.E.Brown lecture in the Town Hall, Arbory Street, on two occasions – one of his lectures being on Manx idioms and the other on "Castletown 100 years ago." ' Charlie reckoned that he belonged to one of the outer Castletown social circles, the inner ones being chiefly inhabited by commissioned officers and clergymen. When he was a young boy there was still a busy market every Friday but the arrival of the railway in 1874 put an end to this age-old institution, 'the farmers and farmers' wives finding a better source of sale in Douglas'. The railway also ended the career of the daily coach that took passengers from the Market Place to Douglas and back, though the carrier's cart for goods lasted another twenty years.[34] With the railway came the building of Victoria Road, and soon afterwards Alexandra Road.

For a time, shipping activity remained healthy, with 16 schooners and eight smacks belonging to Castletown, some of the schooners trading as far afield as the Baltic and Mediterranean. Many of these ships were built in Castletown, and timber for Coole and Qualtrough's boatbuilding yard arrived in Norwegian brigs and brigantines. Thomas Boyd also owned a yard and his brother James ran a rope factory on the quay. Charlie witnessed the building of the schooners 'Ocean Gem' and 'Kate' as well as the 'Progress', built by Coole and Qualtrough. Two open-decked luggers, the 'Arbory' and the 'Wesley' were built in Boyd's shipyard and their crews carried on their conversations mostly in Manx and broken English, always counting the herrings in threes, and in Manx. Local lads could find a job at sea without difficulty and they would go fishing to Kinsale and Crookhaven about April, returning in time for the local herring season. When that finished some boats would then make for the Shetlands and others would sail down the east coast of Scotland, returning through the Caledonian or Bowling canals. No doubt T.E.Brown's central character (and *alter ego*) the fisherman 'Tom Baynes',

127

who told his stories to his shipmates in the fo'c's'le, took shape in the poet's mind from his knowledge of the many colourful characters who populated Castletown harbour in its heyday as a fishing port.

Even Charlie Watterson had seen the harbour 'during a Saturday and Sunday in the herring season so full of schooners, smacks and fishing boats, that you could walk from one side to the other of the harbour on them. They came mostly from St Ives and Penzance, and some from Arklow… Mostly every person in those days, rich and poor alike (provided they were Manx) were buying herrings to salt.'[35] The Karran family from Castletown prospered as owners of a considerable fleet of schooners, registered in Castletown though operating in other ports, and mostly crewed by Castletown men. However, as Charlie pointed out, the advent of steam altered the conditions. Soon all general cargo was carried 'by a wooden steamship called the 'St Mary', built in Port St Mary and owned by the importers and others, [and] it was not long before steamships carried all the cargoes and the sailing ships were doomed'.[36]

Castletown imported coal for the lime kilns at Derbyhaven as well as those at nearby Billown and Ballahot, and there were coal storage houses on the quays. Members of the public requiring coal were served by coal porters who carried heavy bags to any house in the town 'for a copper or two'. One of them, Davie McGill, was also the Town Crier whose announcements and greetings were often accompanied by someone playing 'a melodion or concertina'. Milk was provided by thirteen cow-keepers whose cows frequently wandered up and down the streets and sometimes blundered into private houses. Water, for most working-class people, came from rain-water tubs or wells, for drinking, and from the river for washing.[37] Castletown Regatta provided a memorable day for children and Charlie remembered that 'sailing and rowing boats came from Ramsey and Douglas to compete. A smack or schooner, dressed with bunting, would be anchored outside the Pier Head as a Commodore ship, with plenty of liquid and other refreshment aboard'. Also, 'the Athletic sports were held on the Racecourse….For one of the events a pole was erected and coated with soft soap. Attached to the top was a ham to be climbed for as a prize. This was great fun for the spectators, but not for the unsuccessful competitors'.[38]

A major spectacle was provided by the annual processions of the various 'Friendly Societies' that had been established in the town during the century to assist their members in case of sickness, unemployment or hardship. According to Charlie:

The majority of the members of these clubs wore silk hats and dress coats, known in those days as long-sleeved hats and claw-hammered coats. Each member wore a sash and a rosette and carried a stick surmounted with a shepherd's crook, a javelin, or other design. They were regular swells for the day. The Artificers held their procession on Holy Thursday, assembling one year at the Flat Gate in Queen Street and the next year opposite Beach House, where the late Colonel Carey (the owner of the Calf of Man) resided. This Club would be headed by a brass band and would march through the town, thence to a service at St Mary's ,after that to a dinner at the George Hotel…The Hope and Anchor Lodge of Oddfellows and the Mona Daniel Tent of the Rechabites would have their respective processions on dates selected by themselves. Each of the tents would have two brass bands. Each tent, on the date selected, would assemble at the Town Hall, Arbory Street…and march through the town, sometimes going to King William's College and other times to Lorne House where General Dixon resided; then to a service at St Mary's and afterwards to a dinner at the Town Hall.[39]

Charlie Watterson well remembered Flaxney Stowell, a builder and architect who was also a strong advocate of temperance and who set a good example by living to be 96. In 1902 Stowell published a short book entitled 'Castletown A Hundred Years Ago' in which he recalled that in the early part of the century 'the two brothers Stevenson lived at Balladoole and at Christmas there would be great doings and fine fun going on with balls and masquerades. They built a ball court for the enjoyment of the young people of the town and they themselves entered into all the sports. The guests at the masquerades would sometimes sally forth on to the road and scare the country folk with their fantastic costumes'.[40] In Castletown itself another large house, 'Eldersley', was built by General Cumming who had served with Wolfe at Quebec. He had five sons and four daughters and they added greatly to the social gaiety of the place by giving frequent balls, for which the gentry would come from far and wide. Stowell also encountered T.E.Brown in later years, 'a genial man, so tender-hearted'.[41]

There was no lighthouse on Langness until 1880, and Charlie Watterson wrote that he could remember his father

coming into the house one stormy night, after being out looking after his schooner, saying there had been four shipwrecks during the night. Strange to say, it was a Scotsman, John McMekin, a banker, who was the principal agitator to have the light installed. He kept writing to the Northern Lights Commissioners, pointing out the dire necessity for a light, and was for a long time unsuccessful in his efforts. It must have been both difficult and hazardous for shipping in those days, with no light on

Langness, as when the street lighting of the town was extinguished, one might as well look into a sack as look into Castletown Bay from the sea.[42]

After McMekin's death, T.E.Brown wrote of him in tribute:

- A lovely soul has sought his silent firth,
  Friend of all things weak.
  Go down to that sweet soil you held so dear,
  Go up to God and joys unspeakable.[43]

Flaxney Stowell also made a point of recording that 'terrible wrecks' used frequently to occur on Langness and Scarlett rocks, remembering in particular the fate of ships named 'Maria', 'Fairfield', 'Peggy', 'Tobacco', 'Tea', 'Cotton', and the 'Rum Gulleys'. In 1968 a number of members of the Isle of Man sub-aqua club located the wreck of the 'Racehorse', a brig that had been bound for Douglas on the evening of December 14th 1822 when, confused by the lights from Scarlett House, Captain William Suckling, a cousin of Lord Nelson, set a course that took her onto the rocks at Langness. The crew was rescued by a fleet of small boats manned by Castletown men but there was a tragic outcome when the last boat to return from the wreck capsized with the loss of three lives. This left their dependants in Castletown destitute and may well have strengthened the resolve of Sir William Hillary to found the RNLI.[44]

Queen Street, late 19th century. (Manx National Heritage)

Another ship, the 'John Fairfield', was wrecked at Scarlett in November 1834 after being caught in a storm when on its maiden voyage from Liverpool, bound for Havana: fortunately, on this occasion all the crew and passengers safely reached the shore. According to recent researches:

> The cargo was valued between £40,000 and £50,000. It included bales of calico, broad cloths, webs of linen, hundreds of fowling pieces, gunflints, handsome lamps and Scotch caps and was scattered for miles along the coast. Indeed, shards of well-washed Staffordshire pottery from the cargo can still be found along the coast between Scarlett and Poyll Vaaish. Some of the cargo was recovered but much of it was plundered by the local population. The authorities were slow to respond but when they did some 50 suspected plunderers were sent to Castle Rushen. They were later released among rumours of a cover-up. …In consequence of the wreck, the government accepted the necessity of a lighthouse with a foghorn, which it placed on Langness in order to help prevent a repetition of the wreck on the nearby coastline.[45]

It was a considerable disgrace that the authorities took so long to provide Langness with a suitable lighthouse. The British Government had been aware of the problem since the beginning of the nineteenth century and in 1811 they authorized the building by Thomas Brine of an unlit tower,(later called 'the Herring Tower'), on the seaward side of the peninsula, in the hope that this would provide ships with a point of reference. However, it was useless in bad weather. In 1831, Robert Stevenson, Engineer to the Northern Lighthouse Board, visited the Island and urged that a lighthouse should be built at Langness, but nothing was done because of the reluctance of Trinity House to co-operate. In 1850 the Isle of Man Harbour Commissioners sited a beacon within the old fort on Fort Island, but in most years it operated only in the herring season. When it was at last decided that a lighthouse should be built on Chicken Rock, south of the Calf, in 1868, an elaborate scheme was considered for using this to cast light on the 'Herring Tower' on Langness, but this proved unworkable.

There were at least forty wrecks off Castletown between 1855 and 1880, with the loss of some 100 lives, and this, together with the agitations of John McMekin, at last prompted the commissioning of a new lighthouse at an estimated cost of £8,350 for the land and building. This became operational in 1880 and stood in a courtyard surrounded by cottages, workshops and a gas plant room. The 50-foot tower was provided with a 9000 candle-power light, upgraded to 200,000 candle-power in 1937. It was the last of the Island's lighthouses to become automatic, in 1996, after which its surrounding cottages were sold to a private investor.[46] The cottages, with about thirty acres of land, were bought late in 2004 by Jeremy Clarkson, a well-known presenter on UK TV who had married the daughter of Major Robert Cain, a Manx recipient of the Victoria Cross, but Clarkson caused local dismay in 2005 when he took exception to alleged rights of way which allowed the public to walk very close to his property, and a dispute began which rumbled on for five years with increasing bitterness on both sides.

William Henry Cooper was born in 1870, the eighth of the ten children of Eleanor Clague and James Cooper, a master joiner in Arbory Street who was a son of an English soldier in the Castletown garrison. James Cooper founded his firm of builders and undertakers in 1869 and by 1881 he was employing six men and two apprentices. William attended the Grammar School and 'Finnegan's School' and grew up to be shy and retiring and remained a bachelor living in the family home and working for the family firm. In 1950 he compiled three notebooks of memoirs for the 'Manx Folk Life Survey', which contain information about the people who lived in Castletown in his early years. The fact that he was able to remember the great majority of those who lived in each of the houses in Arbory Street, Arbory Road, Market Square, The Parade, Castle Street, Parliament Square, Chapel Lane, Queen Street, Malew Street and the Crofts shows how small the community still was in the later part of the century and how well everybody knew everybody else. His account of the brothers James and George Quayle, who lived in Queen Street, has the ring about it of one of T.E. Brown's more dramatic yarns:

> They went to the mackerel and herring fishing and in the winter worked for farmers or any other job they could get. James was a bit of a pig and the name of 'Mucker' suited him. I have seen him in the Flatt after he came back from Kinsale and was paid off, spending all his earnings on drink and his mother trying to get some money from him. He would knock her down as often as she ran after him begging for money. He and another man named Clucas were in the Crown Arms on the Quay, drinking and arguing about boat sailing, and they went out and took out an old cranky boat to settle the argument. There was a good breeze of wind and when they got outside the pier head the boat capsized and they were both drowned. Clucas's body was recovered at the time, Quayle's a day or two later.[47]

Chapter Five

THE QUALTROUGHS

C astletown's diminished status in the Island was emphasized early in the 20th century when the visit took place of King Edward VII, the first British reigning monarch to set foot on the Isle of Man. With his wife, Queen Alexandra, he arrived in Douglas Bay on the Royal Yacht on August 24 1901 and he was greeted on board by the Speaker of the House of Keys, A.W.Moore. The next day the Royal Yacht sailed to Ramsey where the King and Queen landed and drove via Bishopscourt to Peel for an open-air lunch in the castle grounds. In the afternoon they drove to Douglas and enjoyed a ride on the electric tramway back to Ramsey, from which they sailed the next morning without so much as a glimpse of the ancient seat of earlier Lords of Man.

Despite the extension of Castletown's boundary in 1883 the 1891 census recorded that the population had fallen from 2,320 to 2,178 in the last twenty years, and this decline continued into the new century, with 1,965 in 1901, 1,817 in 1911, 1,713 in 1931 and 1,536 in 1961. In fact the decline was not as dramatic as that of Peel, which fell from 3,304 in 1901 to 2,483 in 1961 or Ramsey, which fell from 4,729 to 3,789, though Douglas only fell from 19,223 to 18,821[1]. This was a period when the Island's population in general dropped from 54,752 to 48,133, largely owing to the widespread economic depression of the 1930s and the earlier collapse of the traditional occupations of mining and fishing. The Dumbell's bank crash of 1900 damaged many Island businesses and resulted in the loss of the savings of many local people. The most obvious evidence of the bank's demise in Castletown was that its branch in the old House of Keys building was taken over by Parr's Bank.

The years from 1900 to 1914 were nevertheless prosperous ones for the Island in general because the number of annual visitors ballooned to well over 600,000, conveyed to the Island in the impressive fleet of the Steam Packet Company. But with the declaration of war against Germany in 1914 the holiday trade came to an abrupt halt and the Island took on a new role as a place where 'enemy aliens' from Britain could be interned. Lord Raglan was ultimately responsible for the arrangements, which involved the conversion of the former Cunningham's holiday camp in Douglas and then the setting up a vast new camp at Knockaloe, near Peel, which eventually

133

Sir Joseph Qualtrough, 1885-1960. (Manx National Heritage)

accommodated well over 20,000 internees. The war turned Douglas and the
other holiday resorts into ghost towns and ruined the livelihood of the
boarding house and hotel keepers, but Castletown carried on much as before,
with the inhabitants able to feel, for once, that their refusal to cash in on the
holiday trade had at least spared them hardship during the war years. There
was a price to be paid, nevertheless, because 78 Castletown men lost their
lives in the conflict and were commemorated in a Celtic cross memorial
placed against the castle wall in the main square and consecrated (in very bad
weather) in 1923. Able-bodied young men were scarce on the Island during
wartime and in 1916 the Castletown Boys Brigade was asked to join with the
Cadet Force from KWC and some Douglas organizations to provide part of

the Guard of Honour on Tynwald Day. They had to walk to St John's and back, of course. There seems not to have been a Boy Scout troop in Castletown but the Boys Brigade were a smart unit, with their pill box hats and chin straps, white sashes and black leather belts.[2]

Castletown's MHK from 1903 was Lt Colonel George Moore, a military man no doubt to the liking of Lord Raglan at the time when he was undertaking his restoration of Castle Rushen. Moore's home was Great Meadow, on the road to Malew, one of the most ancient estates on the Island. It was mentioned in a papal Bull of 1153 as being among the lands granted by Olaf I to Furness Abbey, the parent of the new abbey at Rushen. By 1703 it belonged to Francis Wilder Moore but he sold it to George Quayle of Castletown and it then passed to the Moores of Billown through marriage. In 1790 Thomas Moore of Billown married Emma Hamilton of Scarlett and they lived in the house at Great Meadow. George Moore, born in 1853, was their grandson. He died in 1919 and his widow lived on in the main house, by then a castellated mansion, until 1928. Her eldest daughter, Mary Moore, inherited the estate and married Robert Riggall, a naval surgeon, and her descendants live there still.[3]

George Moore's death in 1919 prompted a by-election which brought to the House of Keys Joseph Davidson Qualtrough, a young man destined to be the leading Island politician of his generation. He was the son of Joseph Qualtrough Sr, the Castletown shipyard owner who had learnt his trade from his own father, a boatbuilder in Port St Mary. Joseph Senior was elected to the Keys as member for Rushen in 1893 and strongly supported the constitutional reform party, which sought a reduction in the powers of the Lieutenant Governor and a more effective brand of 'Home Rule' for the Island. A tall, handsome, eloquent and impressive man, he was a Rechabite, abstaining from alcohol, and he was a Methodist preacher of whom it was said, when he was about to preach, that 'The Devil will get Hell tonight'. He was also a very shrewd businessman and acquired many properties in and around Castletown. In 1919 the reform party achieved some success when four seats on the Legislative Council became elective and Qualtrough was one of the first elected members, serving also as Chairman of the Harbour Board and Receiver-General, posts which he held until his death in 1933.

His son Joseph Davidson Qualtrough (usually known as 'JD') was born in 1885 in a small cottage on the Derbyhaven side of Hango Hill. Four years later his parents moved to 'Springfield', a newly-built house in Alexandra Road, where they brought up their three sons as well as a daughter who died at the age of five. JD attended Victoria Road School, which was only 150 yards from his home, and moved from there to the Old Grammar School from which he won a scholarship to King William's College, where he rose to be head boy. Although he was well qualified for a university place, his father insisted that he should join the family firm when he left school in December 1903. He soon became, like his father, a Methodist local preacher, resolutely opposed to drinking alcohol and gambling. In 1915 he enlisted in the army, was promoted lieutenant and survived the fighting on the Western Front. While he was being demobbed in 1919 George Moore died, the date for the Castletown by-election for the Keys was announced and JD's father panicked that his son would not get back in time to stand: in fact he arrived in Douglas at 3pm on the day of the deadline for nominations and he was elected unopposed, becoming, at 34, one of the youngest MHKs. In 1923 he married his long-time girlfriend Ethel, eleven years his junior, and they raised four children; though their daughter Mary died at the age of five, as JD's sister had done.

His record in the Castletown elections was remarkable: in 1919, 1924, 1929 and 1934 he was elected unopposed and then, because of the war, there was a long gap until 1946 when he won the seat with 632 votes against Mrs E.M.Harper (228), R.E.Kneen (151) and G.P.MacClellan (94). In 1951 and 1955 he was again unopposed and he died in office in 1960. From his earliest days in the Keys he was a strong supporter of the 'reformers' who sought further reductions in the powers of the Lieutenant Governor, especially in the sphere of finance. Among the many posts he held were Chairman of the Committees of Finance and Constitutional Reform, the Publicity and Electricity Boards, the Council of Education, the Noble's Hospital Management Committee and the Manx Music Festival, and he was a member of many other Boards and Committees as well as a JP. In 1937 he was elected Speaker of the House of Keys and he was appointed CBE and later knighted in 1954. Inevitably he was a dominant and universally known figure in Castletown, where he found time to conduct his chapel choir, act as a Sunday School superintendent and make use of his fine tenor voice in the ranks of the Castletown Choral Society.[4]

Although Qualtrough's main energies were directed towards the interests of the Island in general, he did not hesitate to take up the cudgels in Tynwald on behalf of his constituency. In 1928, at a time of serious economic depression on the Island, the government encouraged local authorities to undertake projects which were likely to maintain employment for those who would otherwise be out of work. In this spirit the Castletown Commissioners decided to carry out improvements to Poulsom Park, which would cost £600. Tynwald was prepared to make an interest-free loan but Qualtrough pointed out that Douglas Corporation had very recently been granted half of the cost of improvements to their harbour. 'What I cannot understand', he told Tynwald, 'is that of this sum Castletown have to pay the whole cost, whereas in the case of this very much larger scheme Douglas gets a grant of one-half. I think, now that we have started on this particular scheme, that all local authorities should be treated exactly alike'.[5] Similarly, in 1931 he found himself coming to the rescue of what remained of the Grammar School he had attended as a young boy.

EDUCATIONAL UPHEAVALS

The National School established in 1822 in a converted warehouse was in need of new premises by the 1830s because of expanding numbers and in 1835 a local petition in Castletown requested that a plot of land near the bridge, in Hope Street, should be made available for a new school building. Permission was granted in 1836 with the proviso that the land would revert to the Crown if there should in the future not be a school on the site. By 1839 the school was open, with 270 pupils, and it was probably about this time that the old 'petty school' ended its career and merged with the new institution.[6] By 1848 there were boys' and girls' divisions, each with five classes. There were lessons in reading, writing and arithmetic and parents were expected to ensure that their children kept the Ten Commandments and were kind to animals. In 1851 an Act of Tynwald permitted rate-assisted education and in 1872 a Board of Education, served by local education committees, was established to provide elementary education throughout the Island. In 1875 the National School was transferred to the authority of the Board, which made Castletown unusual at the time because the elementary schools in all the other towns were run by denominational authorities. By 1895 overcrowding led to the building of a new school in Victoria Road which was used by the boys, while the girls remained in the Hope Street building.

Meanwhile the founders of King William's College had expected that their new school would render the tottering Castletown Grammar School redundant, but this did not in fact happen and it lasted for nearly a hundred years more. Initially this was because George Parsons was an able and determined headmaster and there were 42 boys at his school when he retired in 1855, many of them free place scholars. Then he was succeeded by William Sparrow, another successful schoolmaster from Ramsey, though unlike his predecessors he was not also appointed chaplain of St Mary's. Although the salary was modest the position attracted B.J.S.Lupton to follow him and in 1880 J.T.W.Wicksey, who moved from Peel. He had a Dublin degree in music and was a fine organist, much admired in St Mary's chapel, where 'his arrival at church in top hat, frock coat and twirling a stick, was an imposing sight. He would climb the stairs and walk majestically around the gallery while every face in the pews would be turned upwards to watch his progress'.[7] He had 23 pupils in 1897, though by now all were paying fees of about £4. The school building, however, was clearly inadequate, and Joseph Qualtrough Sr, whose son JD was a pupil there at the time, told a government inquiry in 1897 that to spend money on repairing it would be 'foolish economy'.[8] The closure of the school became unspoken government policy but it proved difficult to kill off under yet another respected teacher, E.T.Shephard. In 1927 and 1928, during the headmastership of J.Ashford Hill, two official inspections found it unsatisfactory and recommended closure. Hill was pressured into moving to another job in Ireland and pupil numbers fell to eight.[9]

The question then arose as to what should become of the modest income of £100 a year, which the school had received from the Barrow trust, if it were to be closed. Most Castletown people wanted the money to fund scholarships to King William's but there were those in Tynwald who argued that the Grammar School had been for the whole Island and that the funds should therefore go to the Education Board. In the Keys this case was eloquently argued in February 1931 by advocate Percy Cowley but J.D. Qualtrough, as MHK for Castletown, appealed to a sense of justice. 'This house', he said, 'was originally a court of justice and in a sense it is so at this moment in that it has to decide between the claims of the people of Castletown and the attempt of the Education authority to seize monies that belong to Castletown'. In a long and detailed speech he then recounted the history of the Grammar School, seeking to prove that the funds it had received had been spent to the benefit of the people of Castletown. He won the day and though the Grammar School was closed in December 1931, its income of £100 a year went to fund scholarships for Castletown boys at King William's.[10]

At the same time the government closed the Catherine Halsall School for girls, by now only a small elementary school, and authorized the payment of its endowments to the former Castletown High School for Girls, increasingly known since 1929 as The Buchan School. Although a number of private boarding schools for girls had flourished on the Island in the 1850s and 1860s they did not last long and in 1874 Sir James Gell's view was that 'at present there is scarcely a superior school for girls in the Island'. He and his wife decided to remedy the situation and approached a friend of theirs, Lady Buchan. As Laura Wilks she had accompanied her Manx-based father Colonel Mark Wilks on his appointment as Governor of St Helena where her beauty elicited compliments from the captive former Emperor Napoleon. She returned to the Island with her father in 1816 and lived with him at the newly-built Kirby Park in Braddan before moving to Scotland on her marriage to General Sir John Buchan. Their only son died in infancy and Sir John died in 1847, leaving Laura a very rich widow with no heir. She was keen to retain her links with the Island and her friendship with the Gells and in 1861 she gave £1,200 to King William's to fund a scholarship in her father's name. When Gell suggested in 1874 that she should do something to help the education of girls, she was more than ready to respond.

Gell was a trustee of King William's and Laura Buchan gave £1,000 in 1875 to fund a school for girls, preferably on the college site, which would benefit from the help and protection of the college. However, although the Principal was sympathetic to the project, the college's own finances were precarious and the trustees could spare little money. Lady Gell chaired a committee to work out the details of the new girls' school and it decided that Lorne House would be an ideal home for it. Unfortunately they could certainly not afford to buy Lorne House at the asking price of £3,000 or even rent it at £120, so that idea fell by the wayside. Fortunately there was a further windfall worth £1,000 from the residue of the estate of Eliza Newton and this enabled a scaled-down school, known as Castletown High School for Girls, to open with seventeen pupils in a rented house at 4, Castle Street, under the headship of Louisa Moss, the sister of the headmaster of the famous Shrewsbury School. Unfortunately initial leadership was poor, headmistresses came and went, the school moved to Bay View House in 1888 and by 1895 there were only four pupils. Under Alice Taylor it expanded to 56 in two years and a move was made to larger premises on the Promenade in 1897. Unfortunately Taylor left in 1899 and the school moved once more, to Bowling Green Road, but languished in the years after the Dumbell's crash of 1900. When Miss Dawson took over as headmistress in 1908 there were only nine day girls in the school but she attracted many more and a move was made to numbers 10 and 12 in Bowling Green Road, the former home of the Gells.

Having dodged a Zeppelin raid during the war, Miss Dawson and her girls prospered, so that there were 56 day pupils and 32 boarders when she retired in 1919. In 1920 the school became a non profit-making limited liability company and continued to expand under Miss M.W.Mathew until threatened by the economic recession after 1929. The trustees appealed to the Manx government, which accepted 'The Buchan School' as it was now generally known, as a Direct Grant School, with 10% of the pupils on free places and it was to this school that the Catherine Halsall endowment was diverted in 1931.

The fortunes of King William's College itself had been mixed since the retirement of Principal Robert Dixon in 1865. He was replaced by Joshua Jones (who changed his name to Hughes-Games in 1880), formerly

Headmaster of the Liverpool Institute, who found under a hundred boys in the school on his arrival and almost doubled this by 1869. He attended the first meeting of the Headmasters' Conference at Sherborne School in Dorset in 1870 and spoke authoritatively there about the teaching of mathematics and science, at which his school excelled in the coming years, gaining 75 awards at Oxford and Cambridge between 1870 and 1890, half of them in mathematics. The British politician William Gladstone visited the school in 1878 and praised its 'flourishing state', while one of the pupils at the time, William Bragg, later became a scientist of world renown, a Nobel Prizewinner and President of the Royal Society. The arrival of the railway in Castletown in 1874 made the school more accessible to day boys and Steam Packet ships became faster and more reliable, so that numbers of foreign boarders remained buoyant. A new chapel, designed by James Cowle, was opened in 1879, the year of the launching of the 'Barrovian' magazine. The college's golden jubilee was celebrated in a mood of confidence in 1883, with 242 boys on the roll and five boarding houses.

In 1886 Hughes-Games was appointed Archdeacon of Man and he was succeeded as principal by Frank Walters, another mathematician, who had been a friend and colleague of T.E.Brown at Clifton. But by 1889 numbers fell to 145 and this precipitated a financial crisis just when Bishop Bardsley openly criticized the College for sidelining Barrow's intention of training Manx clergy. The storm was weathered and money was even found to sponsor the building of a new chapel for the residents of Derbyhaven, opened in 1898. By then numbers had recovered to nearly two hundred, but the vast majority were boarders from 'across'. In 1899 Walters fell ill and died in office, aged 47, and he was replaced by Edwin Kempson, another former Clifton master recommended by T.E.Brown. It was under him that the first General Knowledge Paper appeared in 1905, standardized in 1917 into 18 sections, each with ten questions. Published annually in 'The Guardian' it gained a world-wide following and flourishes still. Benefactions from the Manx philanthropist Henry Bloom Noble provided seven scholarships for Island boys by 1906, and these were much needed because day fees soon reached £15 a term and boarding fees could be as much as £75 a term. Kempson left in 1912 to become a Canon of Newcastle and later Bishop of Warrington and Edward Owen took over at a time when numbers were again low and the school had to face the harrowing years of the Great War, which claimed the lives of 135 of the 546 former pupils who served in the forces.

The public schools were very popular after the war, largely because many people thought, rightly or wrongly, that without the 'officer class' they provided the war might not have been won. During the 1920s numbers rose to a record 312 but fell back drastically to 183 after the effects of the Wall

Street Crash of 1929 cut down the supply of Lancashire boarders. Owen retired in 1930 to be replaced by George Harris, who presided over the school's centenary in 1933 at a time of deep depression and falling numbers. By the mutual agreement of Tynwald and the trustees, King William's became a Direct Grant school in 1934 and received enough state funding to save it from closure. The 168 pupils in 1936 were the lowest number in 30 years, but this was a situation mirrored in many similar schools in the UK during the 1930s, and it left Sydney Wilson, the new principal appointed in 1935, with a formidable task ahead. [11]

RONALDSWAY AND THE 1939-45 WAR

Although King Edward VII had not come to Castletown when he visited the Island in 1901, his successor George V, accompanied by Queen Mary, made up for this lapse in 1920 and they were greeted at Castle Rushen by local dignitaries and presented with a loyal address which read:

We, the High Bailiff, Town Commissioners and inhabitants of the town and district of Castletown tender to Your Majesty our humble duty and heartfelt loyalty. We respectfully welcome to the ancient metropolis of this Island and one-time residence of the Kings and Lords of Man, Your Majesty and your Royal Consort. Since the days of your royal predecessor King Henry III when our ancestors under the rule of Olaf the Second, King of Man, guarded the coasts of England and Ireland, from England's enemies by sea – and lately during the Great War now happily ended – the Manxmen of this district, as elsewhere, have ever striven faithfully to fulfil their duty to their Sovereign Overlord, in the defence of His Honour and of the dignity of his dominions. That Almighty God may spare Your Majesty long to reign over your dominions in peace, prosperity and honour is the earnest prayer of us. [12]

The High Bailiff on this occasion was R.D.Farrant and the Chairman of the Commissioners James Wood Cannell. Since the establishment of the Commissioners in 1884 a number of individuals had been elected Chairman more than twice, including James Mylchreest, John Clague, George Harrington Quayle (1897-1899) and Richard Qualtrough (1914 and 1916-1918), while John William Corrin would dominate the Commissioners between 1928 and 1931 and again from 1943 to 1945. Yet another member of the Qualtrough family, James Alexander, was Chairman in 1927, then again from 1938 to 1939, and finally from 1946 to 1955, while S.B.Taggart held the position in the intervening years from 1940 to 1945.

As modern life became more complicated, and especially as motor cars became affordable, the responsibilities of the Commissioners grew year by year, with the need to maintain, light, clean and police the streets. As a result of Lord Raglan's enthusiasm for motor cars, the first 'Gordon Bennett' race for motor cars was held in 1905 on a course which included Castletown, though in subsequent years courses farther north were used, with the present TT course being established in 1909. By the 1920s motor transport was a fact of life everywhere on the Island and the narrow streets of Castletown became extremely hazardous for motorist and pedestrian alike. Responsibility for the Island roads lay with Tynwald and a Castletown by-pass was planned and executed by the Highways Board and completed by November 1938. It was officially described as being 'four furlongs and 13 poles' in length and drastically reduced the flow of traffic through the town, almost to the point of isolating it.[13]

In 1928 Captain Gordon Olley visited the Island and shortly afterwards founded Olley Air Services Ltd, based in Croydon, which made chartered flights to the grass airstrip which had been established when the Barrow Trust leased some of its Ballagilley land for this use when aeroplanes were in their infancy. Blackpool and West Coast Air Services also used the strip and in 1934 Olley took over the company and also established Isle of Man Air Services, which managed the airstrip facilities. When Tynwald rejected a plan to establish a national airport at Ronaldsway in 1935 Olley took up the challenge himself and leased a further 88 acres of land. Contractors employed 50 men to level and drain the fields and it was at this point that their excavations unearthed the foundations of an Iron Age settlement, together with undisturbed burial grounds and items of pottery, ornaments and hand tools. Experts were called in from the Manx Museum and the finds were carefully recorded and stored.

Two grass runways 720 yards and 940 yards long were ready by the summer of 1935 and a hangar was built the following year, with a workshop and booking office attached to it. There was also a wooden terminal building for passengers, whose number grew from 8,000 in 1935 to 12,000 in 1936. In 1937 the UK's Air Ministry installed a radio station to assist aircraft using the airport, which meant that the de Havilland 'Express', 'Dragon' and 'Rapide' fourteen-seater aircraft could operate more safely on the routes to and from Manchester, Liverpool, Blackpool, Leeds/Bradford, Carlisle, Glasgow and Belfast. The return air fare to Liverpool was two pounds, ten shillings. The increasingly busy landing strip (still grazed by sheep at night to keep the grass short) was operated on land belonging to the Barrow Trust and A. B. Crookall, a local landowner and politician, so there were good reasons why it became known as 'Ronaldsway' rather than 'Castletown' airport. With hindsight, however, this seems a lost opportunity because the Castletown name would have brought greater fame and recognition to the town and possibly redressed some of the initiative seized over the previous years by Douglas.[14]

In 1937 Tynwald agreed to pay £100,000 a year to the UK towards the cost of re-armament to prepare for what many feared was an inevitable conflict with Nazi Germany, and in return the Air Ministry agreed to construct a new grass airfield at Jurby, which opened in 1939 and eventually became the centre for up to eighty Avro-Anson training aircraft. With the outbreak of war Ronaldsway itself was taken over by the RAF and was used by No 1 Ground Defence and Gunnery School, operating Westland Wallace aircraft. It was also one of the few airfields that continued operating civilian flights throughout the wartime period. An extra station was needed for fighter aircraft and by 1942 another airfield had been constructed at Andreas, initially for Spitfires. Then in 1943 RAF Ronaldsway itself was handed over to the UK Admiralty because a further Royal Navy station was needed in a safe location to train thousands of air crew to fly the Barracuda aircraft newly in production for the Fleet Air Arm for use against the Japanese in the South Pacific. Acting under the UK Defence of the Realm Act, which was extended to the Island by Order in Council, a compulsory purchase order was placed on 850 acres of land at Ronaldsway, an area many times larger than the existing airstrip. This consisted of land from Bishop Barrow's Ballagilley farm, the Turkeyland limestone quarry, the Creggans farm, the Balthane farm and above all the Ronaldsway estate itself, which once belonged to William Christian ('Illiam Dhone') and included a fine 17th century farmhouse, which was - regrettably, as it would now seem-demolished.

The contractors, John Laing of Carlisle, brought over hundreds of workmen, many of whom were accommodated in Castletown, and there was plenty of work for local hauliers, who brought sand and gravel from the point of Ayre and elsewhere. Four tarmac runways were built, the main one being 1,400 yards long and intersected by smaller runways. A standard Admiralty-designed control tower was constructed and the Creggans farmhouse became the headquarters of the Admiralty's Works department, housing generators for the whole area, while 12 prefabricated hangars housed the aircraft. While the eastern end of the main runway was being prepared several complete human skeletons were uncovered, together with swords and shields, and it was decided that this must have been the site of the Battle of Ronaldsway in 1275 when 537 Manxmen lost their lives fighting against the Scots. Accordingly the eastern end of the runway was raised in order to leave the battleground undisturbed beneath. The new station, named HMS 'Urley' was commissioned in June 1944 and by January the following year three squadrons were based there, flying between sixty and seventy aircraft a day.[15]

In the late 1930s a highly secret radar system, known as 'Chain Home', was developed in the UK and by 1939 there were nineteen radar stations linked to this system. Two years later there were about 200, including three on the Isle of Man, located at Dalby, Bride and Scarlett. The installation at Scarlett was constructed in 1941 on Scarlett farm and consisted of blast-proof reinforced concrete buildings which included transmitter and receiver blocks, an operations room, a generator house and a semi-circle of 'pillboxes'. There were also barracks and guard posts because each station was operated by about 63 RAF and 60 WAAF officers and NCOs, working four shifts a day to keep it open all day and all night. When they were off-duty these personnel were accommodated in another cluster of buildings erected in Arbory Road in Castletown.

It was important that each station should have a clear view out to sea because the system worked from two large static transmitter aerials suspended between steel masts 325 feet high, which were kept in place by steel guy ropes, and two receiving aerials housed in 240 foot high towers. The system in general was able to provide advance warning of heavy aircraft such as bombers and proved invaluable during the Battle of Britain, but it could not pick up low-flying aircraft or ships. To do this, another system, known as Chain Home Low and more similar to radar, was installed throughout Britain in 1940 with a station on the Island on the top of Mull Hill. In 1944 Scarlett ceased to operate as a Chain Home Station and its buildings were occupied by personnel from the recently opened HMS 'Urley' at Ronaldsway.[16]

After the end of the war, which claimed the lives of 36 Castletown men, including another John Taubman, the Admiralty had no further use for the aerodrome at Ronaldsway on which some £2 million had been spent. Thanks to some diplomatic negotiation by the then Lieutenant Governor, Sir Geoffrey Bromet, who happened to be an Air Vice-Marshal, the Manx Government was able to buy the entire Ronaldsway site and its buildings for £200,000 in 1948. The architect T.H.Kennaugh was commissioned to design a modern civilian airport and the first new buildings were finished in 1951, followed by the main passenger terminal in 1953, opened in June by the UK's Minister of Aviation, Alan Lennox-Boyd. By this time the airport was handling 30,000 passengers a month during the summer and it was for a time ranked as the third busiest in the British Isles after London Heathrow and Northolt, largely because during the 1950s the Island recovered its former status as a major holiday destination.[17]

CASTLE RUSHEN HIGH SCHOOL, 1948

In 1944 the UK Parliament, despite the strains of wartime, passed an Education Act which set up a system of compulsory secondary education for

The modest beginnings of Castle Rushen High School. (Ron Ronan collection)

all children over eleven in a grammar school, if they passed an 'eleven plus' exam, or in a technical school or a 'secondary modern' school if they did not. There is no reason why this system could not easily have been adopted on the Island but it did not find favour with Herbert Fletcher, an Englishman who had been appointed the Island's Director of Education at the age of 36 in 1935. He preferred what was termed a 'comprehensive' school, where all three elements were present on the same campus and no invidious selection exam had to be taken. Suitable school buildings already existed for this purpose in Douglas and Ramsey but not in Peel or Castletown. Since the closure of the old Grammar School in 1931 Castletown children had been required to travel to Douglas for their secondary education and the initial assumption was that this arrangement would continue. Joseph Qualtrough attempted to negotiate the incorporation of King William's and The Buchan into the new system but their trustees were not enthusiastic, so he then looked into the possibility that the Arbory Road domestic buildings of the former Scarlett Chain Home radar installation could be modified to provide a new school.

As Speaker of the Keys as well as MHK for Castletown, Qualtrough was in a strong position to steer the necessary legislation through Tynwald and in April 1947 he introduced a resolution asking that the Isle of Man Education Authority be granted permission to spend £24,000 on establishing a new secondary school for Castletown. The Arbory Road site, he told members of Tynwald,

> comprises a considerable number of substantial brick-built buildings with
> wooden floors and the site has excellent roads, first class drainage, and

the buildings are fitted with electric light. There is enough land for a playing field, the whole comprising 22 or 23 acres, well situated and central for the south of the Island, and the buildings are in every way large enough for classrooms. They will require some small adjustment, the covering in of ways between the classrooms, and the whole is estimated to cost £24,000.[18]

This was recognized to be an ideal opportunity to acquire a new school at a knock-down price and the scheme went ahead. The conversion involved the building of a number of corridors which linked the classrooms and public rooms and 'Castle Rushen High School' was ready to admit its first pupils in September 1948. There were 147 boys and 116 girls, many of whom came by bus from Port Erin, Port St Mary, Colby, Ballabeg, Foxdale and Santon, and their headmaster was Godfrey Cretney, who held up a blank piece of paper at his first assembly to emphasize that everyone was making a fresh start. On May 6th 1949 the school was officially declared open by the British Home Secretary, Chuter Ede. Cretney was a Manxman born but he left after six years to be head of a large comprehensive in Wolverhampton and became well-known in Britain as a spokesman for the virtues of the comprehensive system. He was knighted in 1966 for services to education.

It was never intended that the wartime buildings should be retained permanently and by the end of the 1950s the natural irreverence of pupils had dubbed them 'the shanty town' or 'the dump', a view publicly shared by Cretney's successor as headmaster, John Russell Smith, who during the winter of 1961 had to cope with a hundred burst pipes, a malfunctioning boiler and leaking roofs. A newly built, modern school designed to accommodate 480 pupils was completed in 1962 and opened by Sir Charles Cunningham of the Home Office. He was treated to a concert given by the school orchestra in the new assembly hall, in which they performed the 'Celebration Suite', specially composed for the occasion by the school's director of Music, Harry Pickard.[19] Peel had to wait a good deal longer for its own secondary school, but when this was opened by Queen Elizabeth II in 1979, all the main Island towns had schools which were part of its free comprehensive system.

RICHARD CAIN AND THE CASTLETOWN BREWERY

In Richard Cain Castletown at last found an entrepreneur who could compare with the finest Douglas had produced. He was born in 1862 and was at first apprenticed to the Castletown grocers, Duggan and Mylchreest. Able and industrious, he soon made his way in the business and became its owner, full of enterprising plans for its expansion. When Thomas Sherlock, the co-owner of Castletown Brewery, died in the late 1880s, Cain led a group of Castletown businessmen in making a bid for the brewery and its four tied houses, which included Castletown's Mona Inn, and the shares in the new company were available from November 1890. Once it had been established Cain remained a director and the business made steady progress up to 1898 when a 'Beer Bubble' developed on the Island, following a similar pattern in the UK, because speculators became obsessed with the idea that a fortune could be made out of buying up the existing breweries and amalgamating them into one concern. The driving force behind the new 'Isle of Man Breweries' was Alexander Bruce, general manager of Dumbell's Bank, which was also heavily involved. Many institutions and individuals on the Island were suspicious and critical of the amalgamation but it went ahead despite some strong resistance and Castletown Brewery became part of the new scheme. In the general euphoria top prices were often paid for questionable assets, the whole edifice collapsed with Dumbell's Bank in 1900 and Castletown Brewery, with others, was closed down.

It was rescued in 1904 by Peter Yates (of the Wine Lodges) who paid £3,000 for both the Ballaughton and Castletown Breweries but he soon sold the Castletown section for £4,000 in 1906 to Richard Cain, who had meanwhile restructured his finances. From this point until 1947 he and his sons presided over what might be termed the rise and rise of Castletown Brewery. In 1911 a new building was erected on the site to house two new brewing vats and the company was able to produce some 250,000 bottles of ale a year in addition to draught beer. The war years in fact were a good time for the brewery because the population of the Island had been swelled by about 24,000 enemy aliens in camp at Knockaloe near Peel and they were allowed a drink or two from time to time. During the 1920s profits rose steadily, reaching £2,098 in 1924, and the brewery, which had owned the Station and Union hotels in Castletown from 1906, embarked on a strategy of acquiring some 24 more houses in other towns between 1920 and 1945 as well as the Victoria Hotel in Castletown, which was taken over in 1939.

In 1916 Richard Cain bought the Ballamoar estate in the north of the Island and gave some of his time and attention to being a country gentleman as well as a brewer. In 1919 he entered the Keys as member for Ayre, a seat he held until 1934, and he campaigned for the establishment of an experimental farm at Knockaloe, an all-Island electricity scheme, and the World Manx Association, of which he was the founding president. While he was involved in all these activities he handed over some of the responsibility for the brewery to his sons Wilfred, Harold and James who, to varying degrees, were all involved in its management.

In 1932 Cain pulled off a major publicity success when Prince George

147

Castletown Brewery (right) and the swing bridge. (Ron Ronan collection)

(later the Duke of Kent) visited Castletown Brewery in June that year. According to the historian of the Island's brewing trade:

> The event revealed the growing political and commercial influence of Richard Cain, and the royal connection undoubtedly enhanced Castletown's commercial standing, as a beer entitled 'Prince's Brew' was marketed throughout the Island to commemorate the event....Cain's organization of the visit, involving the whole community, was a commercial triumph, receiving considerable media exposure in an increasing climate of temperance. In the 1930s Castletown Brewery went on to establish itself as one of the Island's premier breweries, along with Okell's of Douglas, because its founder had an uncanny ability of marketing his establishment in a positive light.[20]

In 1934 the Lieutenant Governor, Sir Montagu Butler, turned on a new brew of Castletown Blue Label which was to be sold as 'Governor's Ale'. Other high profile visitors in the 1930s included Sir Derwent Hall Caine in 1936 and the next Governor, (later Earl Granville), in 1938, whose wife was the sister of Queen Elizabeth. In 1936 the brewery was equipped with a new bottling plant and more automation and in 1937 a new boiler was installed to cope with increasing demand for the very popular Blue Label ale, while cans came into use as well as bottles. International recognition came in 1936 with the award of the Blue Riband at the Brewer's Exhibition in London as well as a Cross of Honour and Diploma for the Red Label Pale Ale in Prague and

Pilsen in 1938, while the company's Pale Ale also won first prize at Copenhagen in the same year. Cain wanted to move into the 'take-away' drinks trade, selling direct to the customer, but in this he was for a time vigorously opposed by the temperance movement, led by Methodist ministers who managed to prevent the company being granted the necessary licences until 1938. Nevertheless, by the time war clouds loomed ahead again in 1939 Castletown was 'probably the most dynamic brewery on the Island'.[21]

The war inevitably had its effects. The company had been very successful in marketing its products overseas, but now this became more difficult. Moreover the cargo ship which had operated directly out of Castletown up to 1939 ceased to sail and all supplies had to come through Douglas, which meant added expense. In November 1941 the brewery, which had been painted white, was re-painted a muddy brown colour so that it would not be too obvious a target in the event of a bombing raid. However, as with the first war, the brewing industry prospered in the wartime Island because of the huge increase of population caused by internment of enemy aliens – this time in hotels in the seaside resorts. In addition there was a very considerable influx of service personnel working in the new airfields and training stations established on the Island. By 1944 Castletown recorded an annual profit of £14,481, and paid out a 10% dividend and a 5% bonus. In 1945 5% of the company's products were allocated to troops serving abroad, showing that 'ultimately, Castletown was more ambitious, dynamic and open-minded than its contemporaries, refusing to develop the more insular outlook on trade adopted by their peers'.[22]

Carnival Day, 1946. (Ron Ronan collection)

In May 1945 Castletown bought out Clinch's brewery and three weeks later Heron and Brearley took control of their main rival, Okell's. In July 1945 Richard Cain, by then aged 84, was proud to receive King George VI and Queen Elizabeth at the brewery, shortly after the surrender of Germany in April. The King turned on a special 'Victory Brew' and a large party was thrown for the entire Castletown community. The following year expansion continued with the acquisition of Bramley Brothers' Liverpool brewery and 15 tied houses. However, in July 1947 Richard Cain decided to sell the whole business to Hope and Anchor Breweries from Sheffield for the sum of £450,000. This was partly because he foresaw that a great deal of investment would be necessary in the future to enable the business to compete in a changing world and also because he was by now 86. His eldest surviving son Wilfred was a dedicated brewer but his younger sons Harold and James increasingly nourished political ambitions, which the sale of the company allowed to pursue. Harold served as MHK for Middle from 1958 to 1966 and gave much of his time to public and charitable causes while James served as a Douglas MHK from 1956 to 1966 and his son, James Crookall Cain, rose to be Speaker of the House from 1991 to 1996. Richard Cain, the founder of this influential dynasty, died at the age of 100 in 1963, 'perhaps the most distinguished of all the [brewery] founders in his contribution not only to the brewery but to the life of the Island'.[23]

CASTLETOWN GROWS 1946-1981

Under the chairmanship of James Qualtrough between 1946 and 1955 the Castletown Commissioners had to grapple with several major problems after the war. One was a low population, which was still only 1,749 in 1953. Another was the inadequacy of the town's drainage system, which had been a public health worry for decades. A third was the fact that the by-pass road completed in 1938 had adversely affected local traders as well as users of public transport, because the buses could not negotiate the narrow streets of the town and were instead routed along the by-pass. In 1953 Joseph Qualtrough had come to the conclusion that it was necessary to ask Tynwald to come to the assistance of the town and to vote money for the improvement of the sewerage facilities, at least. 'I am bound to say', he told Tynwald members in January that year, 'that I am reluctant to do this, but I do not think that any part of the Island has been more restrained in its applications for public assistance than Castletown, which has very rarely troubled the Court in these matters. It may be that the whole town are a bit independent, and they can look back on their history with some pride, but ….the town cannot live on history.'[24]

He also explained that:

Castletown in the 1940s, looking very run-down in some areas. (Manx National Heritage)

Castletown at the moment is facing very perplexing problems, which it seems to me can only be solved by a long-term policy. As some members know, the Castletown Commissioners recently applied to the Local Government Board for permission to proceed with a drainage scheme, which scheme involves a new sewer, costing £31,000, in addition to an annual charge of £500 for the provision of an electrical pump – to leapfrog, if I may say so, that troublesome Sand Field, which has always been difficult.....There are no less than four outfalls running into the sea and naturally they are costly to maintain – particularly the main sewer, which carries the principal part of the sewage and runs through the Sand Field. This sand is quicksand; it is always moving. When a trench was cut

151

in it some years ago…the workmen left some pipes in the trench and went to their dinner. When they came back, the pipes were gone. The outfall runs about a half-mile out to sea, over a very stony beach which is subject to the full force of the south-west wind, and it has been very difficult to keep it in repair.[25]

On the issue of the by-pass, he said:

When the by-pass road was built it was quite obvious what the result would be, and I expressed my opposition in the Court at the time, because Castletown was going to be cut off from the main traffic of the Island. That has now come to pass. The by-pass road was essential but its adverse effect on the town has been considerable and there is no doubt that the little local tradespeople have been feeling the effect in a decline of business because the main traffic cannot come in to the town. The Commissioners have been fighting to get the buses into the town. There are serious difficulties which prevent it at the moment owing to the iron bridge and the narrow street, but unless by some means this traffic can be brought into the town the outlook for Castletown is going to be very black indeed.[26]

After almost two years of discussions, enquiries and grumbles from the representatives of other towns that Castletown was getting special treatment, Tynwald eventually voted £39,000 to build a new sewer outfall, pumping station, sewerage and storm water diversions in October 1954, and a long-standing problem was thereby solved. The issue of narrow streets was partially addressed by the construction of Farrant's Way in 1962, though this development resulted in the demolition of many ancient and interesting buildings.[27]

In 1957 Castletown received considerable exposure as a result of a half-hour children's programme for BBC radio's 'Afternoon Out' series presented by the famous broadcaster Wilfred Pickles. 'Castletown is one of my favourite places in this Island', he announced, 'I don't know why, but it reminds me a little of Brittany with its cluster of grey stone fishermen's cottages hugging the water's edge…Then, of course, there is the castle, whose ancient grey walls are mirrored darkly in the still waters of the harbour.' He met Sir Joseph Qualtrough, who showed him Queen Elizabeth's clock, and then he was taken round the castle by one of the guides, 'Mrs Black and her dog Lassie' and shown the main rooms and the dungeons with their instruments of torture. Then Pickles faded out and there was a dramatic re-enactment of the betrayal of Countess Charlotte and the imprisonment of Bishop Wilson. The programme ended with a brief visit to the Nautical Museum in Bridge

House, recently set up in 1951, where Brian Megaw, the Director of the Manx Museum, told Pickles all about the 'Peggy', and he talked to carpenter William Clarke, who maintained it.[28]

Perhaps spurred on by this programme, an article in the Manx press suggested that the attractiveness of Castle Rushen would be increased by the use of 'fittings with dummy figures in period dress and possibly tableaux representing themes from Manx history', and several members of Tynwald woke up to the fact that the castle, which had in 1929 been handed over by the UK to the care of the Manx Government Property Trustees, could be more effectively marketed as a tourist attraction. The lead was taken not by Castletown representatives but by two Douglas MHKs, John Bolton and Clifford Irving. Irving, the persuasive 'Silver Fox', proposed in Tynwald in October 1958 that a committee should be appointed 'to make proposals for the dignified development of Castle Rushen as a national showpiece'. He explained that:

> Purely from the point of view of the people of Castletown alone, (and I believe Castletown is in a near dead state at the moment) this project would be worthwhile. I believe that the one big asset, the one big advantage that Castletown has is Castle Rushen, and I believe as guardians of Castle Rushen, as the government are, we owe it to Castletown to see that the castle is presented in the best possible way not only to visitors but to the Manx people themselves. The important thing with Castletown is to create something that will make people want to go there....We must not be put off by professors of ancient monuments and people like that. They like to see Castle Rushen in its natural state of many hundreds of years ago, but they are small in number. The general public want to go into the castle and have some idea of what went on at a particular period or year, perhaps 1651, which was an important year in the life of the castle.[29]

Few members disagreed with these sentiments and it was accepted that, despite the reluctance of Manx Museum experts, there should be no objection to fake furniture and models as long as they were able to give some idea of what life in the castle had been like in days gone by. In due course a committee was appointed, composed of individuals with a range of expertise, and a more colourful presentation of Castle Rushen became official government policy.

Joseph Qualtrough, who had long been Castletown's champion in Tynwald, died in January 1960 after a remarkable 40 years as MHK for the town and also 22 years as Speaker of the House. He had been the outstanding

153

Manx politician of the century up to then and one of the many tributes paid to him in the Keys and Tynwald came from Charles Kerruish, who was to succeed him as the outstanding politician of the century's remaining years. With the oratorical touch with which he lit up many a Manx debate, Kerruish said:

> This ancient House, in the course of a thousand years, must have paid tribute to many great sons of Manxland, yet few can have rendered more consistent or devoted service to the Manx people than Joseph Davidson Qualtrough. He was a man of vision and clarity of thought. He, more than any other in recent years, sought both to maintain our parliamentary traditions and develop our parliamentary democracy. He was a man of profound culture, who filled every place with distinction. A man, who in any concourse of great men, in the Commonwealth to which we so proudly belong, would not have stood in the shadows. As a Speaker, he was perfect. For a man like that it is difficult to find suitable words to give expression to one's own regard and admiration for his numberless qualities of head and heart. For us all, his passing is a real personal loss. We respected him. We looked to him for guidance whenever we were faced with a difficulty. His example will live in the annals of our history and it will inspire the people who could look up to a great man's example with the utmost confidence for their own guidance and for learning the true tenets and doctrines of selfless service in action.[30]

Entrance to Arbory Street. (Ron Ronan collection)

The resulting by-election was contested by Harold Colebourn (494 votes), J.P.Qualtrough (347) and J.Blackburn (156). Colebourn's defeat of a Qualtrough was rather remarkable because he was a resident of Ballasalla, his career so far had hardly touched on Castletown, and he was a very different sort of person from the late Sir Joseph. A grandson of the wealthy brewer and hotelier Charles Udall, Colebourn was orphaned as a youth, packed off to boarding school in England and then lost an eye fighting in the 1914-18 war. He became fascinated with wireless broadcasting, started his own radio retail and repair business in Douglas and set up a secret transmitter in Ramsey during the 1939-45 war which lured enemy bombers away from their chosen targets in the UK. After the war he set his heart on the establishment of a Manx radio station that would rival Radio Luxembourg and make the Isle of Man a household word throughout Europe but he was thwarted by the UK's refusal to grant the necessary licences. His project for a chair lift across Douglas harbour to Douglas Head did not find favour with the public, though he did manage to get the debates in Tynwald officially recorded.[31] Castletown voters clearly thought well of him because he was re-elected in 1962 with 586 votes, beating off a challenge from Colin Vereker (417) and Mrs M. Faragher (76).

During Colebourn's years as MHK a major new plan was formulated to take Castletown confidently out of the doldrums and into a bright new future. By 1961 the population had dropped yet again, to 1,536, and the Commissioners, chaired between 1961 and 1966 by James Collister, Samuel Taggart, Colin Vereker, Gordon Cubbon and Richard Whittle, proposed to ask Tynwald for permission for a dramatic extension of the town boundaries which would make it at least three times larger. Even though most of the new territory consisted of farm land, except for the Janet's Corner estate, King William's College and the new properties which had been recently built along the Ballakaighen Road, the population would be immediately raised to 2,378 and this would help to increase the revenue from rates. Housing and industrial development were to be encouraged and a new seaside promenade was to be built, with an ambitious 'marine drive' along it, which would cross the harbour on a new bridge and carry traffic to the south of the town. Plans of the scheme were published in the 'Isle of Man Examiner' in February 1962 and it was announced that the authorities 'are hoping to interest a private development company in the erection of a first-class hotel, swimming pool and gardens in the Chapel Lane area where clearance of old buildings has been taking place for some time. An area between Hope Street and Malew Street has been earmarked along with other areas for industrial development'.[32]

The whole scheme depended upon Tynwald's agreement to the boundary

With the milkman, 1950. (Ron Ronan collection)

extension and it fell to Harold Colebourn to shepherd the necessary Bill through numerous debates during 1965 and against very strong opposition from Howard Simcocks, the MHK for Rushen, upon whose territory (and into whose electorate) an enlarged Castletown would encroach.[33] However, the Bill eventually passed and the new boundary was agreed in 1966. The Janet's Corner estate, previously in Malew, had recently been built by the Local Government Board to replace several RAF Nissen Huts (one of which still survives) and seems to have derived its name from the owner of a nearby sweetshop. Work also began on new housing developments at Farrant's Park and in Kissack Road, and from the 1970s onwards the Ballalough area was developed between Arbory Road and the by-pass. As a result Castletown's population rose to 2,671 in 1971 and reached 3,141 ten years later.

The more dramatic aspects of the Commissioners' original scheme never came to pass however, so there was no marine drive or new bridge at the harbour mouth or new hotel by the castle. All this would have involved the demolition of the Old Grammar School and other ancient buildings, and local conservationist were becoming seriously worried about the destruction of so much of the town's historic heritage, which had begun with the construction of Farrant's Way. Accordingly the Castletown Preservation Society was established in 1970 and in 1971 'Country Life', the UK magazine devoted to the preservation of good architecture, among other things, sent one of its journalists, Nicholas Cooper, to take stock of what was happening in Castletown. In a three-page, illustrated article entitled 'Problems of an Island

Retreat', he found that 'Castletown's streets, winding off the Promenade, are narrow and unspoilt. They are notable for their fine Victorian shop fronts, but while these are attractive survivals they are also an index of the economic stagnation that has preserved them'. He felt that Castletown's charm could be under threat if there should be an economic revival because the Isle of Man's planning laws were still based on the UK's Town and Country Planning Act of 1932, 'and the intimacy of the Island's life easily persuades people that further legislation is unnecessary – that things are best arranged by talking things over with old so-and-so. But conditions change faster than people always like to admit, and it is arguable that negotiations can sometimes be strengthened by a bit of law'.[34]

Despite all his hard work in achieving the boundary extension Harold Colebourn lost his seat in 1966 to Colin Vereker (usually known as 'Kim'), who won resoundingly with 685 votes to Colebourn's 309 and J.R.G.Crellin's 301. Vereker, aged 50, trained as an aeronautical engineer before serving in the war with the Fleet Air Arm. A company director and J.P., he was a Castletown Commissioner from 1960 to 1973, serving as Chairman in 1963, 1972 and 1973. He was appointed Chairman of the Airports Board and served on several other boards but in 1971 he lost his seat in the Keys to Mrs Elspeth Quayle (531 votes to 482) with another Qualtrough, H.P., in third place with 352 votes and R.C.Watkin trailing with 218. In 1975 Vereker succeeded his kinsman as the eighth Viscount Gort but he was not successful in his bid for the Castletown seat in the 1976 election, when Mrs Quayle beat him again with a decisive majority of 898 to his 405 and C.Peach's 315.[35] Elspeth Quayle, a landscape gardener by profession, was a JP and served on several government boards, especially Forestry, Mines and Lands, where she was Chair from 1976 to 1981.

Many of Castletown's often conservative and 'respectable' inhabitants were probably uncomfortable about the presence in their midst between 1951 and 1971 of a museum devoted to witchcraft. This was largely the creation of Gerald Gardner, who spent much of his professional life as a customs officer in Ceylon, Borneo and Malaya where he developed an intense interest in magic and witchcraft and began to collect many items connected with cults of various kinds. When he retired to Hampshire at the age of 52 in 1936 he became a member of a southern coven and made no secret of his activities as a 'white witch'. In 1950 he found on the Isle of Man the ideal place to establish a museum to house his large collection of items, the old windmill in Castletown.

Gardner persuaded himself that the mill was mentioned in records in 1611 but this was an earlier corn mill and not his windmill, which was built in 1828 and partially destroyed by fire twenty years later. Gardner liked to tell

157

Singer Dickie Valentine crowning the Castletown Festival Queen, c.1965.(Ron Ronan collection)

the story that after this the 'witches of Arbory' used the mill for their meetings and midnight dances but in fact it was rebuilt and operated until 1873 by the miller John Cain. Certainly it was in a dilapidated state when Gardner and his associate Cecil Williamson renovated and opened it in 1951 as what they claimed was the world's first 'Museum of Magic and Witchcraft'. On the first floor of the building there were two rooms, one representing a magician's study of about 1630 with everything set out for performing ritual magic. The other room was arranged to represent a witch's cottage of the same date. In these rooms there were about 10,000 objects including herbs for making charms or remedies, magical rings and jewellery, the mediaeval magic ring of the Earls of Lonsdale, objects used to ward off the 'Evil Eye', a witch's riding staff (i.e. broomstick), gazing chrystals, and secret manuscripts. There were also details of the burning of Margrett Inequane and her son in Castletown in 1617 on charges of witchcraft, as well as objects and instruments of torture used in witch hunts.[36]

As was intended, the museum, (called by Gardner 'The Witches' Mill') became a major tourist attraction and as such it brought a fair share of custom to the town. It also brought an element of notoriety when the local newspapers reported from time to time the coven activities of Gardner and his friends, which included dancing naked in the moonlight. Gardner died in 1964 at the age of 80 and the museum was inherited by Mrs Monique Wilson, the self-styled 'High Priestess of Witches' who ran it until 1971 when an article about the Mill in the 'National Geographic Magazine' prompted a handsome offer for the entire collection from Ripley International, who owned a series of 'Believe it or Not' exhibitions, and they spirited everything away to San Francisco, no doubt to the disappointment of Isle of Man visitors and the relief of Castletown residents.

SPORT

The Football Association was founded in England in 1863 and the Isle of Man set up its own FA in 1890. A team calling themselves 'Castletown Rovers' played against Douglas Rangers in a league match in 1892, and another, dubbed 'Castletown United' lost 13-1 to a Douglas side in 1894. Temporary local teams came and went until in 1904 a meeting took place at the Town Hall, presided over by a youthful Joseph Qualtrough, where it was decided that 'an Association Football Club should be formed'. In November that year the Club was admitted to the Isle of Man FA and, known as 'the Metropolitans', the team began the season with Qualtrough playing in the first league game, a win over Douglas.[37] A field at Scarlett was the home ground in the first few years and games were often enlivened by what was described as 'rough play' as well as by voluble criticism of the referee. However, a charitable aspect was demonstrated in 1906 by a cycle parade and confetti fete in aid of Noble's Hospital, and a collection for the Titanic Disaster Fund taken during a match in 1912, which raised two pounds and ten shillings. In 1914 the war put an end to league matches, but Castletown ended on a high note, having won the League title for the first time in the 1913-14 season as well as beating Ramsey in the final of the Association Cup.

The league matches started again late in 1919, and it was resolved that 'red shirts and white knickers be the colours for the coming season'.[38] During the 1920s the Club played at home on fields at Scarlett or Shore Road, and were top of the league in 1923,1924 and 1925. In 1923 there was a crisis over the issue of Temperance, which might seem scarcely credible to football supporters of a later generation. Some members of the team announced that they were not happy, when playing away matches in Douglas, to use licensed premises for changing and refreshment, and the matter led to bitter argument and the resignation of several officials. On the other hand, having several 'dry' team members perhaps helped Castletown to defeat their deadly local rivals Rushen United in the Cup Final of 1923.

After these considerable successes in the early 1920s, the Club began to founder somewhat and actually closed down from 1927 to 1928, apparently because of disagreements with the Isle of Man FA. Then came a major row in January 1931 when the Castletown spectators, who had roundly criticized the referee during the grudge match against Rushen United, were accused by him in his report to the FA of invading the pitch in a riotous and threatening manner at the end of the game. The Club denied these allegations but were fined £3, which they refused to pay. The FA eventually suspended the Club in 1932 and because of stubbornness on both sides, the exile lasted until 1937. During this period the only organized football in the town was a competition for the YMCA Cup, not held under the auspices of the FA, which a Castletown team known as 'Park Rangers' won every year. Eventually a meeting of enthusiasts in 1937 voted to apply to join the FA again with a 'clean sheet', and league games resumed in October that year, only to be halted by war in 1939.

Under the Presidency of Joseph Qualtrough the Club was reconstituted in 1946 and the main item on the agenda was the acquisition of a permanent ground, a project enthusiastically supported by George Woods, formerly Commodore Captain of the Steam Packet, and Fred Faragher, Police Inspector of the Castletown Division. By a number of ingenious stratagems, such as dividing the imaginary pitch into small squares on a plan and selling them to benefactors, enough money was raised by the Club to purchase for £650 a plot of land off Malew Road suitable for a pitch only a yard each way smaller than the one at Wembley, as well as a clubhouse (with hot showers), a covered stand to seat 350, and an open stand on the other side of the pitch which could accommodate 650 (demolished in the 1980s when the ground was extended for a second pitch). Everything combined to make 1950 a bumper year for the Club, which won the both the League and the Cup Final and celebrated with the opening of the new stadium on May 2 1950, when an impressive crowd of 3,600 watched an all-Island team draw against South Liverpool, 2-2, after a kick-off by the Lieutenant Governor, Sir Geoffrey Bromet. The Souvenir Booklet commemorating the event claimed that '..Castletown Club has made insular history in respect to the provision of a well laid-out Sports Stadium that will always be a proud possession of the people of Castletown and for the use of the Town. The idea will probably be followed by other towns and clubs, but this will not detract from (our) pioneering pride.'[39]

In 1951 the FA introduced a system of relegation for clubs at the bottom of each division, to add to the excitement, and Castletown managed to finish in the top half of the first division for 32 of the 52 seasons to 2004, winning the League in 1982 and 1999, reaching the Cup Final 12 times, and winning three times. Unfortunately, in the year of the Club's centenary, 2004, fate dealt a hard blow with relegation to the second division, which, alone of all the other Island clubs, Castletown had so far managed to avoid, but they bounced back again for the 2009 season. The Football Stadium also hosts the Castletown Rifle Club, founded in 1908, whose range seems to have been in a cellar in Alexandra Road until the outbreak of war in 1918. Reforming in

1923 the Club moved to a range in a building on the present site of the George Hotel car park and remained there until close links between football players and riflemen led to the building of a new range near to the stadium pavilion in 1979, extended in 1985 as a memorial to B.A.Holt, the Club's patron from 1968 to 1984.

Castletown Cricket Club, which was linked to King William's College in the early years, was several decades old when it became part of the Isle of Man Cricket Confederation in 1930. The war stopped play in 1939 and the Club did not get going again until 1950, when matches were played on KWC's second pitch during the school holidays. For a few years the Club was probably the strongest on the Island, enjoying the support of Syd Copley, KWC's professional who had played Test cricket against the Australians, and its chief rivals were RAF Jurby. However, the Club faded out in the late 1950s and was not revived for a decade, starting up again on a pitch at Castle Rushen High School, and moving to the Football Stadium in the 1970s. Then there was another lapse for a few years until play began again in the late 1980s, this time at KWC, which has been the Club's base ever since, and in the last twenty years it has enjoyed considerable popularity and success. [40]

Castletown has an association with a remarkable cricketing feat which took place in 1899 at Clifton College in Bristol, when a thirteen-year old

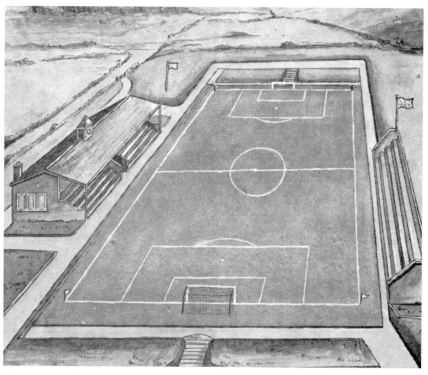

The proposed Sports Stadium at Castletown. **161**

Arthur Collins, the Bristol schoolboy cricketing hero who made 628 not out in 1899 and later married a Castletown girl. (Author's collection)

schoolboy called Arthur Collins scored 628 not out in a junior house match which lasted five days. This still remains cricket's highest individual score and it made Collins a celebrity during his short lifetime. He joined the army after school and in April 1914 he married Ethel Slater, the daughter of a retired army officer living in Castletown. They were married in St Mary's Chapel but Collins was one of the first to leave for France with the British Expeditionary Force when war broke out, and by December he was dead, killed while fighting gallantly. His young widow lived to be over eighty, but she never married again.

Rugby football really caught on in Castletown when some employees of Ronaldsway Aircraft Company founded the Ronaldsway Rugby Club with seven players in 1967. The company withdrew financial support in the late 1980s and at the closing dinner a number of members decided to found the Castletown Rugby Club, and the town Commissioners allowed them to lay out a pitch in Poulsom Park. Another Club, called the Southern Nomads because members are drawn generally from the south of the Island and they have, as yet, no pitch to call their own, was founded in 1982 and they play most of their matches at KWC. In 1971 the Castletown Ale Drinkers Society, which probably contained a few rugby players, came up with the idea of running the 'World Tin Bath Championships' in the harbour, a zany contest now close to its fortieth anniversary. Castletown Hockey Club was established in 1988 by a merger between the existing Celts and Southerners teams, and it soon helped to set up the Manx Hockey Association. The Club is closely affiliated with Castle Rushen High School, using the Astroturf pitch there as well as the indoor training facilities.

The original layout of Castletown golf links was by 'Old' Tom Morris of St Andrew's in 1892 on land on the Langness peninsula which included the 'racecourse', and shortly afterwards the Castletown Golf Links Hotel was built by its proprietor William Johnstone of Salford 'for the convenience of golfers and those wanting a quiet holiday'.[42] In 1979 British and Irish professionals beat Club pros from the USA in a PGA cup contest held on the Castletown course and in 2002 the fifth event on the 'Europro' tour was played there, as were the Duke of York's championships for under 18s in 2003, attended by Prince Andrew. In 2004 the course was ranked 81st out of the 100 best courses by 'Golf World Magazine' and 79th out of 120 by 'Golf Monthly'.

Despite the long association of the name 'Bowling Green' with Castletown, there seems not to have been such a facility in the town until the founding of the bowls club, together with the tennis, swimming and other sporting clubs, in recent times. Sir Joseph Qualtrough had an ingenious theory about the derivation of the Bowling Green name. He argued that Lorne House Hill was an early Tynwald Hill, called 'Howyngren', or 'Hill of the Sun', and that the Manx Gaelic for 'Place of the Sun' is 'Boay yn Gurian'.[43]

D.M. 'Duggie' Brown, later a Castletown resident, was one of the first outstanding Manx TT riders, finishing second in the 1920 Senior race. Between 1939 and 1957 four riders who either lived or worked in Castletown won between them two World Championship level events and four Manx Grand Prix. These were Les Martin, Derek Ennett, George 'Sparrow' Costain and Alan Holmes. In 1954 Ennett won the Junior and Costain won the Senior MGP on a Norton and this inspired the Southern Motorcycle Club to provide a road race in the South of the Island to practice for the MGP. Harold Colebourn was a generous sponsor, and the event took place on July 14th 1955 on the same 4.25 mile Billown circuit still in use, starting on the Castletown bypass and returning to the start via Ballakeighan, Ballabeg Hairpin, Cross Four Ways and Alexandra Bridge.

The name 'Southern Hundred' came from one of the three initial races, which was for 500cc machines and covered 100 miles in 24 laps. Over the years the races became more numerous but shorter, with 16 races spread over 3 days in 2009, the longest over 9 laps. Sidecar races were introduced in 1962, and races for Classic machines in 1987, while from 1991 the Steam Packet Company sponsored more races to tempt some TT competitors to stay on an extra day and thus reduce the number wishing to travel across at the same time. Recent outstanding wins by riders who have lived or worked in Castletown include Steve Moynihan (1971 Junior MGP), Decca Kelly (Lightweight MGP), Jason Griffiths (Southern 100 Championship 1994,1996 and 1997), and Chris Palmer (Ultra-Lightweight TT, 2003, 2004, 2008). In 2008 this race was run on the Billown Circuit and there is a strong feeling in Castletown that races there are fundamentally Castletown's races.[44]

Canon Stenning was President of the Manx Motorcycle Club and ended the prize presentation ceremony at the 1956 Southern Hundred by remarking 'I remember when bikes were bikes and women took their place. See you all in church on Sunday'.[45] One of Castletown's – and the Island's – most influential characters, Ernest Stenning died in 1964, aged 79. He had arrived from Cambridge to teach science at King William's in 1909 and soon became chaplain, a housemaster, coach of most games, and senior science master as well as director of education for the diocese. An enthusiast for road racing, he was an official for the TT races in 1912 and President of the Manx Motor Cycle Club by 1923, as well as being a co-founder in 1923 of the Amateur TT, which became the Manx Grand Prix in 1930. In 1943 he was appointed examining chaplain to the bishop and a Canon of St German's the following year, while at King William's he was appointed vice-principal in 1944. In addition he was a keen antiquarian, writing several articles for academic journals and also finding time to publish, in 1950, a 400-page volume on the Isle of Man in the Hale 'County Books' series. Later in the decade he produced a shortened version of this known as 'A Portrait of the Isle of Man', which sold widely and went through several reprints. In 1954 Stenning became Chairman of the governors at The Buchan School, and in 1958 he was appointed Archdeacon of Man, and in 1959, a chaplain to the Queen. A Freemason since 1914 he also served as Provincial Grand Master for the Island. A tall, imposing figure, and hugely popular, he was a major feature of Castletown cultural and social life for more than half a century.

CASTLETOWN BROWN

James Anthony (Tony) Brown was born in 1950 and educated at Victoria Road School and Castle Rushen High School, after which he qualified as an electrician. Writing in 2007 he recalled:

> The first seven years of my life – from 1950 to 1957 – were lived in Mill Street and my recollections are that it was a busy, lively little street with lots of people living there, and, of course, there was the 'Cosy' Cinema, which was a big part of our lives. Hope Street was also an important part of my life in those days, being just around the corner. It was the 'industrial street' with three coal yards and also leading to Qualtrough's Timber Yard; wagons seemed to go up and down the street all day....We lived

first at No 38 Mill Street, a Castletown Commissioner's house, and it was in such a poor state that, as soon as they could the Commissioners moved our family into No 10 – that was not great either, being a very old property also. When we vacated No 38 it was boarded up and not lived in again until after it was sold by the Commissioners in the late 1970s and the new owner refurbished the property.[46]

In the late 1950s and early 1960s the Commissioners decided to demolish much of Mill Street, while the 'Cosy' Cinema closed down and became part of the Strix factory, so that the whole area became very run-down. In 1976 Tony Brown was elected a Commissioner at the age of 26, declaring that he wanted to help Castletown sustain, develop and secure its infrastructure and business sector as well as to help create and secure business opportunities for the town. He was particularly keen to improve Mill Street but found the way blocked by the imposition of a Public Safety Zone, an area 'identified by the airport that was needed to safeguard the public in relation to aircraft movements',[47] and this prohibited the building of new houses in Mill Street for some twenty years. Tony Brown served as vice-chairman of the Commissioners in 1977 and 1978 and was re-elected in 1979, becoming chairman in 1981. Declaring that he wanted to play a more direct, involved and active part in helping the town and the Island to develop and secure its future he was elected to the Keys in 1981 with 994 votes to the 540 of his rival H.L.Kelly. With his wife he also established 'Tony Brown Electrics' in the town that year, a business that he continued to run in tandem with his political career until 2010.

He won a similar number of votes in 1986 (995), beating N.K.Gale (487) and with the founding of the ministerial system that year he was appointed the Island's first Minister of Health and Social Security, moving to Local Government and the Environment in 1989. This gave him at last the opportunity to do something about Mill Street because the Safety Zone regulations were relaxed and it became possible for his department to buy the Victoria Hotel from Heron and Brearley as well as the 'Cosy' Cinema from Strix, who were moving their factory to new premises. As he explained:

> The way was now open to undertake a major redevelopment of an old area of our town, an area that was in desperate need of investment, and importantly this would mean that instead of using green field sites around our town we could utilize an existing area in the centre and ....bring it back into community life. The Department, under my direct control, finalized the basis of a scheme. I was determined to bring a mix of the community into the centre and I agreed that the scheme should consist of

Chief Minister Tony Brown on Tynwald Day in 2008. (Lily Publications)

three residential components. Phase One was to be Public Sector units to be owned by and under the control of the Castletown Commissioners – this would be in the area of the Victoria Hotel and the old band room. Phase Two was to be first-time buyers houses …on the area backing on to Hope Street behind the Masonic Hall, which had been part of the Strix factory. Phase Three was to be a Public Sector Elderly Persons Sheltered Complex, to be owned and under the control of the Castletown and Malew Elderly Persons Committee, and this was to be on the site of the former 'Cosy' Cinema and main part of the Strix factory running down from Mill Street into Hope Street. I then set about securing the finances within the Government's budget to enable all the redevelopment to take place. All the Department's objectives were realised and today [2007] we have a redeveloped Mill Street, part of Hope Street and part of Malew Street. The project took some ten years from purchasing the first area of land to completion, but it was worth it. [48]

In the 1991 election Tony Brown was returned unopposed and continued in the same ministerial post until he moved to Tourism and Leisure from 1994 to 1996. In that year he was opposed in Castletown by Elsie Pickard (467) and Carol Edge (102) but maintained steady support with 876 votes. He then took over the Ministry of Transport until 2001 when he was returned for Castletown unopposed and served as Speaker of the House of Keys from 2001 to 2006, beating off a challenge in the Castletown seat that year from Roy Redmayne who gained 335 votes to his 915. He was then elected Chief Minister by Tynwald. Inevitably, he has been a major influence on Castletown life during this long period of political service.

Another contemporary Castletown success story has been that of Eric Taylor and his son, John. Eric was educated at King William's and proved to be a gifted inventor, effectively creating the thermostats that would become familiar across the world in many electrical appliances. During the war years he designed thermostats for heated flight suits used by Bomber Command and he used this experience to set up Otter Controls in Buxton after the war to develop the technology. In 1951 he and some friends put up £50 each to open a subsidiary workplace in cramped quarters on the top floors of Bridge House in Castletown, largely to benefit from tax advantages. Otter received a major boost in 1957 with a large-scale order for thermostats for electric blankets and in 1959 Eric's son John, from King William's and also

The far from cosy-looking 'Cosy' Cinema. (Ron Ronan collection)

Cambridge, joined the company. He had inherited the inventive skills of his father, ranging widely across electronics and including his hobby, horology. The company took over the premises of the 'Cosy' Cinema after it closed down in the early 1960s and after Eric Taylor died in 1971 John became the driving force in the business. He built a modern factory in Castletown in 1973 to manufacture and test his new electric kettle controls, called 'vapourstats', and in 1979 he negotiated what proved to be an acrimonious divorce from Otter Controls, establishing 'Strix Limited' in 1981, the name deriving from the Latin for 'screeching owl' [49].

By 1984 there was a Strix factory in Port Erin and that year Edwin Davies, a Manxman, joined the company and later became the major shareholder and chairman. Another factory opened in Ramsey in 1989 and a new Castletown headquarters in the same year. The company acquired Malew Engineering in 1990 as well as Oak Industries in South Africa and set up a branch of the company in Melbourne, Australia. In 1993 a new factory was built at Ronaldsway and a sales office opened in Chicago in 1994 as well as a manufacturing plant in China and sales subsidiaries in Brussels and Moscow, all in 1997. The company's annual revenue surged from about £5 million in 1990 to more than £70 million in 2001 and by this time most electric kettles round the world were equipped with Strix automatic switch-offs. In 2000 the HSBC bank acquired a 40% interest in the company and in 2002 Strix began producing equipment for Moka coffee makers. The whole company was bought by the Dutch bank ABN Amro in 2004 and continued to be the world's leading designer and manufacturer of temperature controls and cordless interfaces for electric kettles and other fluid-heating as well as water-boiling appliances. Strix had a 70% share of the world market for electric kettle switch-offs and for a time it maintained three production factories on the Island, and employed about a thousand people, though by 2009 it maintained only a headquarters in Castletown, with most of the manufacturing taking place in China. [50]

Dr John Taylor left the company in 1999 and became a generous benefactor of educational institutions, in particular Corpus Christi, his former Cambridge college, which he presented in 2008 with a unique time-keeping device of his own design which attracted wide international media attention. Located in a Corpus window on the corner of Bene't Street and King's Parade, the clock has at last encouraged tourists and others to stand with their backs to the fabulous architecture of King's College, looking at Corpus, rather than the other way round. In 2009 the King William's College Society Magazine reported that 'John, in his early seventies, feels that time is being eaten away in an uneven manner. Consequently, on every hour, one hears a chain dropping on a coffin, and he has placed the escapement at the top of the clock with a fearsome beast rocking backwards and forwards and closing its mouth to "eat" time ..'[51]

The fortunes of King William's College, which had nurtured this inventive father and son partnership, managed to improve after Sydney Wilson took over as principal in 1935 at a distinctly low point, with numbers at only 168. Fund-raising appeals led to the enlargement of the main college building and the opening of the Barrovian Hall in 1937. Improved facilities and academic and sporting standards made the school increasingly popular with Island boys and numbers climbed to 285 in 1945, helped by the fact that KWC, unlike many other public schools, was not requisitioned for other uses during the war and many parents of boarders regarded its location as comparatively safe from enemy action.

The trustees were awarded £32,000 compensation for the 188 acres of Bishop Barrow's land which were requisitioned by the Admiralty for HMS 'Urley', and this strengthened the overall financial position. The King and Queen were entertained at the college on their visit to Castletown on July 4th 1945 and by 1947 the trustees felt secure enough to dispense with the Direct Grant and return to independent status. By the time Wilson retired in 1958 there were a record 352 boys at the school, with 24 teachers, and expansion continued under Wilson's successor Geoffrey Rees-Jones, reaching 490 in 1976. However, after that a steady rise in school fees, an increasing trend against boarding, experienced in the UK during the next decade, and an economic recession on the Island during the 1980s, began to have a serious impact on recruitment. In 1987 the trustees decided to make the school co-educational and began to look for boarders in many foreign countries.[52]

The Buchan School, aided by a handsome grant from the Ballamanagh Trust, had in 1940 acquired 'Westhill', an elegant Regency mansion off Arbory Road, and in 1951 numbers reached a record 148, rising further to 267 in 1970. Despite the lack of an endowment, several successful fund-raising appeals led to the steady expansion and improvement of the facilities on the Westhill site and the school numbered 355 pupils in its centenary year, 1975. However, in the following years the same problems that affected King William's reduced the roll at The Buchan, and there was the further problem that its Direct Grant status was due to end in 1991.

After consultations with the trustees of KWC an amalgamation of the two schools took place in 1990, with The Buchan School premises eventually serving as a preparatory school for pupils up to the age of 11, after which they moved to the main KWC campus. In 1999 there were 206 pupils at the Westhill site and 267 at KWC, though only 49 of the total 473 were boarders. In 2000 a new principal, Philip John, who had experience of the

Castletown in the 1990s, looking very much smarter than it did fifty years earlier. (Manx National Heritage)

International Baccalaureate examinations, abolished the traditional 'A' level syllabus at KWC and also initiated an energetic recruitment drive which successfully attracted many more pupils, not least European students, to the Sixth Form. By 2004 the roll had increased to 570 and in the next year or two KWC's impressive 'IB' examination results meant that the school was placed near the top of the British school 'league tables' for the first time.[53]

Meanwhile Castle Rushen High School went from strength to strength in its new buildings. Its popularity led to a steady growth in the number of pupils and extensions were built in 1969 to accommodate 650 pupils, with another series of additions in 1972 to provide for a new estimate of 750. But then the famous wartime 'baby boom' became apparent in the primary schools and the planners began to contemplate even higher numbers. Under Harry Taverner, headmaster from 1976 to 1998, and with the strong support of Victor Kneale, education minister from 1986 to 1990, temporary classrooms at last disappeared, there was an impressive growth in the size of the Sixth Form, and numbers rose above 900. In the school's fiftieth anniversary year, 1998, the academic and sporting results were excellent and a strong tradition of accomplishment in music and the arts had been established. Moreover the list of its distinguished alumni included Sir Miles Walker, the Island's first Chief Minister, and it would soon include one of his successors, Tony Brown.[54]

Although Castle Rushen High School and King William's College prospered in Tony Brown's Castletown, the familiar presence of a working Castletown Brewery disappeared in 1986. After the sale to Hope and Anchor in 1947 the company was restructured and it bought the prominent Fort Anne Hotel in Douglas and also acquired planning permission to build 22 new houses on Victoria Road in Castletown. But it was hard hit in 1950 by a rate revaluation from a Tynwald desperate to increase its income in difficult times, and the rateable value of the premises was raised from £525 to £7,000. Also, there was still considerable opposition from temperance groups and the public in general who felt that everyone in the drinks trade was making too much money because of a lack of price regulation. Annual profits fell steeply in the 1950s from nearly £24,000 in 1951 to just over £14,000 in 1954.[55]

During the 1960s politicians were still convinced that there was too much profiteering in the drinks trade and accordingly Tynwald increased taxes on beer. Then came the new demand for lager, which Castletown Brewery was ill-equipped to produce, and sales of the home-brewed ales fell significantly. The company gradually made the necessary adjustment to the new market conditions and there was a steady improvement in trading during the 1970s. Annual profits exceeded £50,000 in 1975 and rose above £145,000 in 1980 and reached over £206,000 in 1985, though this was at a time of steep inflation. In 1984 strike activity by seamen, the closure of three hotels and a decline in demand for beer owing to a diminishing number of visitors indicated to the brewery trade that the future was going to be difficult and in July 1986 Heron and Brearley, Castletown's biggest rival, made a bid for the company, which was eventually accepted. Although there were no dismissals of the workforce, brewing at the Castletown site stopped almost immediately, in October 1986. In February 1988 the premises were sold for £510,000 and demolished to make way for housing development. In due course the new 'Isle of Man Breweries' set up in 1987 built itself a fine new brewery outside Douglas at Kewaigue, which opened in 1996.[56]

Another historic closure was that of St Mary's, the parish church since 1922. In 1912 the handsome octagonal lantern had to be taken down because it was unsafe and the first Vicar, R.W. Carter, had found it necessary to raise over £1,000 to make further urgent repairs. Some felt that it had served its purpose and should be pulled down and replaced, but where, the Vicar quite reasonably asked, was the necessary £15,000 to come from?[57] In 1954 changes were made internally so that the altar could be more easily seen but by 1975 the roof was leaking badly and a further £1,400 was raised for repairs. Yet the roof still leaked and in 1976 the building was officially declared to be unsafe and had to be closed. Negotiations then began to take place over the Hope Street school, which eventually opened in 1985, not without a maze of legal difficulties and indignant protests, as the parish church of 'St Mary on the Harbour'.

The former church was deconsecrated by Act of Tynwald in 1984 and sold to a developer who converted it into offices, eight on the ground floor and six on a new floor above. One of the more bizarre consequences of the sale was that Tynwald required the remains of Lieutenant Governor Cornelius Smelt to be disinterred and buried elsewhere. His descendants chose St Peter's in Onchan but because Smelt had died in 1832, when there had been a severe outbreak of cholera in Castletown, it was considered that there was some risk of infection from the remains, as the cholera bacteria was thought to be long-lived. So the workmen who carried out the operation were equipped with hooded overalls, neoprene gloves, surgical face masks and Wellington boots.[58]

In March 1989 Sir Laurence New, the Lieutenant Governor, who was a former pupil of KWC, opened Castletown's newly-built Civic Centre and in 1991 Lord Derby unveiled a major reorganization of Castle Rushen's historical presentations. This took place on August 4th and coincided with the launch of 'Manx National Heritage' the new name for the Manx Museum and National Trust, which had been given control over Castle Rushen by Tynwald in 1988. The new displays were imaginative and forward-looking and included the use of models that appeared to talk, no doubt to the satisfaction of Clifford Irving. In 1997 a number of Castletown residents founded their own 'Castletown Heritage' group designed to promote awareness of the town's history and defend it from the worst excesses of developers. The earliest members included Sir David Wilson, a former Director of the British Museum, and his wife, who by then lived in the converted premises of the former lifeboat station on the harbour. Newsletters were produced from time to time which featured articles about the history of the town, and an attempt was made to centralize some of the relevant archive material.

The Old House of Keys, which had been taken over in 1900 by Parr's Bank, subsequently became part of the Westminster Bank, which in 1973 moved out and generously presented the building as a free gift to the Castletown Commissioners that year. The Commissioners moved into it from the former Barracks building but moved out again on the completion of the new Civic Centre. The Old House remained largely unused for a time and attracted the concerned attention of Castletown Heritage members but in 2000 Manx National Heritage took over responsibility for it as part of their Millennium programme and carefully restored it as it would have looked in 1866. In the House members of the visiting public are able to sit round the table as if they were MHKs, under the control of an 'animatronic' Speaker in the chair.

The most spectacular development in the Castletown area since the 1950s has been the growth of Ronaldsway airport. After the opening of the new terminal in 1953 there was a steady increase in the volume of passengers up to 1966, with 408,000 arrivals and departures recorded in that year, then a fall for a few years before another surge to 480,000 in 1973. A decline in the visiting industry as well as an international oil crisis led to a slump in numbers down to 283,000 in 1982, the year of the formation of Manx Airlines, which was able to benefit from business generated by the growing financial sector in the Island. During the 1990s a 20-acre Freeport was established adjacent to the airport, allowing international traders to benefit from the Island's status as a finance centre.

In March 2000 another extension to the main airport was opened, providing a new arrivals area, baggage hall, departure lounge and catering facilities, while the older terminal was refurbished to provide up-to-date check-in facilities and offices. Manx Airlines was taken over by British Airways which eventually sold on to other operators, and in 2004 passenger numbers reached close to 774,000, with airlines operating flights to London, Dublin, Liverpool, Manchester, Birmingham, Bristol, Newcastle, Southampton, Glasgow, Blackpool and elsewhere. The number of departure gates was increased in 2007, and in 2008 work began on an ambitious and expensive programme to extend the main runway by building a rock promontory 800 feet into the sea, and to construct a new control tower challenging John Welch's tower at KWC for dominance over the locality. [59]

On the other side of the road from the airport the Ronaldsway Aircraft Company was established in 1955 by Mrs Jean Burrell, the sister of Ulsterman Sir James Martin, the brains behind the well-known Martin-Baker company which pioneered pilot ejector seats from military jet aircraft. For more than thirty years the Ronaldsway factory (often known simply as 'Martin-Baker') maintained an exclusive relationship with the main company in the UK but after 1989 it began to offer its experience and capabilities to organizations such as Rolls-Royce, BAE Systems, Dowty and Boeing, providing them with a diversity of aero-engine components as well as the original ejector seat equipment. Remaining a family concern, the company steadily developed and expanded, becoming in 2002 the headquarters of RLC Engineering Group, which also has plants in Northern Ireland and Lancashire. It has been a major employer on the Island, with sales in excess of £70 million and over 700 employees recorded in 2007.

LORNE HOUSE AND CALLOW'S YARD

Around 1950, Sir Joseph Qualtrough gave a talk on the history of Castletown and he told his audience:

I think I can begin by saying that the town of Castletown has seen better days. I do not suggest it has come down in the world, for it still retains much of its ancient dignity. But the fact must be admitted that while parts of the Island have gone ahead Castletown has stood still. The tourist industry, which has brought prosperity to other places, has passed Castletown by. This is partly, if not largely, Castletown's own fault. I am old enough to remember the determined opposition of the old Castletown families ….to having anything to do with the 'Trippers' or the 'Cotton Balls' as they used to be called. When I was younger I remember that two parties fought in a deadly battle, one for and one against encouraging visitors. The House of Keys and the Commissioners' elections have been fought on the issue. But the battle was indecisive, to this extent, that the party which stood for progress and development never was able to gain a clear victory.[60]

The census of 2006 revealed that the population of Castletown was only 3,109, 32 fewer than in 1981, and that the 'deadly battle' against development which Qualtrough noted in the 1950s had continued to be fought well into the next century. The biggest contest during these years was over the daring scheme put forward by the Commissioners in 1962, envisaging a new bridge across the mouth of the harbour and a new hotel in the vicinity of the Old Grammar School, which would probably have been demolished. In 2005 it seemed likely that drastic changes would be made by a private developer to Number 5, The Parade, as well as the adjoining historic Balcony House. Supporters of Castletown Heritage rushed to the barricades, complaints were voiced in Tynwald and a considerable row boiled up until the scheme was eventually dropped and both houses were instead sympathetically restored. Some residents of Castletown had also not been at ease when in 2003 most of the town centre was used as an elaborate set for a TV series entitled 'Island at War', which told the story of an imaginary Channel Island occupied by German forces during the 1939-45 war.

In 2005 another entrepreneur came forward with ambitious plans for

Lorne House, 2010. (Patricia Tutt)

The 'Regency' entrance hall and staircase at Lorne House. (Patricia Tutt)

Castletown. This was Roy Tilleard, who was raised in East London and qualified as an accountant, working for almost twenty years in the Unilever organization before starting up his own industrial chemicals business, which he sold in 1990. He then completed a buyout of Deb Group, best known for its Swarfega skincare products, and sold it on in 2004 to Barclays Private Equity. This enabled him to concentrate on his other businesses, including Lorne House Trust, based at Lorne House.

After Lt Colonel William Cuninghame died in 1825, Lorne House had been leased successively to Lieutenant Governors Ready and Hope. However, in 1860 Cuninghame's grandson Patrick wanted to live in it himself and so he did not renew the lease, precipitating the departure of the Governors from Castletown. Patrick lived in the house until his death in 1872, after which, as he was the last of the male line, it was rented out until its sale to the Douglas entrepreneur Henry Bloom Noble in 1893. His trustees sold it on to Surgeon-General Henry Stevenson in 1907 and it was sold again to James Gell in 1919 and to the Proctor-Gregg family in 1928. In 1931 Lorne House was bought by Christian Endeavour Holiday Homes, an inter-denominational organization which provided inexpensive holidays in a religious atmosphere. It opened between Whitsun and the middle of September each year, and guests were able to stay for one or two-week periods.

An annexe was built in the grounds, containing dormitories and bathrooms, and during the 1939-45 war the Manx Childrens' Home occupied Lorne House after their own premises in Douglas had been requisitioned by the Royal Navy. Some 73 children were accommodated in the building, including several sent from the heavily-bombed towns of Liverpool and Coventry. After the war Lorne House was returned to CEHH who continued to operate it until 1972, by which time it was hosting about 100 guests at a cost of £11 a week. In 1972 CEHH requested permission to build in the grounds but this was denied and they sold out to Mannin Industries Ltd, headed by Walter Gilbey, later an MHK. An initial scheme to convert the house into a luxury hotel was dropped and instead it was divided into flats and offices.[61] In 1982 Lorne House Trust, an Investment and Trust company headed by Ronald Buchanan, began to operate from the building, but after his death in 2006 Lorne House was bought by Roy Tilleard, who decided to invest in the building in order to safeguard it from decay and to preserve its historic features. Once it had been extensively renovated, it became the private office for his business activities, including Lorne House Trust, providing company, trust and investment services to entrepreneurial, high net-worth clients.

In October 2005 a Castletown Heritage newsletter told its members that 'Mr Wilf Callow has sold his land running between Arbory Street and Malew Street to a company owned by Mr Roy Tilleard, which has also bought a number of surrounding properties. It has now put up planning application for a large development, principally residential, but with some shops, to be called Callow's Yard. Castletown Heritage has not objected because your committee feels it is the best of all proposals so far for the site'.[62]

Wilf Callow is an interesting example of how, even in dormant Castletown, a local boy with few advantages could make his way. Born in 1926 and brought up in Mill Street and Malew Street, he left Victoria Road School at the age of thirteen and worked for a greengrocer before entering the Merchant Navy as a galley boy in 1943, later serving as a cook until he returned to Castletown in 1946. There was little work available at the time and he took a succession of labouring jobs until he married Marge, a girl from St Helen's who was working in the catering department at King William's. Wilf got a steady job at Martin-Baker's, where he was a machine setter, but he and Marge also opened a fish and chip shop in Ballasalla, where they lived in a tin Nissen hut for a time. Eventually they closed the chip shop on moving to one of the new local government houses at Janet's Corner with their two young children.[63]

The Island's economy showed some signs of stirring in the 1960s and Wilf was able to acquire a house in Malew Street, which he refurbished, and to buy Brewer and Turnbull's shop in Malew Street, which he rented out, while Marge opened a shoe shop in the Street which she operated with her mother. In 1973 the Callows also bought a farmhouse on the Ballamodha Straight, using it as a weekend retreat and as a place to grow fruit and vegetables. Three years later Wilf was able to retire from Martin-Baker's at the age of 50 in order to run his various properties, which expanded to include number 20 in Arbory Street and number 19 in Malew Street. Their gardens were adjoining and therefore provided a link between the two streets, inside the 'triangle'. Wilf was diagnosed with Parkinson's disease in the late 1990s and Marge died after a stroke in 2000, hence the Callow properties were put on the market and attracted the attention of Roy Tilleard who bought them in 2005. At that time many of the shops in both Malew Street and Arbory Street were closed and others were not prospering as businesses, so Roy Tilleard was able to buy up all the properties in Arbory Street from numbers 6 to 28 and in Malew Street from 9 to 21, announcing that he intended to create a multi-purpose shopping, catering and residential complex extending from one street to the other, thereby regenerating business life in the centre of the town.

From the memoirs of William Henry Cooper, born in Arbory Street in 1870, it is clear that the various premises which now comprise the Callow's Yard development had mostly been occupied by small businesses for well over a hundred years. In Arbory Street, number 6 was rebuilt about 1877 for a grocer before becoming a cycle shop that closed down in 1999, and number 8 was a branch of the Bank of Mona in Victorian times before being converted into a shop. Number 10 was occupied by a tinsmith in Cooper's day but served for a time as a post office in the 1990s. Number 12 was a saddler's and boot shop, then a bank, then a milliner's, and finally a newsagent, while 14 was a greengrocer's and 16 a warehouse.[64]

The archway, inscribed 'Castle Rushen Stores' at number 18, was built by T.M.Dodd, a grocer who started business at numbers 19-21 in Malew Street in 1884 and then added this Arbory Street property to his little empire, thereby connecting the two streets. In the early 1990s there were plans to create a shopping arcade in the area from 18-22 Arbory Street through to 17-21 Malew Street, though this did not go ahead. However, it provided an opportunity for archaeologists from the University of Liverpool to excavate part of the area in 1991 and 1992 and discover something about life in the town over the previous few centuries. The dig produced the largest group of 16th and 17th century pottery found up to then on the Island and confirmed that cattle and sheep, rather than pigs, provided the meat diet for townspeople over several centuries. The final report also observed that 'The

The modest office in Castletown harbour of the Douglas-based Steam Packet Company.
(Lily Publications)

Castletown harbour, 2009. (Author)

Castle Rushen Stores assemblage is probably most remarkable for the recovery of four butchered dog vertebrae from a late context, reflecting perhaps the extreme poverty of certain residents in the town during the 18th or 19th century.'[65]

Number 20, Arbory Street, was a substantial three-storeyed, five-bay building in which James Taggart established a millinery business in the 1880s which proved so successful that 'Taggart's hats were a synonym for the best in millinery and were worn all over the Island'.[66] In the 1920s Taggart sold out to John Christian Moore, who also retailed carpets and furniture. Numbers 22 and 24 were both shops but number 26 was a cottage with a large doorway leading to a passage through to Arbory Street. T.M.Dodd built an archway here, inscribed 'AD 1898', as an alternative entrance to his Malew Street premises. The last house in Arbory Street to be occupied by Callow's Yard is number 28, which was bought by R.Corlett, who, according to Cooper, 'erected storage sheds in the garden and bought houses in Malew Street so that he could take gardens to erect stables, etc.'[67] So it can be seen that over time a number of properties in Arbory Street became linked with those in Malew Street, with access to both streets and with gardens or yards in common.

In Malew Street, Callow's Yard starts at number 9, which was historically a confectioner's shop, connected to a restaurant at number 11, while number 13 was in turn a baker's, a boot shop and latterly a dentist's surgery. Number 15 was built by Cooper's father about 1887 when he was working as an apprentice with him, to the designs of Daniel Cregeen, a Manx architect and engineer. Later known as 'Peveril House' it is one of the tallest houses in Castletown, built of red brick with yellow brick facings and a moulded frieze, and standing three storeys tall with dormer windows. According to local historian Eva Wilson, 'The red brick would have come from Ruabon in North Wales. The yellow brick came from Flintshire, where it was taken as return ballast goods in the Island's ore trade with North Wales.'[68] Number 17 was a shop owned by the Rothwell family for three generations before becoming the workplace of 'Bill the Barber'. Numbers 19 and 21 were the main premises of T.M.Dodd, a large shop selling groceries, wines and spirits, and behind them were a mineral water and bottling factory with access to Arbory Street. William Clague Wilson, (1900-1999) said in an interview towards the end of his life that Dodd's shop

was quite wide and large, on the right they dealt with provisions, bacon, butter, eggs and large cheeses and so on, on the left were general groceries. The staff were men, five or six of them, I remember they wore white coats down to their knees. In the middle of the shop was a rack with a display of fancy goods, such as chocolates and fancy ginger biscuits, things like that. The upper part of the office, where the lady clerk sat with her books – her name was Ada Sayle – was glassed in with a window in it. Tom Dodd was the only grocer in the Island, as far as I know, who ever had a connecting system between the shop assistant on the floor and the lady in the office, whereby the invoice and the money was put in a cup, [and] a string was pulled which propelled the cup along the cable to the office.[69]

In the Callow's Yard scheme, number 21 has been converted into a Manx Electricity Authority substation, which involved new high-voltage cables being laid to it from the harbour and the consequent temporary closure and digging up of Bank Street. The substation, in addition to providing the electricity required by the new development, also serves the whole of Castletown.

When Roy Tilleard first unveiled his plans for Callow's Yard, the news came as something of a bombshell in Castletown and opinion became, and remained, divided as to the merits of the scheme. Some conservationists feared that historic features would disappear, some local residents were unhappy at the prospect of months of disruption, and others feared that the

Georgian Castletown. (Lily Publications)

Callow's Yard. (Lily Publications)

'tone' of Castletown would be changed for ever. On the other hand, many people welcomed the project as a visionary scheme that could bring the town great benefits. Roy Tilleard refused to be blown off course by his critics or be daunted by the many problems, scheduled and unexpected, which inevitably arose, and by the middle of 2009 Callow's Yard had taken shape and was close to completion. It consisted of 28 apartments and houses to be rented out as though they were hotel rooms, as well as about 30,000 square feet of retail outlets, including shops, several restaurants, a coffee shop, a food hall, an art gallery, a function room, a jazz club, an atrium and a central, multi-purpose arena. At an open meeting held at the site in May 2009 and attended by some 120 guests, Roy Tilleard told his audience that Callow's Yard would bring transient people with money to spend into the town. There can be little doubt that at the start of the 21st century neither Arbory Street nor Malew Street were the thriving thoroughfares they had once been, and the hope is that Callow's Yard will restore vitality and prosperity to the heart of an historic town.

References

CHAPTER ONE (PAGES 10-45)

1.   E.H.Stenning, *Portrait of the Isle of Man*, p38.
2.   Ibid.
3.   See David M.Wilson, *The Vikings in the Isle of Man*, pp 38-46.
4.   George Broderick, transcriber and translator, *Chronicles of the Kings of Man and the Isles*, folio 34 verso.
5.   Broderick, f.40 recto.
6.   W.C.Cubbon, *Excavations at Ronaldsway*, 1935, in Proceedings of the Isle of Man Natural History and Antiquarian Society, Vol IV, p153.
7.   Broderick, f.43 v., f.44 r., f 44 v.
8.   Broderick, f. 48 r., f 48 v.,f.49 r.
9.   Broderick, f. 49 r.
10. A.Rigby, Castle Rushen, *A Historical and Descriptive Account*, p75.
11. Edward J. Cowan, *The Last Kings of Man*, in the 2006 page proofs of Vol 3 of 'A New History of the Isle of Man', p 112.
12. A.Rigby, *Castle Rushen*, in Proceedings, Vol I, p347.
13. A.M.Cubbon, *The Mediaeval St Mary's Church*, in Proceedings, Vol VII, pp 307-340.
14. Broderick, f.50 r., and A.W.Moore, *A History of the Isle of Man*, Vol 1, p213.
15. Broderick, f.50 r.
16. Stenning, *Portrait*, pp100-102.
17. Ibid, p103.
18. Rigby, Proceedings, Vol 1., p349.
19. This is the official view of Manx National Heritage according to information on public display in Castle Rushen in 2010.
20. Moore, Vol 1, p213.
21. Ibid.
22. Moore, Vol 2, pp763,764.
23. J.R.Roscow, *The Development of Sixteenth Century Castletown*, in Proceedings, Vol X, No 4, pp 306,308.
24. Ibid, p313.
25. Ibid, pp 313-314.
26. Ibid. p312.
27. Ibid.
28. Hinton Bird, *An Island That Led*, Vol 1, p7.
29. Roscow, p315.
30. Ibid, p307.
31. Mark Solly, *The Derby House,* Castletown Heritage Newsletter No7.
32. Roscow, p313.
33. Stenning, *Portrait*, p104.
34. Roscow, p316.
35. David Craine, *Manannan's Isle*, p15.
36. Ibid, p16.
37. Moore, p253.
38. J.R.Roscow, *The Development of Castletown*, 1601-1703, in Proceedings, Vol X1, No 1, p5.
39. Moore, p247.
40. Ibid, p353.
41. Stenning, *Portrait*, p148.

42.   Roscow, *Proceedings*, Vol X, p213.
43.   Michael Hoy, *A Blessing to this Island*, p3.
44.   Moore, p254.
45.   Ibid, p251.
46.   Ibid, pp 278-279.
47.   Ibid, pp 283-284.
48.   Ibid, pp 300-301.
49.   Ibid, p380.

CHAPTER TWO (PAGES 46-81)

1.   E.H.Stenning, *The Original Lands of Bishop Barrow's Trustees*, in
        Proceedings, Vol 4, p129.
2.   Ibid, p123.
3.   Moore, pp 463-465.
4.   Hoy, p3.
5.   Bird, pp 8,9.
6.   Hoy, p3.
7.   Ibid.
8.   Bird, p13.
9.   Bird, p28.
10.   Stenning, Proceedings, Vol V, p129.
11.   Ibid, p131.
12.   Ibid. pp 130,132.
13.   Hoy, p5.
14.   Roscow, Proceedings, Vol XI, p14.
15.   Ibid, p15
16.   Bird, p67.
17.   Andrew Johnson, *The Old House of Keys*, in Proceedings, Vol XI,
        No 2, pp 223, 224.
18.   Ibid, p225.
19.   Bird, pp 68,69.
20.   Roscow, *Proceedings*, Vol XI, p16.
21.   Moore, pp 409,410.
22.   Ibid, p410.
23.   Ibid, pp 410-412.
24.   A.W.Moore, *A History of the Isle of Man*, Vol 2, p775.
25.   A.W.Moore, *Manx Worthies*, p71.
26.   Ibid, p72.
27.   Ibid.
28.   Moore, Vol 1, p495.
29.   W.R. Sergeant, *Castle Rushen Gaol*, in Proceedings, Vol VI, p278.
30.   Moore, Vol 1, p496.
31.   N.Mathieson, *The Governors during the Atholl Lordship*, in
        Proceedings, Vol VI, No 1, p48.
32.   Moore, Vol I, p454. See also a more detailed account of the Duke's
        visit in C.W.Gawne, *Controversy*, pp 23-26.
33.   Mathieson, *The Governors*, p50.
34.   Ibid, pp 56,61.
35.   S.Miller, *My Misfortunes Press So Hard Upon Me*, Proceedings, Vol XI, No 4, pp 557-560.
36.   George Waldron, *The History and Description of the Isle of Man*,
        1744, pp5,8.
37.   P.W.Caine, *John Stevenson II*, Proceedings, Vol IV, p260.
38.   Ibid, p256.
39.   Ibid, p259.
40.   T.M.Moore, *Some Social Aspects of Castletown in the 18th and 19th
        Centuries*, in Proceedings, Vol VII, pp 686-705.
41.   See my *Governors of the Isle of Man*, p9.

42. Ibid, p10.
43. Ibid, pp 19-22.
44. John Feltham, *A Tour through the Island of Mann in 1797 and 1798*, pp 266-269.
45. Sergeant, p280.
46. Ibid, p284.
47. Ibid., p285.
48. Ibid, p286.
49. Bird, pp72-74.
50. Ibid, p102.
51. Ibid, pp97,98.
52. Ibid, p106.
53. See Journal of the Manx Museum, No 44, Sep 1935 Vol III, p 41.
54. Bird, p142.
55. Ibid, p144.
56. T.M.Moore, p701.
57. Bird, pp 94,263.
58. Ibid, p228.
59. T.H.Kelly, *Castletown Methodist Church 150th Anniversary, 1834-1984*, p3
60. Ibid, p4.
61. J.I.West, *John Wesley in the Isle of Man*, in Proceedings, Vol VI, pp 24,26
62. T.H.Kelly, p6 and J.D.R.Kewley, *Buildings in the Isle of Man by Thomas Brine*, in Proceedings, Vol XII, No 1, p151.

CHAPTER THREE (PAGES 82-107)

1. Johnson, p226.
2. Kewley, pp 147,148.
3. Johnson, p228.
4. Ibid, p229.
5. Ibid, p230.
6. Moore, Vol 2, p541.
7. John Gelling, *A History of the Manx Church*, 1698-1911, pp 21,37,43,38.
8. Ibid, pp 59,60.
9. Kewley, p148.
10. N.Mathieson, *Old Inns and Coffee Houses*, in Proceedings, Vol 5, No 4, pp 429,430.
11. Moore, Vol 2, p580.
12. Mathieson, *Old Inns*, p430.
13. John Kitto, *Historic Houses in the Isle of Man*, p105.
14. P.G.Ralfe, *Notes on Old Castletown*, in Proceedings, Vol III, p215.
15. Theodora Roscoe, *Dorothy Wordworth visits the Island*, 1828, in Journal of the Manx Museum, Vol 5, No 69, p114.
16. T.M.Moore, p699.
17. A.W.Moore, Vol 2, pp 568, 569.
18. Ibid, p572.
19. Ibid, and Ralfe, p216.
20. Basil and Eleanor Megaw, *John Quilliam of the 'Victory'*, in JMM Vol V, No 7, p67.
21. W.S.Cowin, *An Old Castletown Banking House*, in Proceedings, Vol V, pp 73-79.
22. *The Nautical Museum*, MNH pamphlet.
23. Ibid.
24. Moore, *Manx Worthies*, pp 86,100.
25. Gawne, *Controversy*, pp 60-61.

26.   Craine, David, *The Potato Riots*, in Proceedings, Vol IV, p567.

27.   Ibid, p568.

28.   Ibid, p572.

29.   Ibid, p573.

30.   Ibid, p577.

31.   DW, *Governors*, pp 24-8.

32.   Hoy, pp 9-29.

33.   DW, *Governors*, pp 34-35.

34.   Patricia Tutt, *Lorne House*, pp 1,2, 28, 32.

35.   Ibid. pp 40-42.

36.   DW, Governors, pp44,45.

37.   Quoted in Eva Wilson, (ed) The *'Town Clark's'* Castletown, pp 89-90.

CHAPTER FOUR (PAGES 108-132)

1.   L.S.Garrad, *Red Herring Houses at Derbyhaven and South Quay*,
        Douglas, in Proceedings, Vol IX, pp 133,134.

2.   DW, *Governors*, pp 52,53.

3.   Johnson, p239.

4.   Ibid, p240.

5.   Autobiographical memoir by John Moore Jeffcott in Manx National
        Heritage Library, reference ms 09642.

6.   *Isle of Man Times*, 20.5.1892.

7.   NMP Manx Year Book, 1906, p7.

8.   See the map of the town boundaries in David G. Kermode, *Offshore
        Island Politics*, p384.

9.   Hansard Reports of the debates in Tynwald and the House of Keys,
        Vol 14, p377 and The Isle of Man Victorian Society Newsletter, No 84 pp19,20..

10.   Hansard, Vol 12, p466.

11.   Hansard, Tynwald Court, 28.10.1896.

12.   Hansard, Vol 16, p110

13.   Hansard, TC, 3.2.1903.

14.   Hansard, Vol 23, p832.

15.   Hansard, Vol 8, p213.

16.   Hansard, TC, 12.5.1896.

17.   Hansard, TC, 10.10.1911.

18.   *Mona's Herald and Fargher's Advertiser*, 8.7.1896.

19.   Hansard, TC, 24.1.1899.

20.   Moore, Vol 2, p708.

21.   Crumplin, Tim, and Rawcliffe, Roger, *A Time of Manx Cheer*, pp 13,
        76,77.

22.   Dollin Kelly, (ed.), *New Manx Worthies*, pp 374-375.

23.   Gelling, p72.

24.   Ibid, pp72,73.

25.   Ibid, p190.

26.   Ibid, pp206-218.

27.   Sergeant, p289.

28.   Ibid, p290.

29.   Ibid, p292.

30.   *New Manx Worthies*, pp 412,413.

31.   House of Keys Summary of of Minutes of Public Proceedings,
        16.10.1928.

32.   See my *T.E.Brown, His Life and Legacy*, for a full account of Brown's
        career.

33.   T.E.Brown in *Castletown*, an advertising leaflet, c1895.

34.   C.C.Watterson, *Old Castletown*, in Proceedings, Vol V, No 11,
        p100.

35.   Ibid, p103.

36.   Ibid.
37.   Ibid, p112.
38.   Ibid, p111.
39.   Ibid, p110
40.   Ibid, p21.
41.   Ibid, p37.
42.   Ibid, p104.
43.   Quoted in J.D.Qualtrough, *Castletown, some notes on its history*, from the website 'A Manx Notebook' compiled by Frances Coakley.
44.   Pat Skillicorn, *Pennies for the Poor*, Castletown Heritage Newsletter No 8.
45.   Ibid.
46.   John Hellowell, *A Tour of Manx Lighthouses*, pp 57-58.
47.   Eva Wilson (ed), *William Henry Cooper's Castletown*, p76.

CHAPTER FIVE (PAGES 133-183)

1.   Kermode, pp 5,384.
2.   See *William Clague Wilson remembers his childhood and youth in Castletown*, in CHN no 4.
3.   John Kitto, *Historic Houses in the Isle of Man*, pp 59-60.
4.   *New Manx Worthies*, pp 375-378.
5.   Hansard, TC, 19.10.1928, p39.
6.   Bird, Vol 2, pp 242-243.
7.   Gelling, p167.
8.   Bird, Vol 2, p93.
9.   Ibid, p194.
10.   Hansard, HK, 17.2.1931, pp 261-263.
11.   Hoy, pp 31-84.
12.   Manx National Heritage Library, F73/IX, p49.
13.   Hansard, TC, 1.11.1938, p49.
14.   Gordon Kniveton, (ed.) *A Chronicle of the Twentieth Century*, Vol 1, p145.
15.   Ibid, p189.
16.   Alan Cleary, *Chain Home Radar at Scarlett*, CH Newsletter, No 5.
17.   Kniveton, p20.
18.   Hansard, TC, 15.4.1947.
19.   Kniveton, Vol 1, p240, Vol 2, pp 63,64.
20.   Crumplin, p160.
21.   Ibid, pp 172,173.
22.   Ibid, p190.
23.   Ibid, p45.
24.   Hansard, TC, 21.1.1953, p315.
25.   Ibid, p313.
26.   Ibid, p314.
27.   Hansard, Vol 72, pp 28-42.
28.   From a transcript of the programme in the MNHL, ref MD52.
29.   Hansard, TC, 21.10.1958.
30.   Hansard, HK, 19.1.1960.
31.   *New Manx Worthies*, pp 97-99.
32.   *Isle of Man Examiner*, 22.2.1962.
33.   Hansard, HK, 11.5.65.
34.   *Country Life*, 29.4.1971, pp 10,11.
35.   T.Sherratt, *Isle of Man Parliamentary Results*, 1919-1979. (ms in the Tynwald Library).
36.   See G.B.Gardner, *The Story of the Famous Witches' Mill at Castletown*, (pamphlet).
37.   Colin Moore, *Built for Success*, pp 5,6.

38. Ibid, p18.
39. Ibid. pp 36-43, and *Castletown Metropolitan AFC* , Souvenir
    Booklet, 1950, pp 2,12,23.
40. My thanks to Syd Cringle and Peter Baker for information about the
    early years of the Cricket Club.
41. See my *A Season's Fame* for an account of Collins' remarkable
    innings.
42. *Castletown*, an advertising leaflet, c.1895.
43. Qualtrough, *Castletown*, op cit.
44. G.B.Trustrum, *Castletown and Motorcycle Road Racing*, pp 1,2.
45. Ibid, p 3.
46. Tony Brown, *Past and Present Mill Street and Hope Street,Castletown*, in
    CHN No 15, Nov 2007, p22.
47. Ibid, p24.
48. Ibid, p26.
49. From the official website of Strix, Ltd.
50. Ibid.
51. *King William's College Society Magazine*, 2008, p38.
52. Hoy, pp84-132.
53. Ibid, pp114-141.
54. J. Atkinson and W.C.Callister, *Castle Rushen High School*, 1948-
    1998, pp 25-79
55. Crumplin, pp 207-227.
56. Ibid, pp 222-274.
57. *Manx Church Magazine*, November 1923.
58. *Manx Life*, October 1985.
59. From the official website of Ronaldsway airport.
60. Qualtrough, *Castletown*, op.cit.
61. Stowell and Buchanan, *Lorne House*.
62. CH Newsletter, No 12.
63. *Manx Independent*, 28.11.08.
64. Eva Wilson (ed.), *William Henry Cooper's Castletown*, pp 30-34.
65. P.J.Davey and others, *Excavations in Castletown, Isle of Man, 1989-1992*,P140.
66. Eva Wilson, (Cooper), p34.
67. Ibid, p35.
68. Ibid, p86
69. Ibid, pp 87,88.

Bibliography

PROCEEDINGS OF THE ISLE OF MAN NATURAL HISTORY AND ANTIQUARIAN SOCIETY.

Caine, P.W., *John Stevenson II* , Vol IV, pp 252-262.

       The place-name Rushen, Vol V, pp 390-392.

       The re-erecting of Castle Rushen, Vol IV, pp 604-606.

Cowin, W.S., *An Old Castletown Banking House,* Vol V, pp 70-86.

Craine, David, *The Potato Riots,* Vol IV pp 565-577.

Crowe, Nigel, *Manx Houses of the Seventeenth Century, A Hidden Heritage?* Vol XII, No 1, pp 65-96.

Cubbon, A.M., *The Mediaeval St Mary's Church, later the Grammar School,* Vol VII, pp307-341.

Cubbon, W.C., *Excavations at Ronaldsway, 1935,* Vol IV, p 151.

Curphey, R.A., *The Castletown Artificers' Friendly Society,* Vol VII, pp164,180.

Garrad, L.S., *Red Herring Houses at Derbyhaven and South Quay, Douglas,* Vol IX, pp133-135.

Johnson, Andrew, *The Old House of Keys,* Vol XI, No 2, p223.

Kewley, J.D.R., *Buildings in the Isle of Man by Thomas Brine,* Vol XII, No 1, p 147.

King, B.A., *HM Sloop of War 'Racehorse',* Vol IX, pp 3-9.

Mathieson, N., *Old Inns and Coffee Houses,* Vol V, No 4, p 411.

       The Governors during the Atholl Lordship, Vol VI, No1, pp 46-53.

Miller, Stephen, *My Misfortunes Press So Hard Upon Me,* Letters from George and Theodosia Waldron to Sir Hans Sloane, Vol XI, No 4, pp 557-563.

Moore, T.M., *Some Social Aspects of Castletown in the 18th and 19th centuries,* Vol VII, pp 686-705.

Ralfe, P.G., *Notes on Old Castletown,* Vol III, p 208.

Rigby, A., *Castle Rushen,* Vol I, pp 51-52.

       The Chapel on St Mary's Island, Vol I, pp 131,415.

Roscow, J.R., *The Development of Sixteenth Century Castletown,* Vol X, No4 p 301.

       The Development of Castletown 1601-1703, Vol XI, No I, pp 5-28.

Sergeant, W.R., *Castle Rushen Gaol,* Vol VI, pp 278-294.

Stenning, E.H., *The original lands of Bishop Barrow's Trustees,* Vol V, pp 122-140.

Watterson, C.C., *Old Castletown,* Vol V, No II, pp 99-113.

West, J.I., *John Wesley in the Isle of Man,* Vol VI, pp 15-27.

OTHER ARTICLES

Brown, Tony, *Past and Present Mill Street and Hope Street, Castletown,* in Castletown Heritage Newsletter, No 15, pp 22-27.

Cleary, Alan, *Chain Home Radar at Scarlett,* CH Newsletter No 5, 1999.

Megaw, Basil and Eleanor, *John Quilliam of the 'Victory',* Journal of the Manx Museum, Vol V, No 7, pp 77-81.

Qualtrough, J.D., *Castletown, some notes on its history,* on website *A Manx Note Book,* ed. Frances Coakley.

Roscoe, Theodora, *Dorothy Wordsworth visits the Island, 1828,* in Journal of the Manx Museum, Vol V, no 69.

Skillicorn, Pat, *Pennies for the Poor,* CH Newsletter No 8, 2001.

Trustrum, G.B, *Castletown and Motorcycle Road Racing,* ms. 2009.

Wilson, Eva (ed) *William Clague Wilson remembers his childhood and youth in Castletown,* in CH Newsletter, Vol 4.

BOOKS

Atkinson, J. and Callister, W.C., *Castle Rushen High School, 1948-1998,* 1998.

Bird, Hinton, *An Island That Led*, two vols, privately printed, vol 1, n.d., Vol 2, 1995.

Craine, David, *Mannanan's Isle*, Manx Museum and National Trust, 1955.

Cringle, Terry (with others) *Here is the News*, The Manx Experience, Douglas, n.d.

Davey, P.J., and others, *Excavations in Castletown, Isle of Man, 1989-1992,* Liverpool University
          Press, 1996.

Duffy, Sean (ed.) *Medieval Period, 1000-1406,* Vol 3 of 'A New History of the Isle of Man',
          Liverpool University Press (page proofs only, 2006).

Crumplin, Tim, and Rawcliffe, Roger, *A Time of Manx Cheer,* The Manx Experience, 2002.

Feltham, John, *A Tour through the Island of Mann in 1797 and 1798,* Bath, 1798.

Gawne, C.W., *Controversy, The Isle of Man and Britain 1651-1895*, Manx Heritage Foundation, 2009.

Gelling, John, *A History of the Manx Church 1698-1911*, Manx Heritage Foundation, Douglas, 1998.

Hellowell, John, *A Tour of Manx Lighthouses*, 1998.

Hoy, Michael, *A Blessing to this Island, The story of King William's College and The Buchan School*,
          special annotated edition, 2006.

Kelly, Dollin, (ed), *New Manx Worthies,* Manx Heritage Foundation, 2006.

Kermode, David G, *Offshore Island Politics*, Liverpool University Press, 2001.

Kitto, John, *Historic Houses in the Isle of Man*, 1990.

Kniveton, Gordon, (ed) *A Chronicle of the 20th century*, Vol 1, 1999, Vol 2, 2000.

Moore, A.W., *A History of the Isle of Man,* two vols, London 1900, Manx Museum and National
          Trust reprint, 1997.
          Manx Worthies, Douglas, 1901.

Moore, Colin, *Built for Success*, Castletown (Metropolitan) A.F.C., The
          Centenary History 1904-2004, 2004.

Rigby, A., *Castle Rushen, A Historical and Descriptive Account,* Douglas, 1927.

Stenning, E.H., *Portrait of the Isle of Man,* Robert Hale, 1958, 1965 edition.

Tutt, Patricia, *Lorne House, A Manx Survivor*, Lily Publications, 2010.

Stowell, Flaxney, *Castletown 100 years Ago,* 1902.

Waldron, George, *The History and Description of the Isle of Man,* London, 1744.

Wilson, David M., *The Vikings in the Isle of Man,* Aarhus University Press, 2008.

Wilson, Eva, (ed.), *William Henry Cooper's Castletown,* Castletown Heritage, 2005.
          The 'Town Clark's' Castletown, Castletown Heritage, 2009.

Winterbottom, Derek, *Governors of the Isle of Man since 1765*, Manx Heritage Foundation, 1999.
          Profile of the Isle of Man, Lily Publications, 2007.
          T.E. Brown, His Life and Legacy, The Manx Experience, Douglas, 1997.

PAMPHLETS

Brown, T.E., *Castletown*, an advertising leaflet, *c.*1895.

Castletown Metropolitan AFC, 1904-1950, souvenir booklet, 1950.

Gardner, C.B., *The Story of the famous witches' mill at Castletown,* 1963.

Kelly, T.H., *Castletown Methodist Church 150th Anniversary, 1834-1984.* 1984.

Manx National Heritage: *Castle Rushen*
          Rushen Abbey
          The Nautical Museum
          The Old House of Keys

Stowell, Layton, and Buchanan, Ronald, *Notes on Lorne House*.

Winterbottom, Derek, *A Season's Fame,* Bristol Historical Association pamphlet, 1991, 1999
          reprint.

WEBSITE

Coakley, Frances (ed) *A Manx Note Book, www.isle-of-man.com/manxnotebook*

Index